Praise for *Imagining Our Neighbors as Ourselves*

"*Imagining Our Neighbors as Ourselves* will instruct and delight any reader who cares even a little about art, imagination, and humanity. Mary McCampbell is a faithful, loving guide who will teach you things you didn't even know you needed to know, and this is a book you won't even realize you needed until you've read it."

—Karen Swallow Prior, research professor of English and of Christianity and culture, Southeastern Baptist Theological Seminary, and author of *On Reading Well: Finding the Good Life through Great Books*

"Educating toward sanctified imagination is a growing movement and a much-needed antidote to the scarcity mindset of a fear-driven culture. In *Imagining Our Neighbors as Ourselves* Mary McCampbell opens our vista to a feast of literature and movies for our edification, and she even invites us back to *Mr. Rogers' Neighborhood*. From Douglas Coupland to C. S. Lewis, from Flannery O'Connor to Toni Morrison, Mary McCampbell paints a landscape of mystery, hope, and splendor for our imagination to be fed and to be nurtured toward the New Creation."

—Makoto Fujimura, artist and author of *Art+Faith: A Theology of Making*

"Psychologists' fairly recent findings that empathy can be developed even during adulthood should give us a bit more hope amidst this polarized nation and complex world. Empathy, compassion, and interconnectedness seem impossible as we flip through some major cable news networks today. Yet diligently, McCampbell takes the ingredients of the familiar and invites us on a theological and experiential journey to self and neighbor compassion. McCampbell uses the artistic tools of literature and television, for example, to move us from navel-gazing to looking outward to neighbor. In her book, both storytelling and story analysis, from film to Holy Scripture, inspire and equip us to grow what seems so lacking today: empathy. I'd encourage readers to move through the text slowly, learning from the phrases and insights, and even vicariously from McCampbell's style of engagement with the arts, to strengthen their empathy muscle."

—Christina Edmondson, psychologist, cohost of the *Truth's Table* podcast, and author of *Faithful Antiracism: Moving Past Talk to Systemic Change*

"Mary McCampbell has given us a vision of a flourishing community: one full of art, music, film, and fiction that tells the stories of who we are and the diverse gifts we bring to the table. Her book will have us opening our eyes to more clearly see those who are different from us—either because of gender, skin color, ability, or political opinions—as our neighbors. Through the stories we encounter in her work, we will be drawn toward a fuller knowledge of what love means. As McCampbell shows us, love looks like a welcoming table."

—Jessica Hooten Wilson, Louise Cowan Scholar in Residence,
University of Dallas, and author of *The Scandal of Holiness:
Renewing Your Imagination in the Company of Literary Saints*

"*Imagining Our Neighbors as Ourselves* is a rare and precious book. Mary McCampbell explores a vast web of texts—from fiction by Graham Greene, Toni Morrison, and Douglas Coupland to television drama including *Better Call Saul, Friday Night Lights*, and *The Walking Dead*—with wit, rigor, and an eye for theological depth. She shows how the arts frequently 'model the way of empathy' and, in turn, encourage a compassionate and imaginative response to life itself. This is a compelling and quietly urgent book that embodies the creative empathy it finds in literature, film, and music."

—Andrew Tate, Reader of Literature, Religion, and Aesthetics, Lancaster
University, and author of *Contemporary Fiction and Christianity*

"Mary McCampbell sees so widely and so well, with uncanny depth of feeling for what is and for what ought to be, that she understands the crucial way the imagination is meant to give us eyes to see what is in fact the truth of our existence. Artful and thoughtful, remarkably eloquent and literate, she has seen the best films and read the best novels and short stories, skillfully drawing on her years of paying attention to what matters most to all of us as we wrestle with the mystery of suffering and of beauty. She graces the reader by inviting us to learn over her shoulder and through her heart. *Imagining Our Neighbors as Ourselves* is a very good book by a very good teacher—a book for every serious student of art and, even more, for every serious human being."

—Steven Garber, Senior Fellow for Vocation and the Common
Good for the M. J. Murdock Charitable Trust and author of
The Seamless Life: A Tapestry of Love and Learning, Worship and Work

"Everyone thinks they understand empathy, until they really dig into it. Mary McCampbell does that good work for us here, enriching us with a better understanding of ourselves, others, and God. Her brilliant analysis of poems, novels, short stories, films, and television shows will leave you with a new list of rich stories to encounter, as well as a renewed conviction to relentlessly love others, after the heart of God. Embracing entertainment, but never merely entertained, McCampbell excavates a vast range of contemporary narratives, revealing great depths of human need, care, and value."

—Joseph G. Kickasola, professor of film and digital media, Baylor University, and author of *The Films of Krzysztof Kieślowski: The Liminal Image*

IMAGINING OUR NEIGHBORS AS OURSELVES

IMAGINING OUR NEIGHBORS AS OURSELVES

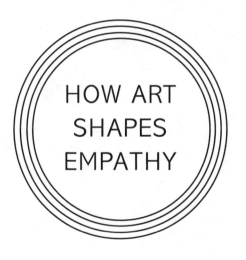

HOW ART
SHAPES
EMPATHY

Mary W. McCampbell

Fortress Press
Minneapolis

IMAGINING OUR NEIGHBORS AS OURSELVES
How Art Shapes Empathy

Unless otherwise noted, Scriptures are taken from the Holy Bible, New International
Version®, NIV®. Copyright © 1973, 1978, 1984, 2011 by Biblica, Inc.™ Used by
permission of Zondervan. All rights reserved worldwide. www.zondervan.com The
"NIV" and "New International Version" are trademarks registered in the United
States Patent and Trademark Office by Biblica, Inc.™

Scripture quotations marked (KJV) are taken from the King James Version.

Cover design: L. Owens

Print ISBN: 978-1-5064-7390-1
eBook ISBN: 978-1-5064-7391-8

For my mother, Frances Walker McCampbell.
Thank you so much for teaching me the way of empathy.

CONTENTS

INTRODUCTION

The Imagination as a Means to Love

Hate Is a Failure of Imagination

In his 1940 novel, *The Power and the Glory*, Graham Greene's beleaguered whiskey priest has been jailed alongside a very "pious" woman who is repulsed when she finds out that he is a "bad priest" who craves a drink more than anything, even "more than God."[1] He attempts to show her kindness, to which she responds, "The sooner you are dead the better."[2] The comment silences the priest, and as he sits pondering the darkness of his own soul and the spite within hers, his thoughts lead to some of the most powerful words ever written about the necessity of Christian empathy: "When you visualized a man or a woman carefully, you could always begin to feel pity. That was a quality God's image carried with it. When you saw the lines at the corners of the eyes, the shape of the mouth, how the hair grew, it was impossible to hate. Hate was just a failure of imagination."[3] Like so many other prophetic artists, Greene reminds us that to love, we must first be able to effectively imagine the lives of others, striving to recognize the image of God in them. In doing this, we begin to feel the weight of our own responsibility, one for another, just as the whiskey priest does when looking at a woman who hates him: "He began to feel an overwhelming responsibility for this pious woman."[4] As the priest looks at the pious woman, he is close enough to see her features, to focus on her likeness. But he also needs to use his imagination to envision what it might be like to be her, so full of anger and judgment. His proximity makes this possible, and although he is a self-avowed "bad priest," he understands both the challenge and the embodied reality of Christ's command to love our neighbors as ourselves.[5] His capacity to extend grace is both intentional and supernatural as he imagines his jail-cell neighbor both truthfully and compassionately.

1

Novelist Michael Chabon agrees that imagination is a necessity if we want to empathize and treat others with compassion: "To me, imagination is key to morality. If you can't imagine what it is to live in someone else's head, then you're more likely to hurt them."[6] A constricted imagination that has not been fed on goodness, beauty, and truth can cause damage to our neighbors, leading to objectification or dehumanization rather than empathy and compassion. When encountering differences in the other, we have a natural tendency to place a makeshift label on them in order to fit them neatly into our ordered understanding of reality. Empathy can only grow when we actively work against this default tendency. As Chabon implies, our malnourished capacity for empathy is connected to an equally malnourished imagination. The smaller our world is—our circle of like friends, our limited environment, our entertainment choices that reflect what we think we already know—the more malnourished our imaginations will be. When this is the case, we are less likely to empathize. Holding onto the jagged edges of reality—rather than airbrushing them to fit our own agenda—is essential if we are to try to honor the humanity of another.

The arts have an almost mystical capacity to teach a sort of attentiveness that forces us to slow down and look beyond brokenness, comprehend its cause, and disclose the image of God in the other. Engaging in the arts can help expand our small worlds and our capacity for empathy as our imaginations are enriched, populated by both the differences and sameness of the human experience. This can lead to a sort of graciousness and patience as we follow a story, a song, a painting to its often surprising conclusion. The arts can be formative, even apocalyptic, as they help us move aside the veil and reveal the complex beauty of fallen human beings.[7] The intentionality that it takes to surrender a bit of our comfort and self-centeredness is also an act of spiritual formation leading toward deeper, richer love for our neighbors.

WHAT IS CHRISTIAN EMPATHY?

In recent years, the term *empathy* has been in vogue. Psychologist Paul Bloom defines empathy as "the process of experiencing the world as others do, or at least as you think they do. To empathize with someone is to put yourself in her shoes, to feel her pain."[8] Empathy is distinctly different from sympathy in that sympathy usually positions us above the other, looking down on them and feeling sorry for them. Empathy asks us to feel what they feel, thus subverting the power differential. Textbook empathy as Bloom defines it only goes so far. Although empathetic identification is a good thing, empathy needs a context and motive for it to help us love our neighbors according to Christ's terms and, ultimately, his sacrificial example.

The Christian understanding of empathy is connected to Christ's teaching on the two greatest commandments: "'Love the Lord your God with all your heart and with all your soul and with all your strength and with all your mind'; and, 'Love your neighbor as yourself.'"[9] Of course, these two loves are intricately connected, as we cannot possibly love our neighbors in a Christlike way without being connected to Christ, the source of love. Christian empathy asks us to be both self-sacrificial and intentional as we reach beyond our usual circles and experiences to identify with those who are outcast, misunderstood, abused. We fail to love God when we neglect to see and cherish the *imago Dei* in other human beings. But this sort of love and its corresponding empathy are very difficult, and we find ourselves often resorting to stereotypes and dismissing the sacredness of other lives, usually out of the impulse to first serve and protect ourselves.

Christian empathy moves beyond both instinctual emotions and prescriptions for how to be a good person. The incarnation of Christ is the most complete, profound embodiment of empathy in history. Christ "became flesh" to share in our existential experience of being human, including our sufferings, as he lived among us.[10] There are many scriptural examples of this, but perhaps one of the most moving is Christ's response after the death of his friend Lazarus in the Gospel of John: "Jesus wept."[11] Christ knew that he would raise Lazarus from the dead, so his weeping was not for his friend's utter end. Instead, he wept with us and for us, lamenting alongside Lazarus's grieving sisters, feeling their pain as well as the tragic impact the curse of death has on all human beings. His weeping was the God-man's act of compassion and empathy, shared mourning for the unavoidable pain of the fallen human condition. In his crucifixion, Christ's capacity for empathy was complete. As he took on human sins and suffered for them, he felt the weight of human grief, despair, and self-inflicted pain. Unlike Christ, we cannot ever fully understand the mind or existential experience of another, yet we are commanded to love them like we would love ourselves. This is an incredible, superhuman feat, and we need imagination to help bridge the gap between ourselves and the other.

"The Good Samaritan" and the Sacred Function of Stories

As we grow our imaginations, we need stories that can convict us of our own sins of omission or commission, enabling us to see the beautiful, complex world of our neighbors as we look beyond ourselves. In showing us how to both identify with our neighbors and bridge the gap between them and ourselves, Christ tells a story of an unexpected empath, the Good Samaritan in Luke 10:25–37. You might remember that this story was told in response to the questions directed at Jesus by an expert in the law. Like the rich young ruler, this man asks Jesus what he must "do to inherit eternal life."[12] Christ responds with a question, asking the expert in the law what was written in the law. The expert correctly responds with these words: "'Love the Lord your God with all your heart and with all your soul and with all your strength and with all your mind'; and, 'Love your neighbor as yourself.'"[13] Jesus admonishes him to follow these laws in order to live. But that is not enough for the religious leader; he wants to confound and humiliate Jesus, so he asks him, "And who is my neighbor?"[14] Christ responds with the story of a man who lays on the side of the road in desperate need of help after being attacked by robbers. Two respected Jewish religious figures, a priest and then a Levite, pass by the wounded man, ignoring his need. Not only do they ignore the man, but they both intentionally "[pass] by on the other side" in order to avoid him. If he is out of sight, he is out of mind.[15] The next traveler, a Samaritan, sees the injured man and "[takes] pity on him," not only bandaging his wounds but lifting him up, placing him on his donkey, and taking him to an inn in order to care for him.[16] He could have just given him money or seen to his wounds and left. Instead, he takes the man in his arms, journeying alongside him, even spending the night at the inn to tend to his needs. The next day, he pays the innkeeper to care for the robbery victim, also offering to pay him more money if the cost of care is greater than what has been paid. After telling the story, Jesus asks the one questioning him yet another question: "Which of these three do you think was a neighbor to the man who fell into the hands of robbers?"[17] When the law expert answers, "The one who had mercy on him," Christ commands him to "go and do likewise."[18]

Christ *commands* the law expert and anyone listening or reading to be more like the Samaritan by showing compassion and following the way of self-sacrifice rather than the way of self-advancement. It is very important to consider the players in this story: two highly regarded Jewish religious figures and one outsider, a Samaritan. As civil rights activist Howard Thurman explains in his sermon on this parable, the Samaritan lived "on the other side of the tracks" both literally and figuratively.[19] Not only was he ethnically different from the Jewish man, but his religious beliefs were considered heretical, syncretistic, and in Jewish eyes, disgraceful. Yet this perceived outcast, this nonbeliever, is the only one in the story who acknowledges the glorious humanity of the injured man. The religious leaders don't want to get tangled up in his affairs; perhaps they are in a hurry or don't want to put themselves at risk. But the Samaritan takes the risk. He slows down, reaches down, and pulls a fellow image bearer up.

Thurman emphasizes that this act of compassion is about a shared human kinship: "We are not related to his position. We are not related to his race. We are not related to his creed. We are not related . . . really, we are not related to his need. But before you disagree, think about it a little. We are not related to his need. We are related to him. To him!"[20] Like the whiskey priest in Greene's novel, another of religious society's outcasts, the Samaritan sees that he is responsible for the man before him because they are connected at the most core level. Thurman continues, arguing that, in its essence, the sacrificial love of the Samaritan echoes the unconditional love of Christ:

> He means that when I love, I go beyond the good and the evil in the object of my affection. I deal with the person, not with the fact that he is lovable or unlovable—if there's such a word—not with the fact that he's gifted or not gifted, not with the fact that he's healthy or unhealthy, not with the fact that he's worthy or unworthy, that he's kind or unkind. All of that becomes secondary. The primary thing is that when I say, "I love," it means that I'm involved in an encounter that leads from the core of me to

the core of you, past all the good things I know about you, all the attractive things I know about you, beyond all of the bad things I know about you.[21]

At the moment that the Samaritan sees the robbery victim on the side of the road, he does not focus on his differences, but he acknowledges their core connection as human beings. He looks beyond the fact that this helpless man probably hates him and that if the situation was reversed, he would quite possibly follow the lead of the priest and Levite, literally walking on the other side of the road in order to avoid a Samaritan. In his analysis of the parable, Pope Benedict XVI emphasizes the subversive nature of Christ's teaching on the concept of "neighbor." The cultural understanding of "neighbor" before the teaching of this parable referred specifically to "the closely-knit community of a single country or people."[22] But in the story, the "limit is now abolished," and "anyone who needs me, and whom I can help, is my neighbour."[23] In a very beautiful, very countercultural manner, Christ shows us that one conventionally seen as an "outsider" is the one who has a heart that "sees where love is needed and acts accordingly."[24]

DIVINE HOSPITALITY

The Good Samaritan's act of empathy is also a divine act of hospitality for the "least of these," someone outside of his ethnicity, religion, and social group.[25] Practicing this kind of radical empathy is also showing hospitality to Christ himself. This practice was taken very literally by Benedictine monks during the Middle Ages. According to *The Rule of St. Benedict*, each monastery is to have a porter stationed at the front gate whose sole vocation is welcoming guests. The porter is not just a doorman; his job is to show embodied hospitality to Christ himself when he comes to visit: "Let all guests who arrive be received like Christ, for He is going to say, 'I came as a guest, and you received Me.' And to all let due honor be shown, especially to the domestics of the faith and to pilgrims."[26] The Benedictine porter is commanded to be humble, with "the head bowed or the whole body prostrated on the ground in adoration of Christ, who indeed is received in their persons."[27] All guests should be treated with dignity, respect, and kindness—but especially "in the reception of the poor and of pilgrims the greatest care and solicitude should be shown, because it is especially in them that Christ is received."[28]

Christian hospitality and empathy go hand in hand, for in order to empathize with one another, we have to be willing to create space or, as Christina Pohl puts it, "make room" for the other mentally and emotionally, just as the Benedictine porters have physically done for their visitors.[29] The more we can imagine ourselves in the shoes and lives of the other, the more we can transcend the constructed, disruptive barriers that often distract us from true human connections. According to Pohl, the act of true Christian hospitality has always been "subversive, countercultural" because it is the act of "transcending social differences and breaking social boundaries."[30] But it can be very difficult to transcend social differences unless we increase our proximity to those who are different, intentionally working to see life through their eyes. In reading, watching, and listening to the stories of others, we enrich our imaginations, creating space for honoring the sacredness in other human beings, no matter how different they are from us.

Honoring the *Imago Dei*

The foundation of all Christian hospitality is the practice of seeing the image of God in other human beings, and this intentional practice is also the gateway to greater empathy. All humans, as Blaise Pascal explains, are glorious in their status of image bearers, even in the midst of their "wretchedness," a result of the fall.[31] Creating space and time to see the intrinsic glory of the other is an act of grace and love, an attempt to see them as Christ sees them. The more we employ this sacred practice, the more we rest in the amazement of our Creator, sensing the beauty and wonder of humanity, created in his image. As C. S. Lewis explains in *The Weight of Glory*, "Next to the Blessed Sacrament itself, your neighbor is the holiest object presented to your senses."[32] Lewis reminds us that, according to the law of Christ, "it may be possible for each to think too much of his own potential glory hereafter; it is hardly possible for him to think too often or too deeply about that of his neighbor."[33] If we intentionally pause to contemplate the glory, beauty, and potential that the image of God carries with it, the result is a divine encounter that leads to a heart transformation of humility and joy. Lewis continues, emphasizing the individual, glorious potential of the other: "The dullest and most uninteresting person you talk to may one day be a creature which, if you saw it now, you would be strongly tempted to worship."[34] Sadly, this glory is often misused, appropriated as an object of worship, turning a neighbor into an idol rather than a coheir of the image of the Creator. On the flip side, the glory that God's image carries with it can easily be ignored or debased.

The healthiest way to respond to the glory residing in fellow image bearers is to see it as Christ's presence within them and honor him by showing love and empathy toward the other. If our default setting is selfishness or a tendency toward idolatry, then it takes something beyond the natural to enable us to be gracious, empathetic, and loving. The Victorian poet Gerard Manley Hopkins very much understood human brokenness, especially the natural tendency to see the world through dark, self-colored lenses. Hopkins's perception was not just that of a fallen human being; it also took on the life-altering shade of clinical depression. More than anything, his illness caused him to struggle to see the image of God within himself. His poems often read like psalms, describing the beauty of a world that is "charged with the grandeur of God" or the devastating pain of feeling abandoned by God.[35]

Through this pain, however, he acknowledges the supernatural source of love for the natural world, other human beings, and the self. In "As Kingfishers Catch Fire," Hopkins focuses on the one quality that defines the behavior and identity of a variety of creatures: "Each mortal thing does one thing and the same."[36] In the poem's second stanza, he relates this to the created purpose of human beings—to do justice and to extend grace:

> I say móre: the just man justices;
> Keeps grace: thát keeps all his goings graces;
> Acts in God's eye what in God's eye he is—
> Chríst—for Christ plays in ten thousand places,
> Lovely in limbs, and lovely in eyes not his
> To the Father through the features of men's faces.[37]

The only way that we, as humans, can begin "to act justly and to love mercy and to walk humbly with your God" is to do this through the power of Christ.[38] A human being must love herself by seeing herself as what she is in God's eye: "Christ."[39] And this same Christ is also in those neighbors that she encounters: "For Christ plays in ten thousand places / Lovely in limbs, and lovely in eyes not his."[40] When we see the "features of men's faces," we see both the Father and the Son, the creators of sacred humanity.[41]

No Room at the Table

Yet these glorious features, the reflection of God's own image, are so often maligned by those who should be able to see their beauty and worth. Reading about the holy humanity of those who have been unjustly treated can wake us up to the need to look more closely at our neighbors' faces. As Jeremy Begbie has noted, engaging the arts can help confront and replace dehumanization with rehumanization.[42] This transformation can occur both for the artist and their audience as they see God's glorious image in the story's abused characters. In Alice Walker's short story "The Welcome Table," we see the devastating results when Christian hospitality and empathy are absent. At the beginning of Walker's story, an elderly Southern Black woman enters a small country church full of white worshippers, sits quietly in the back, and bows her head to pray. Within moments, the church falls silent, and several members of the congregation walk back to her row, bend down, and interrupt her silent prayer by asking her to leave. Eventually, they grab underneath her thin, feeble arms and show her out of the building, unwilling to see her image-bearing status. Instead, they look in condescending anger at her, seeing only "cooks, chauffeurs, maids, mistresses."[43] They also see her as a threat. When glancing at her small, withered face, they "saw jungle orgies in an evil place," and some were "reminded of riotous anarchists looting and raping in the streets."[44] Instead of recognizing a fellow Christian, noting the glory of her sacred being, the congregation only sees objectifying labels created by their own fear and desire for power. She is a cancer that could spread; she must be rooted out.

If the parishioners of the church had been practicing Christian hospitality informed by empathy, they would have seen Christ in their visitor and proceeded to honor her. Denying this respect is an insult to the Creator. In Matthew 25, Christ makes it clear that denying the needs of our neighbor is a denial of Christ himself, for "truly I tell you, whatever you did not do for one of the least of these, you did not do for me."[45] When looking at one another, we must see Christ himself;

his unconditional hospitality and deep empathy are the heart of Christian subversion in a world that often despises perceived difference or weakness. Both Christian hospitality and empathy "resist boundaries that endanger persons by denying their humanness."[46] And in Walker's story of an elderly Black Christian being rejected in the house of the Lord, the author ironically points out that "the protection and promise of God's impartial love grew more not less desirable as the sermon gathered fury and leashed themselves upon their penitent heads."[47] The congregants are so deeply entrenched in their man-made doctrines of exclusivity, extended only to those who fit their superficial mold, that they deny Christ himself in their actions.

"The Welcome Table" is named after an African American spiritual that laments a lack of Christian hospitality and justice and longs for inclusion and equity. The unknown enslaved author cries out for a place at the "welcome table," where finally, finally he can "tell God how you treat me" after withholding his own vengeance and waiting for God's justice.[48] At the "welcome table," the final feast of the Lamb, justice will be done and the "least of these" will be welcomed.[49] In fact, they will have seats of honor. Langston Hughes's powerful 1925 poem, "I, Too," also echoes a desire for true hospitality, a place at the table, a longing that will be met only when Black Americans are seen as glorious, worthy human beings. The speaker in Hughes's poem ironically uses the term *brother* to describe himself, a poignant reminder that all human beings are part of the same family.[50] Although he is a "brother," he has been assigned a substandard place in the greatly deprived white Christian cultural imagination of Jim Crow America. Because the *imago Dei* is not fully acknowledged in this "darker brother" as he works in a white person's home, he is sent to "eat in the kitchen" rather than given a place at what Martin Luther King Jr. referred to as "the table of brotherhood."[51] Yet one day, his beauty and the beauty of his people will be seen, acknowledged, respected, admired. At this point, those who banned him from an earthly "welcome table" will feel shame for their lack of love, moral imagination, and empathy.

THE ARTS AS A PROPHETIC MEANS TO GROW EMPATHY

The congregants in Alice Walker's story and the employers in Langston Hughes's poem both have constricted imaginations, nurtured only by their immediate circle of friends who look, talk, live, and believe as they do. This is tragic, as the ability to imagine is directly connected to the ability to know how to read the world and other people, not just for knowledge, but for wisdom that bears the fruit of love. In order to shift the limited perceptions of these small-minded characters, they need to be shaken up and encounter a prophetic understanding of reality that shatters their illusions. This is what all human beings ultimately need—a prophetic awakening that injects color, life, and reality into our dulled minds and hearts. In his classic work of Old Testament theology, *The Prophetic Imagination*, Walter Brueggemann explains that human beings longing for acceptance and approval can easily be conditioned by the powerful offerings of the in-control status quo, what he refers to as the "empire" or the "royal consciousness."[52] The ideology of the empire easily fits our desires to domesticate our lives and surroundings, making ourselves more comfortable by creating a cocoon of like thinkers who look and live the same way we do. But this is not the way of the Gospels, not the way of loving our neighbors as ourselves. Brueggemann focuses on two things that the poetry and stories of the prophets show us how to do: (1) subvert the status quo by speaking truth and critiquing the unjust way things are and (2) reenergize ourselves by grounding our understanding of truth and hope in Christian doxology. In other words, the "empire" mindset wants us to feel as if things are fine the way they are so that there is no need for change. This keeps the most powerful and socially acceptable in control, often by ignoring or trampling on their less powerful neighbors. But the prophetic message tells us that one of the best ways to critique the false promises of heaven on earth is through lament and mourning. This lament is, however, not without hope, as it is founded on the truth of a gospel kingdom that promises regeneration, a means to see with new eyes and hear with unclogged ears.[53] Brueggemann emphasizes that the very language of the prophets is poetic language, the language of metaphor, which challenges the constricted guidelines of the empire, offering an alternative reality rooted in the way of the kingdom of God.[54] Of course, the artworks discussed in this book are extrabiblical, not themselves directly divinely inspired, yet they are often prophetic in their capacity to critique what is dehumanizing and false, to create a space for empathetic mourning, and to provide language that points toward the future fullness of humanity. In this sense, art that challenges our limited understanding of our neighbors and attempts to highlight the God-given glory within them is prophetic, a means to enriching our imaginations.

PROPHETIC EMPATHY IN FICTION

Our tendency to resist the prophetic call for reality, compassion, and empathy is so normalized that it is often invisible to us. In her essays, Flannery O'Connor refers to normalized sins as "distortions," and she believes that we are so firmly entrenched in our denial of sin that it sometimes takes a form of violence to prophetically wake us up.[55] O'Connor's stories often contain self-righteous, self-satisfied, and spiritually blind Southern cultural Christians whose pride prevents them from being able to see the wonder and sanctity of the *imago Dei*. For instance, in "Revelation," Mrs. Turpin sits in a doctor's waiting room humming along with Christian radio tunes, thanking God in her mind that she is not a Black person or the "white trash" that she observes in the waiting room alongside her.[56] She is smugly unaware of her racism, classism, and self-righteousness, yet because of it, she cannot truly see her neighbors as they are. In O'Connor's most widely read story, "A Good Man Is Hard to Find," the protagonist is a similar character, an elderly white Southern woman who sees her own self-worth in the fact that she is a "lady," a Southern belle who knows how to dress appropriately and possesses good manners.[57] In this sense, she has uncritically absorbed the shallow value system of the "empire."[58] She manipulates her family into driving to her chosen vacation destination, and on the way, she unintentionally causes the family to have a car accident. Standing on the side of the road, the family encounters the serial killer only known as The Misfit and his band of ragtag assailants. In the most poignant section of the story, the grandmother is left alone with her killer, trying to manipulate him with empty, false praises such as "You're a good man!" and "You have good blood in your veins!"[59] The Misfit does not buy it, and neither do O'Connor's readers.

But the narrative shifts in a mysterious and beautiful way when the grandmother begins to speak of Jesus. Initially, she is using the name of Christ in the same hollow way that she has used her social status. But quite surprisingly, The Misfit begins to admit that he longs to know whether Jesus truly "raised the dead," as he recognizes that this possible reality is the defining factor of truth and meaning—or the absence of both: "'Jesus was the only One that ever raised the dead,' The Misfit continued, 'and He shouldn't have done it. He thown everything off balance. If He did what He said, then it's nothing for you to do but thow away everything and follow Him, and if He didn't, then it's nothing for you to do but enjoy the few minutes you got left the best way you can—by killing somebody or burning down his house or doing some other meanness to him. No pleasure but meanness,' he said and his voice had become almost a snarl."[60] As he continues speaking, The Misfit's voice "cracks" and the grandmother's "head clears"; she is finally able to look beyond herself in order to see and hear his pain.[61] At this moment, she reaches out and touches him, exclaiming, "Why you're one of my babies. You're one of my own children!"[62] Unlike her previous conversation with The Misfit, this endearing cry comes from a place of honesty, compassion, and empathy rather than a place of manipulation. The hypocritical old socialite puts her life even more at risk by choosing to show love to someone who is deemed unlovable; she sees him as a member of her own family. Like the whiskey priest who felt an "overwhelming responsibility" for the "pious woman," the grandmother feels "responsible for the man before her and joined to him by ties of kinship which have their roots deep in the mystery she has merely been prattling about so far."[63]

According to the author, the grandmother "does the right thing, she makes the right gesture."[64] The grandmother's "right gesture" is manifest when she begins to see the image of God in her captor's face. O'Connor further explains that the grandmother's response is "a gesture which somehow made contact with mystery."[65] The deep mystery of Christ's love and our shared family connections come together in this moment of profound empathy and selflessness. If you know the story, you know that O'Connor does not provide us with a formulaic feel-good ending: The Misfit immediately shoots and kills the grandmother when she gently touches him. He recognizes the change in her and feels threatened by it, knowing that if he begins to acknowledge the very "mystery" that empowers her compassion, he would have to change his life, to transform, to "thow away everything and follow Him."[66] In his tender song written from the point of view of The Misfit, Sufjan Stevens claims that the grandmother's actions leave him "creased."[67] His soul receives a permanent wrinkle that will hopefully never straighten out, and it just might save him. The most famous line of the story speaks to The Misfit's paradoxical spiritual sensitivity: "'She would of been a good woman,' The Misfit said, 'if it had been somebody there to shoot her every minute of her life.'"[68] In the pivotal moment at the end of the encounter between the old lady and her killer, the grandmother truly sees The Misfit, and in seeing him, she loves him. This is not a natural action but a supernatural one. How hard would it be to love your very real enemy, the man holding a gun on you and your loved ones? The grandmother is transformed in this moment, overlooking the immediate threat to her life in order to focus on the glorious personhood of an image bearer.

O'Connor's story is ultimately about the need for an impassioned empathy that can only occur through the power of the very "Mystery" that has created us all in his image. In "A Good Man Is Hard to Find," it takes an act of abrupt violence to shake the grandmother into submission as she looks past her idolatrous categories of class, comfort, and appearance. O'Connor saw all human beings, including herself, as hardheaded and hard-hearted, so often blind and deaf to the needs of those around them. The grandmother's imagination only created space for considering the holy humanity of the depraved Misfit when she was thrust close enough to see and hear his suffering.

INTENTIONAL EMPATHY

Although O'Connor frequently uses violence to usher in a prophetic moment, human beings are, of course, created to have the capacity to develop a more empathetic imagination without being subjected to violence. But we need to spend time intentionally learning the patience and attentiveness that can enable us to see and hear the glory in our brothers and sisters. O'Connor's hypocritical grandmother did not recognize her spiritual blindness and deafness until it was almost too late, but a dramatic encounter with the other led to her change. The arts provide us with admittedly less drastic opportunities for encountering, listening to, and truly seeing our neighbors. As we read, watch, or listen to the story of another, we can begin to discern the spiritual "kinship" between image bearers.[69] The intentionality that it takes to surrender a bit of our own default self-centeredness is a sacrificial act of spiritual formation.

Engaging with art that prophetically wakes us up can become a regular part of our spiritual formation, jolting us from our typically self-concerned spiritual stupors. In his oft-quoted Kenyon College commencement speech, author David Foster Wallace argues that self-centeredness is "our default setting, hard-wired into our boards at birth."[70] He issues a charge to the graduates, asking them to think about the real-life, human value of their liberal arts education. In doing this, he connects critical thinking with the capacity for empathy. He then candidly relates how the self-centeredness that is at the core of human beings can lead to an internal emotional outburst when standing in line at the grocery store: "And who are all these people in my way? And look at how repulsive most of them are, and how stupid and cow-like and dead-eyed and nonhuman they seem in the checkout line, or at how annoying and rude it is that people are talking loudly on cell phones in the middle of the line. And look at how deeply and personally unfair this is."[71] The painful honesty of Wallace's words reflects the inner frustration many of us feel when encountering nameless others in our way. He then challenges the graduates to recognize their self-centeredness while working to acknowledge the pain suffered by others as a large part of seeing their humanity. He knows, however, that it is "extremely difficult to stay alert and attentive, instead of getting hypnotized by the constant monologue inside your own head."[72] The default setting is all too easy, and its existence is invisible unless intentionally acknowledged: "If you're automatically sure that you know what reality is, and you are operating on your default setting, then you, like me, probably won't consider possibilities that aren't annoying and miserable. But if you really learn how to pay attention, then you will know there are other options. It will actually be within your power to experience a crowded, hot, slow, consumer-hell type situation as not only meaningful, but sacred, on fire with the same force that made the stars: love, fellowship, the mystical oneness of all things deep down."[73] It is fascinating to hear Wallace speak of the "sacred" and "meaningful," as he did not subscribe to any specific religious faith. At the same time, his words about the "mystical oneness" sound Buddhist, or perhaps unknowingly, they echo some of O'Connor's referencing of the "Mystery" that engenders kinship between human beings. Regardless of his professed core beliefs, Wallace claims that recognizing the fragile, broken, and beautiful humanity in another person, even just a seemingly random person at the supermarket, is a sacred act. He then connects the way we see other human beings as determined by what or whom we worship, because "in the day-to-day trenches of adult life, there is actually no such thing as atheism. There is no such thing as not worshipping. Everybody worships. The only choice we get is what to worship."[74] Wallace explains that if we are worshipping money, beauty, and fame, as well as worshipping other human beings as we use them as objects for fulfillment, we will fail to be attentive. These types of worship are all variations of that "default" setting, a natural adherence to the empire mentality.

Common Grace Abounds

Although Wallace prophetically diagnoses the symptoms, he does not use theological terminology or provide a lasting remedy. This prophetic speech is also a reminder that not everyone who has a heart that "sees where love is needed and acts accordingly"[75] is a follower of Christ. In choosing a Samaritan as the example to follow in his parable, Jesus shows us that all humans are made in God's image, and because of this, even those who are not believers can do good things, speak truth, and show kindness. The figure of the Good Samaritan is a reminder that common grace abounds and that we can learn good things from our non-Christian neighbors. Sometimes our non-Christian neighbors are better neighbors than we are, and God can use them to teach us. Like David Foster Wallace, they may have a prophetic sensibility, and the Lord can use them to teach truth, grace, and mercy—even if they do not understand that he is the Beginning and the End of these things.

Reading as Loving

Engaging in narratives through reading, watching performances (film, television, theater), and listening to music enables us to flex the muscles of our imagination as we enter the story of the other. While engaging the arts, we often find human commonalities while privileging the stories of others, connecting back to our shared *imago Dei* being. Although we have these rich opportunities to grow emotionally and spiritually for the sake of expanding our empathy, we have been culturally trained as consumers to treat our practices of reading, watching, and listening as mere acts of consumption in order to get a quick fix of enjoyment.[76] We gravitate toward narratives that we like, and we take what we want out of them for the sake of entertainment. Although these tendencies are very natural, this form of reading does not stretch the imagination in a way that helps us see ourselves more clearly or learn to love our neighbors more deeply. It is a stumbling block to the kind of mature spiritual formation that leads to deeper empathy.

At the beginning of each of the college courses that I teach, I emphasize that the authors of the books we are reading—whether the books were written in 1603 or 1994—are human beings created in God's image. These image bearers have something important to say to us, and if we submit ourselves to their voices, we will have the privilege of seeing life through their eyes. Scott Huelin calls this practice a "hermeneutics of hospitality," the act of charitable interpretative reading that will enable us to "listen and receive."[77] Huelin also reminds us that, as readers of culture, we are also sojourners, strangers entering a unique and foreign "country" each time we open a book, watch a film, or listen to a new song.[78] We have been invited in, and we need to be attentive, gracious guests. In this sense, the act of attentive reading is an act of love itself. These encounters have the potential to lead to an enriched, informed imagination and a transformed heart and mind.

IMAGINING OUR NEIGHBORS AS OURSELVES

Charitable reading, watching, and listening is a discipline that can lead to the development of a more empathetic imagination. Some texts—be they film or literature—model the way of empathy for us as we witness the before and after of a central character's transformation once they have started to truly love their neighbors. Prophetic works of art that help us empathize must also present the human condition accurately, resisting the popular trends toward romanticism or cynicism.[79] When we encounter the complexity of the human experience through watching the transformation of fictional characters, we also see the potential for goodness, beauty, and truth in other human beings. At the same time, we can be convicted by the raw honesty of our darkest motives being reflected on the page or screen—and this conviction can lead to empathy with those who share our condition. Good art challenges us into having eyes to see our neighbors, and many times, these neighbors look, speak, and live very differently than we do. Sometimes they might even be considered our enemies. But art that feeds our imagination in the way of empathy always reminds us that these human beings are complex, beautiful, and worthy of love. Their worth lies not in what they do but in how and why they were created. Art that enables us to imagine our neighbors as ourselves continually points back to the greatest Artist. The Source of creation has gifted many artists with the prophetic ability to speak the truth in creative, challenging, life-altering ways. In reading, watching, and listening to their offerings, we have the blessed opportunity to expand our minds and our hearts for the sake of empathetic love.

Chapter One

ART AS A MODEL FOR THE EMPATHETIC IMAGINATION

How Stories Reflect Our Longings

In her reflections on writing "A Good Man Is Hard to Find," O'Connor reminds us that the real heart of writing is found in the "lines of spiritual motion" that mold and reveal the hearts of her characters—lines that are "usually invisible."[1] In light of this, she cautions us against "misreading" her most well-known story, "A Good Man Is Hard to Find," by looking for and at the wrong things: "And in this story you should be on the lookout for such things as the action of grace in the grandmother's soul, and not for the dead bodies."[2] O'Connor is referencing our cultural training to crave sensation and focus merely on the rudimentary, visible plot rather than seeking to lift the veil that discloses the invisible, yet most real, spiritual dimension. The form of any traditional narrative invites readers and viewers on a journey that leads us to a final disclosure of truth and meaning. Our desire for an ending is an eschatological one as we lean toward the promise of both resolution and revelation.[3] These moments of final disclosure are directly related to either a change in a character or a change in *our* perception of a character. Without this, we would have no stories. Although we have been conditioned by many mainstream blockbuster movies (and other forms of streamlined entertainment) to focus on special effects and pretty faces, the real meat of any worthy story lies in the reader/viewer's deepened understanding of the motives and morality of a character that leads to change, conflict, or stasis.

In O'Connor's work, violence often precedes these moments of deepened understanding, shocking both her characters and her readers into an apocalyptic moment of self-exposure and discovery of the earthly and heavenly Other. The most important character changes in "A Good Man Is Hard to Find" are not the deaths of its secondary characters but the shifting internal landscapes of both the grandmother and The Misfit. These characters, like the story's readers, have had their spiritual sensitivities numbed—so much so that sin, be it the grandmother's religious hypocrisy or The Misfit's nihilism, has become normalized. Regarding this instance and many others, O'Connor famously says that "you have to make your vision apparent by shock—to the hard of hearing you shout, and for the almost-blind you draw large and startling figures."[4] The artist must make the invisible—the truly important spiritual lines of reality—visible by shocking us into attentiveness.

O'Connor's storytelling methods, both her construction of plot and her development of eccentric characters, are wonderfully stylized and extreme. But not all stories use literal violence to lead us to the final moment of revelation. On some level, however, a sort of violence, dissonance, and disruption must occur in the form of an internal or external conflict that leads to character change. Like the reader, a character must be shaken up, disrupted, perhaps even forced into seeing a new reality or state of being. And these various forms of character change guide readers into unexpected revelations about the characters.

Perhaps every viewer has watched a television show, made initial judgments about which characters she did or did not like, and then become deeply stirred upon learning their backstories and witnessing unexpected behavior. I remember when several of my most culturally savvy friends recommended the television series *Friday Night Lights* to me, and I could not imagine having any interest in a show about a high school football coach, his players, his family, and the small town that sees Friday-night football as an essential component of the good life. This all seemed so familiar, so boring, so shallow. My own high school's football team won state championships under the guidance of my best friend's father, a decorated and highly respected coach. Although I did attend one football game my freshman year, eager to ascend the high school hierarchy by showing my support of the untouchable players and their bubbly cheerleader girlfriends, my attentions and allegiances soon switched to makeshift punk rock shows, wearing all black, and boycotting all things relating to high school football and school spirit. Because of this, I thought that I knew the people depicted in *Friday Night Lights*, and my childish high school prejudices seeped into my adult perceptions of both people and art. Even so, I took the plunge and soon fell in love with the Taylor family and participated in their growth as I, along with Coach and Tammy Taylor, learned the painful backstory of the annoyingly Byronic Tim Riggins; discovered that Tara, the popular bad girl, just wanted to be unconditionally loved; and so on.[5] Watching this show and growing to love these characters truly convicted me. As much as popular, white, suburban folks are certainly not often thought of as unfairly othered in contemporary American society, they had been othered for a long time in my own mind. I had forgotten to remember that God's image resides within them in their status as complex, glorious human beings. *Friday Night Lights*, a masterfully drawn portrait of beautiful yet broken small-town Texas inhabitants, is just one example of the way the narrative structure of a good work of art teaches us how to be more patient, understanding, empathetic, and loving.

Like O'Connor's seminal story and *Friday Night Lights*, there are many works of art that go beyond just asking us to empathize with their characters. They provide a parabolic model for the practice of empathy, illustrating intent, action, and final impact. Central characters in works of art as seemingly disparate as the nineteenth-century poem "This Lime-Tree Bower My Prison," contemporary films *A Beautiful Day in the Neighborhood* and *Lars and the Real Girl*, and minimalist short story "A Small, Good Thing" each model the act of sacrificially loving their neighbors as themselves, taking us step by step through the sometimes painful yet always redemptive process. In looking closely at each of these, we can see how engaging these transformative stories can be a means to love.

"THIS LIME-TREE BOWER MY PRISON"

The classic Coleridge poem "This Lime-Tree Bower My Prison" is a primer on the transformation of the imagination for good rather than evil. If all would take time to read, contemplate, and act upon the deeply Christian assertions of this poem, perhaps conversation would be more kind, productive, and loving. Coleridge's poem is a short narrative that instructs readers how to follow what Christ deemed the second most important commandment, to "love your neighbor as yourself."[6] Coleridge uses the poetic form to take us into his own mind, making himself vulnerable as he exposes his tendency toward envy, resentment, and even hate. This focus on the truth of a selfish yet very human knee-jerk response allows us to bear witness to his change of mind and heart as he begins to see his neighbor through the eyes of empathetic love. In loving his neighbor with a transformed imagination, he is also learning how to better love God.

In a note directly preceding Coleridge's poem, he writes that his dear friends Charles and Mary Lamb had come from London to visit him in the Lake District. The poet spent joyful hours mapping out their adventures together, yet shortly before his friends' arrival, he had an accident and injured his leg, preventing him from going on their shared outing. Instead, he is left alone to ponder his misfortune, albeit in a glorious setting that he fails to notice. The more he imagines his friends' explorations, the more resentful and self-pitying he becomes, and we soon see the famous Romantic poet in his most raw emo phase. "This Lime-Tree Bower My Prison" is a record of Coleridge's emotional and spiritual journey as he moves from anger to contemplation, to wonder, to love.

The poem has a wonderfully whiny start as Coleridge shows readers the power that emotion (in this case, bitterness and anger) has on human perception: "Well, they are gone, and here I must remain, / This lime-tree bower my prison!"[7] Although a lime-tree bower (in the British Lake District, no less) is traditionally associated with the idyllic rather than the carceral, the pouting poet sees it through distorted lenses of disappointment, jealousy, and resentment. He becomes even more dramatic as he fumes over the fact that these are friends who he may never more "meet again"—especially as they have chosen to leave him to his prison while enjoying the beautiful settings of the countryside "of which I told."[8]

Coleridge's self-pity commingles with near hatred of his friends as he imagines all of the fun things that they are doing, the "beauties and feelings" that they are experiencing without him.[9] In typical Romantic fashion, he also imagines the comfort he could find in future years, remembering his time as a "worshipper of Nature" alongside his visitors.[10] His sense of temporal grief becomes increasingly dramatic as he imagines having no shared memories of this day in the future years when "age had dimm'd mine eyes to blindness!"[11] Of course, his feelings of disappointment and even anger are understandable. They reflect the inherent selfishness in the human heart, the feelings that we often have but rarely share with others. And this acute, momentary hatred of his friends also springs from his own hurt and insecurity. He feels betrayed and used as his friends "wander in gladness . . . to that still roaring dell, of which I told."[12] How dare they enjoy this day without him, the architect of its delights? He even wonders if he might never see them again as he spirals more deeply into self-pity.

But the narrative soon shifts, following a sudden change in Coleridge's perspective. Once he begins to imaginatively visualize the delight upon his friends' faces and remembers especially Charles's great love of nature (which he has longed for while in the city), the poet's feelings abruptly change. He thinks fondly on the "gentle heart" of his friend "to whom no sound is dissonant which tells of Life."[13] Coleridge must remind himself that he loves his friend deeply, and he begins to empathize with Charles as soon as he is able to envision himself in his friend's place, enjoying nature after many years pent up in the soul-crushing city. Coleridge begins to forget himself, focusing on Charles's great joy, and this newly acquired empathy also leads to the poet's own happiness: "A delight / Comes sudden on my heart, and I am glad / As if I myself were there!"[14] Once his imagination has somehow dispelled his hatred and anger, he can see that the lime-tree bower that he is sitting in is no prison. Rather, it is a thing of great beauty. He realizes that his immediate environs are gifts in themselves that have been ignored as he has "not mark'd much that has sooth'd me."[15] His perception shifts dramatically, and he is now able to both empathize with another and see reality more clearly.

Although Coleridge is not sharing these experiences with his friends, he is able to imagine as if he was—and his love for his absent visitors becomes selfless rather than self-serving. Coleridge, unlike fellow Romantic poet William Blake, does not deify the imagination. In Coleridge's writing, there is a deep connection between the spiritual realm and the imagination—and the imagination cannot be used *correctly* to enable us to see more clearly until it is somehow connected to that larger spiritual reality. This happens in "This Lime-Tree Bower" as the poet understands the sacredness of his friends' own love of nature—and this manages to take him outside of himself. In this deeply personal poem, we see that the imagination can be either destructive or edifying, leading to hatred or to love. The poet chooses the way of love via empathy and, in doing so, instructs his readers how to do the same.

It is important to note that when the poet has been hurt, he also has the potential to cause hurt. Thankfully, he does not share his anger and bitterness with his friends, and his emotional and spiritual transformation takes place before he encounters them again. Although Coleridge has not been severely abused by his friends, he feels that he has been. And even this minor injury launches him into an initial reaction of resentment and anger. Although this poem is about the poet's own movement from anger to empathy toward others, it is also important to consider that he needs compassion and understanding himself, even if his responses come from pain rather than love. Although his anger becomes irrational, his status as a glorious image bearer never diminishes, and extending empathy to him only comes by acknowledging this.

A Beautiful Day in the Neighborhood

The 2019 film *A Beautiful Day in the Neighborhood* explores the intentionality it takes to acknowledge God's image in and develop empathy for someone whose history of abuse and neglect leads him to patterns of abuse and self-protective cynicism himself. Although the popular film is about legendary children's show host Fred Rogers, it is not a movie for children. The story starts with the familiar sounds and sights of the *Mister Rogers' Neighborhood* set, including bright colors, trolley music, and the iconic, cheerful host taking off his cardigan. Despite this opening scene, viewers soon realize that the film will not be focusing on Mr. Rogers's show. The nostalgic opening is a framing technique employed to introduce the *real* story of a friend of Mr. Rogers, a reporter for *Esquire* magazine named Lloyd Vogel. The first image we see of Lloyd is both comical and alarming. On his storyboard, Mr. Rogers shares a photo of Lloyd's battered face and troubled eyes among the cheerful images of familiar puppet characters. The ever-compassionate host then says the following to his viewers: "Someone has hurt my friend Lloyd—and not just his face. He is having a hard time forgiving the person who hurt him. Do you know what forgiveness means? It's a decision we make to release a person from the feelings of anger we have against them. Sometimes it's hardest to forgive the ones we love."[16] Although Mr. Rogers's tone and pattern of articulation sound as if he is speaking to children, he is actually speaking to the members of the adult viewing audience that, in reality, probably struggle more with forgiveness than do the children for whom his television show was intended. Lloyd Vogel is an adult who has been deeply hurt and, we soon learn, lives with the relational and psychological consequences of this wounding, eventually collapsing under the weight of them. But for now, we only see the deeply sad eyes and wounded face of a man who Mr. Rogers describes, not as an abuser or a jerk, but as a human being who endured pain that led to even more pain. Because of this framing technique, viewers are asked to view Lloyd, a very unlikable character, through the kind, understanding, and gracious eyes of Fred Rogers.

The narrative shifts to Lloyd's perspective as he grudgingly attends his sister's wedding along with his wife and infant son. Soon after Lloyd arrives, he encounters his father, and Lloyd is unwilling and unable to engage in any sort of small talk with him. Lloyd's estranged father, Jerry, has obviously had a bit too much to drink, and he almost immediately mentions Lloyd's mother, whose suffering and death shaped Lloyd's childhood. With little hesitation, Lloyd swings at his dad, and the two engage in a fistfight, leaving Lloyd's face bloody and bruised. At this point, Lloyd is an unlikable character, partially because of our minimal knowledge of his story. But Mr. Rogers's words are a reminder that there is more than meets the eye here: "Someone has hurt my friend Lloyd—and not just his face."[17] His attention to Lloyd's pain is a reminder that Lloyd, although wounded, is someone worthy of friendship and compassion.

The scene quickly changes, taking us back to Mr. Rogers's television set, where he asks his viewers, "Have you ever felt the way Lloyd does? So angry that you want to hurt someone or yourself? I know I have."[18] He proceeds to tell the story of how he was bullied for being chubby as a child. In this beautiful scene, Mr. Rogers practices a type of emotional attachment, even with his anonymous viewers. He claims to "look through the lens of the camera to a single child, trying to be fully present to their needs."[19] Fred Rogers makes it a practice to be intentionally present in all his encounters with other humans, both through a television camera and in real life. His practices of attachment are reminiscent of what psychologists Daniel J. Siegel and Mary Hartzell call "attunement" and "coherence."[20] When a parent is "attuned" to their child, they can enter the child's state of mind in order to understand their needs: why he is crying, why she is sad, and so on. From this first step, a parent can then provide a sense of "coherence" for the child by renarrating their experiences in order to make sense of their emotional reaction. In this instance, children will feel safe, supported, and loved. *A Beautiful Day in the Neighborhood* highlights the way Mr. Rogers practices a form of attachment by sharing his own childhood trauma, forging a connection among himself, Lloyd, and the children viewing as he makes himself vulnerable while relating a like experience. This is a form of empathy, a determined effort made to relate, connect, and humanize. The more viewers learn about Lloyd's life, the more they understand his anger and neglect issues with both his father and his young wife. Lloyd's father abandoned him, his sister, and his mother after she was diagnosed with a terminal illness. Jerry had been cheating on his wife even before the diagnosis, and he finally decided to leave once he learned of her fate. The two children then had to care for their mother, witnessing her painful death. This abandonment and complete lack of attachment is at the very heart of Lloyd's trauma, manifesting itself as anger and withdrawal.

In the film, Mr. Rogers is a guide for learning how to be attentive enough to the wounded other to develop empathy even while they are angry. Lloyd contacts Mr. Rogers's staff in order to do a brief interview with him, although he is not delighted to be interviewing the host of a "hokey kids' show."[21] Lloyd's reputation as a harsh critic and a hothead journalist precedes him, and we learn that Mr. Rogers is the only person contacted by *Esquire* willing to be interviewed. Lloyd reluctantly accepts the assignment. A few days later, Lloyd is surprised by a phone call from Fred Rogers, who tells him that "the most important thing in the world to me right now" is "talking on the telephone to Lloyd Vogel."[22]

When Lloyd first encounters Mr. Rogers in person, he witnesses the show host giving his undivided attention to a child sent by the Make-A-Wish Foundation. The child appears withdrawn, even frightened, until Rogers physically bends down and speaks to him on his level, relating the child's fear to his own. The show's producers are frustrated because he practices these kinds of behaviors daily, always causing production to fall behind schedule. Rogers's gentle attention soon turns to Lloyd and, in particular, Lloyd's bruised face. He sees the pain in Lloyd's eyes, and he draws a fragment of his story out of him, patiently waiting for the rest to be revealed. This patience is, in itself, a spiritual practice, instructive for both Lloyd and the film's viewers.

As Lloyd interviews Mr. Rogers on several more occasions, his trust slowly grows, although it is often laced with cynicism about Mr. Rogers's niceness. This cynicism turns to protective anger when Mr. Rogers introduces him to his famous puppet, Daniel, and then asks Lloyd about the ragged stuffed toy from his nursery days. On finding out that Lloyd was given a stuffed rabbit by his mother, Rogers kindly presses for more details, turning his interview into an exploration of Lloyd's damaged childhood. At this point, Lloyd erupts in anger, this space of his wounded soul too tender to touch. Like so many of us, in his anger, Lloyd uses irony as a defense mechanism, exclaiming, "It's been a real pleasure!"[23]

Although Lloyd abruptly dismisses Fred and leaves his apartment, this does not alter Fred's calm, kind manner when again speaking with Lloyd. Directly before the scene of Lloyd's angry outburst, we see a clip of Mr. Rogers on the *Arsenio Hall Show*, where he says that his focus is to let those in his audience know that "each one of us is precious."[24] Although Mr. Rogers does not overtly say this, viewers know that the empathy he continually extends toward Lloyd stems from a generous capacity to imagine Lloyd's own broken childhood, even when seeing the unresolved pain. These actions are also instructive, as this work of art reminds us that seeing the "precious" value of each life is a deliberate action.

Mr. Rogers hopes for Lloyd to know that he is "precious," just as he hopes this for his child viewers. In a sadly comic scene, Mr. Rogers's manager, Bill, tells Lloyd that "he loves people like you."[25] When Lloyd asks him what kind of person Bill thinks he is, Bill simply asks, "You don't care for humanity, do you?"[26] Lloyd's experiences of abandonment and abuse have led to deep distrust, yet his cynicism is viewed not as a threat by Mr. Rogers but as an opportunity to help

Lloyd see that he is indeed "precious." A friend of the real Fred Rogers, priest Henri Nouwen, explains, "If you know you are Beloved of God, you can live with an enormous amount of success and an enormous amount of failure without losing your identity, because your identity is that you are Beloved."[27] Lloyd Vogel relies on protective cynicism to distance himself from others, knowing that relationships can fail, burn, and hurt. Like all children, Lloyd would have seen his parents as models of God in his life—and, devastatingly, one of them abandoned him, throwing him into an adult space of managing his dying mother's suffering. It makes sense that Lloyd does not feel "beloved of God" or of most human beings, including his own family.

Fred Rogers's own profound capacity for empathy, both in real life and then reflected in film, was influenced by his relationship with Henri Nouwen, a personal hero whom he met in 1984 and developed a friendship with over the next twelve years. In a sense, Rogers was mentored by Nouwen, and he claims that the priest helped him "grow into a thoughtful person who cares about the essentials of life."[28] At one point, Rogers wrote to Nouwen about his own feelings of pain and betrayal in response to a negative article that had been written about him. Nouwen's response contained the kind of empathy and attachment techniques that we see in Rogers's own behavior: He tells Fred that receiving a letter like this would have hurt him as well. He then encourages Fred not to argue with the author of the article, knowing that "some of the criticisms we simply have to suffer and see as invitations to enter deeper into the heart of Jesus."[29] The letter ends with Nouwen writing, "Let us pray for each other, that we remain faithful and not become bitter and that we continue to return to the center where we can find the joy and peace that is not of this world."[30] In her film, director Marielle Heller creates a realistic portrait of Rogers's real-world faithfulness while narrating and teaching the truth of his intentional acts of love.

In Tom Hanks's portrayal of Rogers, we see a man who exudes both joy and peace. He is not merely nice; he is deeply kind, centered, and not easily shaken. This leads Lloyd to ask Fred's wife, Joanne, what it is like to be married to a "living saint."[31] She explains that both she and Fred dislike this label because Fred's centered peace and empathic behavior are the result of a practice. Rogers was not born this way; he worked at it very intentionally for many years, thus habituating an inner calm that radiates true kindness. Joanne's explanations of

Rogers's practice again sound very much influenced by Nouwen's own monastic practices: "He reads scripture, he swims laps, prays for people by name, writes letters . . . hundreds of letters."[32] In this simple list, viewers are reminded that the practice of praying for others and writing letters for their benefit is a way to "in humility value others above yourselves."[33] Seeing the outcome of this practice is moving, convicting—and perhaps most importantly, instructive. While watching, we follow Fred's pattern of empathizing with Lloyd. This exercise, if reflected upon and repeated, can become transformational in the lives of viewers.

Although Lloyd is deeply unkind to Fred, Fred manages to focus on the hurt he sees in his friend rather than his own hurt. Like Coleridge, he can transcend an oft-normal focus on the self to truly see the pain and need of the other. He also actively chooses to see the beautiful things within Lloyd and acknowledge them, label them, and increase their visibility. When Lloyd asks Fred if it is too much of a "burden" to listen to other people's problems, Fred thanks him for asking, noting that he is "grateful" for Lloyd's "compassion."[34] Fred remembers both the hurt and the compassion as he comforts Lloyd when learning that his abusive, estranged father has been hospitalized.

Avoiding the present realities of his painful past, Lloyd chooses to travel to Pittsburgh to see Fred Rogers rather than stay at the hospital with his family. But perhaps a visit with Fred is actually a way to deal with his past, his pain, and his own estranged father. As Lloyd and Fred sit across from each other in a Chinese restaurant, Fred encourages Lloyd to "take a minute to think of all the people that loved you into being."[35] They both sit silently, Lloyd's head bowed, all eyes in the restaurant upon them—a famous man and a sullen man-child. The camera slowly moves back to Mr. Rogers's face, and he looks into the camera, directly into the eyes of the film's viewers for most of the long, full minute. At the end of that time, Lloyd's face, which has long been hardened with resentment, fear, and pain, is finally covered with tears. His hardness begins to soften. Rather than embarrassing Lloyd by noting his tears, Fred says, "Thank you for doing that with me. I feel so much better," thus shifting agency back to Lloyd.[36]

The tears continue to flow as Lloyd finds his wife, who is understandably angry, and reveals the source of his own pain while confessing the ways in which he has damaged their relationship because of it.

He weeps while she embraces him. Just as Mr. Rogers has made space for Lloyd's difficult, often chaotic feelings, Lloyd begins to make room for his own feelings. Once he can see himself more clearly, his capacity to see others begins to grow. Miraculously, he has a beautiful final moment with his father, who, on his deathbed, sincerely apologizes for his cruelty. Jerry's voice is full of grief for the years spent without his children: "I'm just now starting to figure out how to live my life."[37] Jerry is redeemed by the love he received from his son, who is redeemed by the love that he receives from Fred Rogers. And as we watch this film, we see the method, the action, and the result of Mr. Rogers's capacity for loving a seemingly unlovable neighbor. Like the children of Mr. Rogers's show, adult viewers also feel seen, loved, and heard because, to some extent, every human being is like Lloyd—broken and angry. In seeing the way love transforms, not in an abstract, ethereal way but as a result of real-life, concrete behaviors, we are inspired to learn to love in a similar way.

With Jerry's final words, viewers are once again reminded that Mr. Rogers's lessons about learning to manage our emotions, learning to love ourselves and others, and learning to make room for the glory and wonder of the other are all things that it takes a lifetime to learn. Human beings are the best when we realize that we need to become more like children: "Truly I tell you, unless you change and become like little children, you will never enter the kingdom of heaven."[38] In doing this, we acknowledge our neediness and, hopefully, learn to trust. The film ends with Mr. Rogers's well-known mantra: "You made today a very special day by just being you. There is no one in the world like you, and I like you just the way you are."[39] These words, relaying the sacred truth that all human beings are "beloved of God," help rehumanize those who, like Lloyd, have been dehumanized.[40] In *A Beautiful Day in the Neighborhood*, Mr. Rogers's children's lessons are the result of an intentional, habitual practice of empathy, and they lead to an attachment that breathes life into those who listen, including the members of the film's audience.

"A Small, Good Thing"

Another powerful and quiet narrative that teaches us how unexpected yet intentional attentive listening can lead to empathy is "A Small,

Good Thing" by minimalist short story author Raymond Carver. Carver's story is a harrowing and tender depiction of grief, loneliness, and the conflict that can develop when these two deep human sadnesses are not recognized. It further illustrates the ways that a narrative can instruct us and shape us into thinking beyond ourselves. Unlike *A Beautiful Day in the Neighborhood*, this story does not contain an obvious hero who has spent years learning the means to deeper, more Christlike empathy. "A Small, Good Thing" takes readers in a jarringly different direction, showing how empathy is possible even when dysfunctional, wounded humans crash into each other. It is possible for the initial violence of word and deed to transition into a kind of healing.

Carver's story begins with a happy young mother visiting a bakery to order a birthday cake for her son, Scotty, who will be "eight years old next Monday."[41] The child's mother, Anne, feels slightly uncomfortable in the baker's presence because "the baker was not jolly."[42] Yet in his awkward silences, the baker does create space for her words, her presence: "He wiped his hands on his apron as he listened to her. He kept his eyes down on the photographs and let her talk. He let her take her time. He'd just come to work, and he'd be there all night, baking, and he was in no real hurry."[43] Ann leaves quickly after giving him the order.

On Monday, Scotty's birthday, he is walking to school with two friends when he is hit by a car. The driver waits to see that Scotty stands up, and then he drives away, taking no responsibility for the accident. The "birthday boy," as Carver calls him, walks home after the accident and tells his mother what just occurred.[44] She is understandably alarmed, and soon after Scotty renarrates the accident, he collapses on the couch, unresponsive. Anne and her husband, Howard, spend days by their son's bedside in the hospital. The doctors assure them that everything looks "OK," yet they are puzzled about why he is not waking up.[45] Scotty's doctors continually assure his parents that he is not in a coma, and Howard eventually takes some time for a break from the hospital to go home. As soon as he walks through the door, the phone rings. At the other end of the receiver is an angry voice wanting to know why the birthday cake has not been picked up. Howard responds with anger of his own, says he has no idea what the caller is talking about, and hangs up.

The days drag on, and Scotty's state does not improve. When Ann finally decides to take her own break from the hospital and go home, she is on the receiving end of a set of harassing calls. "Have you forgotten about Scotty?" the voice on the other end of the line asks.[46] Panicked, she calls the hospital to see if something has happened. It hasn't. She rushes back to the hospital only to see Scotty open his eyes for a few moments and then breathe his last breath. The doctors claim that it was a "hidden occlusion," virtually impossible for them to catch. The chief doctor tending to Scotty, Dr. Francis, embraces both parents, apologizes, and almost breaks into tears himself.[47]

When the bereaved parents return home, it is not to peace and quiet. The phone begins ringing again. On the other end, an embittered voice growls, "Have you forgotten about Scotty?"[48] He calls over and over; it seems like a deranged joke. Ann finally realizes who has been calling: the baker. In the midst of their unimaginable grief, Ann and Howard rush to the bakery to face the "bastard" who has been harassing them.[49]

Thus far, the plot has been unusually gripping for a Raymond Carver story. Carver is a minimalist in the tradition of Ernest Hemingway, an author who writes stories with most of the discernible complexity under more obvious, thin surfaces. When reading Carver (and Hemingway), readers are asked to stretch themselves, to read between the lines, to imaginatively fill in the gaps, so to speak. What is left unsaid is often more important than what is said. Yet in this story, Carver constructs perhaps his most detailed narrative, inviting readers into the grief of this small family's tragedy. The plot is simple but clear, and most of it, thus far, is obvious even to a casual reader. But what happens at the end of the story reminds us that our initial reading—of literature, of life, of the other—is most likely shallow and always incomplete.

When Ann and Howard step into the bakery, they hear the lonely whirring of the machinery that was in the background of all of the disturbing calls they had received. The "not jolly" baker is surprised to see them in the middle of the night. Clearly alarmed, he asks them to leave because the bakery is closed.[50] Ann lashes out at him, explaining through tears of passion, anger, and grief that they had just lost their son, Scotty, the intended recipient of the cake. She even tells the baker, "I wanted to kill you . . . I wanted you dead."[51] The baker's next movements are unexpected—and the most important ones in the story: he clears a table, pulls up three chairs, pours coffee, and brings some piping hot, freshly baked cinnamon rolls to lay before the couple. He creates space for his guests both physically and emotionally, offering unforeseen hospitality. Before they eat, he tells the couple how very sorry he is, that he has forgotten how to be a human being, that now he is only a baker: "I am not an evil man, I don't think. Not evil, like you said on the phone. You got to understand what it comes down to is I don't know how to act anymore, it would seem."[52] Although drawing attention to himself, he also shares the grief of the former life he has lost—or the possibility of that life. He explains that he has no family, no kids—but that even all of this is no excuse for his behavior on the phone. Again, he apologizes and asks for forgiveness.

Next, the baker offers Ann and Howard some of his rolls, telling them that they probably need to eat something and "keep going" because "eating is a small, good thing in a time like this."[53] He is right. Ann and Howard have not properly eaten in days, and they certainly have not savored the comfort and warmth of fresh, filling food. The cinnamon rolls are warm, the icing runny. They begin to eat, and he encourages them to eat more: "There's all the rolls in the world in here."[54]

Carver tells us that "Ann was suddenly hungry" and eats three rolls. As they eat, the baker begins to talk: "They listened carefully. Although they were tired and in anguish, they listened to what the baker had to say. They nodded when the baker began to speak of loneliness, and of the sense of doubt and limitation that had come to him in his middle years. He told them what it was like to be childless all these years. To repeat the days with the ovens endlessly full and endlessly empty."[55] The baker shares both his bread and his deep sadness. Every celebratory cake that he had made was a reminder of his own emptiness, lost possibilities, absences. Only in sharing his own pain, making himself vulnerable, could he carry the couples' grief and offer them comfort in the form of food and space. In these moments, the baker, Ann, and Howard learn to listen to each other. The cinnamon rolls feel almost sacramental, an offering and a shared, small joy alongside their profound trauma. The baker hands the couple a loaf of bread, asking them to smell it: "It's a heavy bread, but rich."[56] They smell it, they taste it, and they eat and eat. As they feast on this heavy, rich bread, Ann and Howard "talked on into the early morning, the high, pale cast of light in the windows, and they did not think of leaving."[57]

These final words of Carver's story are ones of warmth, comfort, and a shared experience of both vulnerability and safety. Although the baker initially acted out of anger and unknowingly caused more pain, his confession, act of contrition, and invitation for shared space create community rather than division. He is a lonely man who fears he has forgotten what it is like to be human, yet he rehumanizes himself by becoming vulnerable and doing the one thing that he knows how to do well: making and sharing bread and cinnamon rolls. It is important to remember, once again, that doing "for one of the least of these" is actually serving Christ, transforming these small acts of giving into something almost sacramental.[58] The baker's feeble offering is reminiscent of the widow's mite in Luke 21.[59] Perhaps Christ's response to an act like the baker's would be similar to that when the woman poured perfume on his body in Mark 14: "She did what she could."[60] Of course, there is no evidence that the baker in Carver's story is intentionally giving to Christ; readers know nothing of his faith or absence thereof. Regardless, this "small, good thing" that he does for the couple is an example that readers can follow. The baker's act of creating a space, both in his shop and in his imagination, to listen to this grieving couple is a model of the ways in which our own imaginations can also be transformed by slowing down, becoming attentive, and truly listening. The story itself is a means to love because it asks readers to slow down and be attentive while modeling the empathetic community that is created as a result of a transformed imagination.

LARS AND THE REAL GIRL

The spiritual and emotional awards of slowing down and listening are also highlighted in Craig Gillespie's 2007 film *Lars and the Real Girl*. In the film, viewers see the impact of both a family and a church community making space for someone whose pain has isolated him. Like the baker, each member of this community must be intentional in their choices to do so. Yet in Gillespie's film, the focus is also on the way that imagining the plight of a deeply broken individual in order to love him is something that requires both time and sacrifice.

Film scholar Craig Detweiler rightfully refers to this quirky yet deeply endearing film as a "postmodern parable" about childlike faith and love as well as a "heartfelt portrait of the kingdom of God in action."[61] This is not the sort of description one would expect from a Christian scholar writing about a film that contains a blow-up sex doll as a main character. The sweetness of the film is an unexpected, refreshing contrast to the viewers' anticipation of the vulgar and profane.

The film's protagonist, Lars, is a lonely, isolated young man who lives in the garage of his childhood home, mostly avoiding his colleagues, his family, and the cute young woman in the office who has a crush on him. At first, his character seems delightfully off-kilter—but his alternate understanding of the world soon proves to be delusional. Lars's brother, Gus, and his pregnant sister-in-law, Karin, live in the main house in front of his garage home. Karin is a very caring soul, always trying to connect with Lars, even to the point of nearly tackling him in the driveway in order to force him into accepting a dinner invitation. One evening, an uncharacteristically smiley Lars shows up on the doorstep of the main house to tell Gus and Karin about the out-of-town female visitor who has come to see him. She does not speak very good English and she is in a wheelchair, Lars tells them, attempting to prepare them for her differences.

But there was no way that they could have possibly been prepared to meet Bianca, the subject of Lars's giddy devotion: Bianca is an anatomically correct mail-order sex doll. She wears a fishnet top and has full, partially parted lips. The doll is beautiful—but she is made of plastic. Lars does not seem to notice this. As he sheepishly whispers in her ear and tells his family that she is a "missionary" just taking a break to "see the world," they realize that Lars believes she is a real woman.[62] It is fair to be nervous about the direction this film could go; it is a story about a man and a sex doll, after all. But Lars's innocence and gentleness transform a literal commodified object, created for self-derived pleasure, into a deeply cherished and respected companion. Lars tells his brother and sister-in-law that Bianca is "very religious," so he would like for her to stay in their spare bedroom rather than his apartment.[63] He even asks them to help clothe and bathe her so that he does not violate her chastity.

While with Bianca, Lars acts like a child, spending time reading to her from his hidden treehouse in the woods, pampering her, and giggling in a state of love and wonder. As the film continues, Karin and Gus grow more concerned for Lars's mental health and, as a result, encourage him to take Bianca in to see a doctor, where she ends up getting weekly treatments. In reality, the person receiving medical care is Lars, who sits and chats with psychologist Dr. Dagmar while he waits during Bianca's supposed treatments. When she speaks to Lars's family, Dr. Dagmar explains that Lars is having delusions and that the best way to help him is to play along, to let things work themselves out naturally. She believes that the delusion is a result of a longtime decompensation based on past traumatic circumstances.

We soon learn that the very childlike and childish Lars lost his mother during his birth. He carries around a blanket that his mother knit for him just before she died, and during a symbolic moment, he insists that pregnant Karin wear the blanket around her shoulders because of the cold. Karin's pregnancy must have triggered the unresolved grief of Lars's mother's death and the memories of the years of loneliness that he spent with a deeply despairing hermit father. During Lars's childhood, his older brother, Gus, left home quickly, abandoning Lars to suffocate in the sad loneliness of their father's house. In this painful context, Lars's delusions make sense. He is afraid of human relationships to the extent that human touch literally burns his skin. Like Lloyd Vogel, he is a man whose cold childhood did not contain the safety of attachment.

The arrival of Lars's companion presents an opportunity both to his family and to the community. What do you do when a family member or neighbor clings to a delusion in order to protect himself from the deep wound of abandonment? With Bianca, Lars is happier and seemingly more alive than anyone has ever seen him. But Gus and Karin are, understandably, both concerned about Lars's mental state and their own reputation. At one point, Gus asks, "What will people say?"[64] He is also very eager to fix Lars, as if there is an on/off switch that can compensate for years of trauma. Karin is more concerned about making sure that Lars is unharmed, both mentally and emotionally. Quite a Herculean effort, they both pretend to believe that Bianca is a real woman, and this leads to Lars feeling both happy and secure.

Lars's security also comes from his involvement in his local church. At the beginning of the film when Karin invites him to a family breakfast, he declines because he must attend a church service. His encounter with Karin is in the dreary, snowy early morning, a contrast to the warmth and communal comfort of the church, where he plays with action figures, partially listening to the sermon. Before church dismisses, the priest says these words: "We need never ask 'Lord, what should I do?' The Lord has told us what to do. Love one another. Love is God in action."[65] And to a large degree, the film is about "love" being "God in action." It shows us "the kingdom of God in action" as the church members gather around Lars, loving him in both an unnatural and unusual way.[66]

Although the priest tells the congregation that they should never ask, "Lord, what should I do?" the congregants perhaps never imagined having to make such a bizarre set of intentional relational decisions.[67] It's one thing to learn to love another human being; it's another thing to feign love for a sex doll to enact your love for your neighbor. When Karin and Gus first meet with the priest and church members, there is a great deal of anticipated confusion, chaos, and resistance. They don't want Lars to bring Bianca to church. Some of them don't want anything to do with Bianca and Lars. But then one member reminds the others that every family in the church has some sort of hidden, shameful dysfunction. Of all communities, the church should be the most welcoming place for a hurting person, a societal misfit, to go for love and support. The body of Christ should have the intentional capacity to acknowledge the tragedy of broken humanity while retaining an intention to collectively strive for holiness. When that bold and compassionate church member reminds the others of these things, it is reminiscent of Christ telling the angry crowd, "Let any one of you who is without sin be the first to throw a stone," silencing the voices of self-righteousness.[68] The priest of Lars's church then asks his parishioners the classic question: "What would Jesus do?"[69] And in the very next scene, we see Bianca sitting in her wheelchair next to a squeaky clean, beaming Lars and his bewildered family.

This uncomfortable, absurd, yet parabolic image is a visual reminder of the countercultural nature of the church's job to love the seemingly unlovable. As Pastor Mary Hulst notes in *Think Christian*, churchgoers are accustomed to putting on their Sunday best both literally and spiritually in order to appear acceptable in front of Christian brothers and sisters. She asks, "Don't you sometimes want to walk into worship unshowered and unshaven, pushing your 'doll in a wheel-chair' and just have people love you right there in the moment?"[70] The answer, of course, is a resounding yes. Although making great efforts to disguise perceived abnormalities and deficiencies, all human beings want to be loved unconditionally if/when these are on display. And as we learn more about how to love our neighbors as we love ourselves, we must recognize and honor this desire, this intrinsic deep need, in those around us.

The focus of *Lars and the Real Girl* is just as much—perhaps more—on the reactions of Lars's family and community to his vulnerability than it is on Lars himself. In fact, viewers are never able to get into Lars's head. They do, however, come to understand some of the nature of his pain via his actions, his symptoms, his story, and the diagnosis from his doctor. Similarly, in our day-to-day reality, we cannot venture inside the head of another human being. We must love them even in our ignorance just because, in God's eyes, they are infinitely loveable. Lars's community does just this.

At first, the community's acceptance of Bianca seems dangerously enabling, perhaps even collectively delusional. But as Lars's family and congregation follow the doctor's advice and continue to contemplate what Jesus might do in this situation, the spell begins to break. The first signs of healing appear as Lars's colleague Margo, who has had a crush on him for some time, extends her hand to shake his, and he accepts, no longer feeling burned. As time moves on, Lars reports that Bianca is very ill and must be admitted to the hospital. His church family sends flowers and takes turns sitting with a grieving Lars as Bianca slips away from his imaginary world. When she dies, the congregants plan and attend an elaborate funeral.

All these things appear ridiculous on the surface. And in the eyes of the world, they are ridiculous. But then again, Christians are asked to love sacrificially in a way that the world often finds absurd. *Lars and the Real Girl* is a story about greater love springing from great weakness, pain, and brokenness. As the film ends, Lars leaves Bianca's graveside and invites the ever-faithful Margo to join him for a walk. His church community has truly "loved him into being."[71] The film forces its viewers into the uncomfortable space of Lars's community and family, and they are also asked to imagine who Lars, the image bearer, is as a person, beyond his bizarre obsession. As a powerful piece of art, *Lars and the Real Girl* pushes us into the space of sacrificial love, challenging us to drop labels and shift categories, using our imaginations to see who Lars is and can be.

Each of these works of art resists a sort of cynicism and operates out of a deep faith in the inherent God-given value of human beings, however broken they are. Nancy Oliver, the screenwriter for *Lars and the Real Girl*, observed that, leading up to the time that the film was made, "there were a lot of movies that were dark, edgy, sarcastic and sometimes mean-spirited."[72] In a quiet act of empathetic rebellion, she decided to "write about compassion and goodness, something that was sincere, because I wasn't seeing that anywhere."[73] The acts of "compassion and goodness" in "This Lime-Tree Bower My Prison," *A Beautiful Day in the Neighborhood*, "A Small, Good Thing," and *Lars and the Real Girl* define each narrative as the product of a selfless empathy that leads to personal transformation for its recipients. These contemporary parables model the movements of an empathy that is informed by an active, generous, compassionate imagination that is broadened rather than constricted, making space for the experience, pain, and plight of the other.

Chapter Two

EMPATHY FOR THE WRETCHED AND GLORIOUS HUMAN CONDITION

The Existence of God Implies the Existence of Human Nature

"Hell is other people," writes French philosopher Jean-Paul Sartre in his 1944 play, *No Exit*.[1] In describing the experience of three damned souls locked in a room together, his hyperbolic language is reflective of a hollow human anthropology, devoid of anything sacred or shared. Sartre, an atheist and existentialist, did not believe in the existence of an actual hell—yet his play holds theological interest, especially when considering what he believes about the human condition. Sartre taught that human nature does not exist because, in order for there to be a shared likeness among human beings, a grand designer, God, would have to exist. Like Friedrich Nietzsche, Sartre believed that because the idea of God is no longer needed (and that the real God never existed), the concept of human nature is also meaningless. Both God and human nature were erroneous tools created to make sense of reality, only living in the constructed world of ideas.

Sartre is onto something significant here. He recognizes that the existence of God must imply inherent similarities between all human beings. If God is real, then we are intricately connected, forged in his shared image. In the lecture "Existentialism Is a Humanism," Sartre argues that humans have ultimate freedom, that their "existence precedes their essence," which means that they define themselves by the choices that they make.[2] Although there is some limited truth to

41

this view, Sartre denies the idea of the sanctity of life in claiming that a human being only has worth if he or she chooses to do so. If all humans are made in God's image, however, they have inherent value regardless of the choices that they make. Sartre alleges that humans have ultimate freedom because there are no "signs or omens" to direct our choices, and we choose who we want to be completely.[3] But he does not rejoice in this. In fact, he says that we are "condemned to be free" because there is no right or wrong way to choose, no guidance, and no limits to protect us from destroying ourselves and others.[4]

Sartre's thinking is helpful in its very precise logic: If God is dead, then we are in a wasteland of broken communication and failed relationships—nothing works without the commonality of our shared origin. But if God exists, then we are more connected than disconnected; we all share the image of the divine, and this fact is endlessly mysterious, rich, and beautiful. Because God does exist, we do share a nature, and this is a large part of the reason that we have the capacity for empathy. In order to better love our fellow human beings, we need to understand not only their individual needs but also the interconnected ways in which humanity shares both aches and joys, glory and sin. One of the first steps to expanding the imagination toward the love of our neighbor is to reflect upon the collective human condition—both our place in the universe and our spiritual disposition.

The Arts Reflect the Complexity of the Human Condition

The arts have a significant capacity to enable us to see the beauty and limits of human beings by placing them under a microscope. As we look at the screen, turn the page, or listen to the chorus, we see, read, and hear ourselves in the voices of our neighbors. The artist's role is prophetic as she creates stories that enable us to deepen both our sadness for humanity's fallen state and our joy in its beauty and richness as it collectively reflects God's image. Intentionally witnessing the ebb and flow of the human condition by engaging the arts can prime us for enlarging our capacity for empathy. In seeing stories of the flawed, inconstant humanity of others, we see both ourselves and our neighbors, concurrently depraved and sacred. Flannery O'Connor's hilarious short story "A Temple of the Holy Ghost" highlights the capacity we each have for being both spiritually aware and deceived at the same time. In this story, the pendulum swing of the human condition is very apparent, yet the very awareness of its off-kilter trajectory tilts toward hope. C. S. Lewis's favorite piece of his own writing—the novel *Till We Have Faces*—and the music of Sufjan Stevens both trace the ways that the human tendency toward narcissism disguises itself as love. AMC's series *Better Call Saul* pinpoints the connection between family trauma and self-deception, emphasizing that toxic outside forces can impact our existential reality in tragic ways. Last of all, Lorraine Hansberry's classic play *A Raisin in the Sun* explores the ways that toxic social structures and dehumanizing socialization can also cause humans to deny the dignity within themselves. The protagonist in each of these narratives searches for an identity while simultaneously deceiving themselves into thinking that they are fine—they are in desperate need of a prophetic awakening. While journeying alongside the characters wrestling into and out of reality, these works of art help us craft a more complex, nuanced Christian anthropology. That complexity leads to deeper graciousness, understanding, and empathy for our shared plights as human beings.

THE "WRETCHEDNESS" AND "GREATNESS" OF HUMAN BEINGS

Before engaging these works directly, it is helpful to look at both the intricacy and vastness of the human condition through the lens of philosopher Blaise Pascal's writing. Long before Sartre's antitheological discussion of the absence of human nature, French mathematician and philosopher Pascal challenged the common cultural understanding of human beings as either wholly good or bad, rejecting these categories as reductionist, incomplete, and dehumanizing. Pascal's reading of Scripture led him to see human beings as both "great" and "wretched."[5] For Pascal, human "greatness" reflects God's image in us: our conscience / moral compass, our creativity, our desire for love and community, our need to worship. Our "wretchedness" is our frailty, our fallen nature, and our tendency to deny our utter dependence on God.[6] The pendulum within every human being continuously swings both ways, and the process of sanctification begins with an awareness of this arc both within ourselves and in our neighbors. The more we are aware of our own fickle natures and the constant movement of the inner pendulum, the more we have the capacity to imagine the reality of other human beings who are joint members of this condition. The natural human tendency is to see the complexity of our own nature and forgive ourselves while, at the same time, flattening out the nature of those around us, labeling them as either good or bad, and choosing to accept or reject them.

Honest, complex art can help us understand what it is like to live in someone else's head in order to develop a more informed love for them. But the starting point is to ask not what *they* are like but what *we* are like, working to understand the commonalities of our collective natures. According to Pascal's diagnosis of the human condition in *Pensées*, one starting point is to understand the nature of our shared "wretchedness": "The greatness of man is so evident, that it is even proved by his wretchedness. For what in animals is nature we call in man wretchedness; by which we recognize that, his nature being now like that of animals, he has fallen from a better nature which once was his."[7] When any human being operates purely pragmatically out of a sense of either survival or self-interest, this leads to a constriction of the imagination, focusing mainly on the self, the material world, and the next step for advancement. And in doing this, the recognition and appreciation of God's image are tarnished. We must use our imagination in order to see God's image in others and even in ourselves, because its reality transcends the easily accessible senses. We cannot perceive God, a spiritual being, with our senses, and we need to reach beyond our senses to begin to comprehend his image in humanity. The arts provide us many opportunities to practice recognizing God's image in others.

Our individual conscience is greatly informed by stories, as we long for transformation and righteousness. In the absence of the imagination that can both create and dwell upon stories, we become more like animals when we ignore the natural pull to acknowledge God and operate according to a conscience that echoes his precepts. This is acknowledged in the postapocalyptic zombie series *The Walking Dead* when the most morally aware character of the series, Dale Horvath, issues a challenge to the show's ragtag group of survivors: "The world that we know is gone. But keeping our humanity—that's a choice."[8] So much of the series explores what it looks like to keep or lose "our humanity." But in order to try to preserve humanity, the survivors need to understand what "humanity" is. While seeking to understand the true nature of humanity, they ultimately push back against Darwinian claims that humans are just more rationally developed animals. In the series, although the zombies are the obvious enemies, they are inhuman, and killing them is not a moral choice. But many survivors are also quick to pull the trigger on fellow human beings. According to Dale's assessment, following this path begins to erode their "humanity." At one point early in the series, former sheriff and group leader Rick Grimes claims that "we need to be willing to lay down our lives for each other if it comes to that."⁹ Grimes iterates that being human is more than just surviving. It is also having empathy and compassion, sometimes to the point of extreme sacrifice for others. This is the "greatness" of which Pascal speaks, the *imago Dei* in every human being. Grimes's comment is an allusion to Christ's words in John 15:13: "Greater love has no one than this: to lay down one's life for one's friends." In the show's portrayal of a brutal survival-of-the-fittest mentality as well as the hope for retaining and even growing this thing called humanity, *The Walking Dead* examines the pervasive wretchedness and greatness of our lives, always in tension, always competing.

Pascal continually acknowledges the tension between the great and the wretched when describing the paradoxical state of the human condition, emphasizing the "tangled knot" of our existence: "What a novelty, what monsters! Chaotic, contradictory, prodigious, judging everything, mindless worm of the earth, storehouse of truth, cesspool of uncertainty and error, glory and reject of the universe."¹⁰ In these sets of seemingly contradictory extremes, Pascal illustrates that we are far too complex and too inherently contradictory to begin to understand ourselves: "Man is beyond man."¹¹ Anyone who claims to understand herself, let alone God, has been seduced by pride's false promises. There is only one way to remedy this chaotic reality, according to Pascal: "Listen to God."¹² God can be heard in our frustrated stillness, our moments of defeat in our attempts to understand ourselves. In his most famous quote, so often paraphrased in sermons and elsewhere, Pascal writes that the root of all human misery is an inability to sit alone in a room. With all our might, we do not want to examine our own wretchedness. Even more, we fear the weakness we feel upon examination that then propels us toward God. But according to Pascal, this is the sacred way, the paradoxical way, the only way. We must use our imaginations as we remember, reflect, and sit still in our honesty. We come to the truth by revisiting and piecing together our own narratives and then extending that grace to others. It takes great effort and intentionality to delve into our own stories and then be able to lightly hold the stories of others, seeing our shared likeness with eyes of empathy and compassion.

PROPHETIC ART RESISTS OVERSIMPLIFICATION

Prophetic art can help us become curious, stretch our imaginations, linger upon the apparent tensions of the human condition. But there is also a great deal of popular art that flattens human beings into one-dimensional caricatures, muting the presence of either the *imago Dei* or our fallen nature—often presenting what David Dark calls a "triumphal cupcake ending" that resolves the tensions between these two aspects of our nature according to a dishonest, simplistic formula.[13] In this sense, many of us have been trained to apply simplistic formulas to other human beings and to ourselves. But humans cannot be solved according to their own devices, and as Pascal notes, even when we do cling to truth, we quite quickly resort to our old patterns of wretchedness. On one point, both Blaise Pascal and Friedrich Nietzsche agree with each other: human beings continually deceive themselves. Unlike Nietzsche, however, Pascal believes that the only path toward clarity and revelation is through submission to God, the very humility and submissiveness that Nietzsche would call the root of self-deception.

"A Temple of the Holy Ghost," *Till We Have Faces*, *The Age of Adz*, *Better Call Saul*, and *A Raisin in the Sun* are each works of art that help readers, viewers, and listeners understand more about what Pascal sees as the constant "inconstancy" of the human condition.[14] Rather than relying on feel-good formulas, they expose self-deception while leaving space for the possibility of hope and redemption. They creatively inform our imaginations with the constant coexistence of human beauty and error, leading us away from a tendency to caricature. The internal struggles of all the characters in these works of art share several common traits: the desire for approval, the search for identity, the desperate need to be loved. Of course, these are some of the deepest human desires and the ones that we both long for and, simultaneously, fear. Although the desire to be loved and love itself are part of what Pascal sees as our "greatness," like every other aspect of human existence, they are easily tainted and perverted. This is especially true when we examine the ways that pride is, at its base, a paradoxical mixture of both rebellion and the desire for approval. As we watch the downfall of these characters, still knowing their goodness, we are watching ourselves. And the more that we dwell in the awkward spaces between the now and the not yet, the flailing goodness and promised hope of sanctification, the more we can imaginatively identify with these characters.

"A Temple of the Holy Ghost"

In her dark, satirical stories, Flannery O'Connor shocks us into imagining the gap between good and evil within ourselves and within others. She knows, like Pascal, that we do not want to sit alone and think of our natural state; we are addicted to distractions that have become normalized—so much so that they are the everyday stuff of formulaic daily life. As we follow the trajectory of her stories, we are jolted into seeing dark, conflicted tendencies within all human beings, including the religious, the criminal, and even the child. O'Connor often underscores the gap between orthodoxy and orthopraxy, even asking us to redefine what orthodoxy is as we remember the words of James 2: "Faith by itself, if it is not accompanied by action, is dead."[15] We see this clearly in "A Good Man Is Hard to Find" in the character of an elderly woman resting upon her superficial laurels of class and race. Only when she comes face-to-face with death and a man who could be her spiritual son does she see the marred, forgotten image of God within him and within herself. Some of O'Connor's most biting satirical portraits seem to be fashioned after their author herself. This is a valuable example as she guides us through pointing the finger not just at others but at ourselves. In seeing our own flaws and contradictions, we can more easily extend that empathy to others. For instance, like O'Connor, Hulga, the central character in the story "Good Country People," is a brilliant young woman who grew up in the Deep South, out in the country, but made her way to a prestigious university. Hulga has gained a PhD in philosophy and finally feels justified and appreciated when in community with her academic peers and away from those "good country people" who she believes are, at least intellectually, beneath her.[16] Because of a medical condition, Hulga must move back down South and live with her mother, among the very community that she had tried to escape. O'Connor was also a country misfit, a brilliant Roman Catholic in heavily Baptist Southern Georgia. Like Hulga, O'Connor was able to attend and teach at a prestigious university away from the South and then, because of a health condition, had to come back to live with her mother in the country.

In "A Temple of the Holy Ghost," a brilliant, precocious, prideful, and imaginative little girl who is referred to only as "the child" is another O'Connor stand-in.[17] Like O'Connor, the child lives on a farm in the Deep South, and her Roman Catholic family is quite a minority among the neighboring homegrown Southern Baptists and Pentecostals. Like the author who created her, the child loves to make fun of people, and both her intelligence and her pride play a big part in this. As O'Connor endearingly mocks herself, she opens her readers up to the possibility of self-critique, helping them bridge the gap between their flawed selves and their flawed neighbors. O'Connor's sassy stand-in is both self-righteous and comically cruel—and she knows it. When talking about the two female cousins visiting her family while on holiday from their Catholic school, the child's inner voice relays her true feelings: "They were practically morons and she was glad to think that they were only second cousins and she could not have inherited any of their stupidity."[18] O'Connor's honest portrayal of the child's inner monologue is significant: she exposes the deeply critical, often hypocritical attitudes that many of us share. The child continues by shamelessly mocking her cousins' two suitors who are not Catholic and have ambitions to be Church of God preachers, something that the child scoffs at because "you don't have to know nothing to be one."[19] The boys do not know the Latin mass like she does, and when they sing a song from their worship context, she stamps her foot and screams, "You big dumb Church of God ox!"[20] The child's tendency toward arrogant snark, either out loud or in her mind, is at the same time offensive, hilarious, endearing, and recognizable. We see ourselves in her just as O'Connor crafted her after her own "inconstant" image.[21]

As prideful and mean-spirited as the child can be, O'Connor also emphasizes her deep sensitivity to spiritual matters. Although she gleefully mocks her cousins, her peers, the man with a fat neck who drives the taxi, the Baptist preacher, and pretty much anyone else who annoys her, she stops short of mocking anything that she considers sacred. The two Catholic school cousins laugh while reminiscing about the nuns telling them to ward off any sexual advances from young men by saying, "Stop sir! I am a Temple of the Holy Ghost!"[22] O'Connor writes that the child "didn't see anything funny in this."[23] While the girls turn blue with laughter, the child becomes quiet, contemplative. And then she realizes that the phrase "I am a Temple of the Holy Ghost" completely transforms her way of thinking about herself: "It made her feel as if somebody had given her a present."[24]

In this moment, the child is devout and feels a deep sense of spiritual conviction. She is also very self-aware, knowing that "she was eaten up with the sin of pride, the worst one."[25] In all her complexity, she is a profound, transparent picture of the human condition. She lives in the tension of a deep sensitivity to the things of God and an inability to stay in that space for long, for she continually ignores the image of God, "the temple of the Holy Ghost," in others by mocking them. She also says "perfunctory" prayers because that is what a young Catholic is supposed to do—but this ritual often leaves her unfulfilled: "She took a running start and went through the Apostle's Creed and then hung by her chin on the side of the bed, empty minded."[26] Sometimes her prayers are prideful and sidestep the meaning that each human being, not just her, is considered a "Temple of the Holy Ghost." She knows that she could never be a saint because of her acknowledged and deeply ingrained pridefulness but believes "she could be a martyr if they killed her quick."[27] Readers see the inside of the child's wild imagination as she envisions being thrown to the lions for martyrdom and the same lions falling at her feet, converted after an interaction with her. Even her desire for martyrdom is ultimately prideful. The child has a strong sense of what is right and true, yet she continually follows an internal subtext that elevates herself above others. The child is all of us, even the devout. In seeing ourselves in her, we can also imagine the shared inner struggle of our neighbor, imprinted with the same mercurial condition. Even though we see the child's flaws, we also see her goodness. And in this, we both relate to and empathize with her.

Unsurprisingly for any O'Connor story, the child has a jolting spiritual revelation that springs from a very unlikely source. One evening, her cousins are giggling as they talk about an exhibit that the local men are going to see in a traveling "freak show."[28] Women and children are not allowed to see the person in the exhibition tent: they are part man and part woman, and they bear all to prove it. The child does not find mocking this person as funny, and as she drifts into sleep, she dreams of the hermaphrodite telling a crowd, starved for spectacle, that "God done this to me, and I praise Him."[29] The hermaphrodite continues, saying, "A temple of God is a Holy thing."[30] Over and over, the child's unconscious mind ruminates on the fact that even this supposed "freak" is a "Temple of the Holy Ghost." The child's vivid unconscious imagination is a source of love, even empathy. In a few days' time, the child and her mother take the cousins back to the convent, and they arrive in the middle of the mass. As the priest lifts the host, the broken body of Christ, the child is profoundly convicted as she connects the sacred body of Christ to the Temple of the Holy Ghost, God's presence and image within her and within those whom she so relentlessly mocks. O'Connor writes that "her ugly thoughts stopped, and she began to realize that she was in the presence of God."[31] She fervently prays, "Hep me not to be so mean. . . . Hep me not to give her so much sass."[32] After this pivotal, transformative moment, the child and her mother get back into the taxi, and her mind immediately slips into a mockery of the rolls of fat on the driver's neck. The child is transformed, but she still retains the very wretchedness that we all do. She both loves the image of God in herself and hates it in others. This difficult recognition is the first step in the development of empathy. We must be honest about our shared human condition, which includes a resistance to empathy, if we are to love our neighbors as ourselves. Just as the child's orthodoxy and orthopraxy are often, in day-to-day life, disconnected, so are ours. But O'Connor's story captures our imagination as it turns a mirror upon us. When the child has these sobering moments, she recognizes that to mock everything is to ignore the sacredness of all that God has created, especially human beings, the Temples of his Holy Ghost. And she presents a similar opportunity for the reader.

TILL WE HAVE FACES

Like "A Temple of the Holy Ghost," C. S. Lewis's 1956 novel *Till We Have Faces* is a dark yet deeply redemptive exploration of the almost instinctual tendency for human beings to privilege our feelings and pleasures over the sake of our neighbors' well-being. Lewis creates a fictional narrative to explore the dismal truth of human self-love that transforms into a bright, concrete hope in the capacity for real, empathetic love. The only way to this final step is through honest self-reflection. In Lewis's retelling of the myth of Cupid and Psyche, the author crafts a convicting, sobering narrative about the ways that self-interest and emotional greed can be disguised as love.

The story's protagonist is Orual, the unlikely eldest princess of Glome, the novel's imaginary kingdom. She is deeply aware of her lack of physical beauty and a frequent victim of her father's rage. *Till We Have Faces* is written as a testimony, the running account of Orual's record of resentment against the pagan gods of Glome, especially the all-consuming and faceless Ungit, whose darkly jealous love is the opposite of Christlike love. Orual is an admittedly miserable, self-pitying character, but her life changes when her youngest sister, Psyche, is born. Psyche is so beautiful and sweet that Orual is enchanted by her grace and loveliness, wanting nothing more than to protect her. But as Psyche grows older, her beauty and charm become dangerous for the entire royal family as townspeople begin to worship her, even claiming that they were healed upon encounters with her. The town's worship of Psyche is short-lived due to the negative reaction of the gods, and when the jealous gods demand a sacrifice in exchange for lifting a curse, the entire kingdom enthusiastically demands that Psyche be offered up to the frightening "God of the Mountain."[33]

Psyche's forthcoming death is far more upsetting for Orual than it is for Psyche herself. Psyche has a deep peace and sense of calling that lures her toward this mysterious exchange. At one point, Psyche explains to her sister that not only is she willing to be turned over to the gods, but she also actually craves it: "The sweetest thing in all my life has been the longing—to reach the Mountain, to find the place where all the beauty comes from."[34] At this point, Lewis begins to reveal Orual's cruel and manipulative heart to his readers (although she is still blinded by delusions of her own goodness). Orual believes that she loves Psyche more than anything—but Lewis continually emphasizes that Orual's love of Psyche is not love at all; it is an act of possession and desperation. It is a love of the feeling of loving another, an idol, and the hollow core of Orual's fragile identity. The evening before Psyche's journey up the mountain, Orual cries, "Oh cruel! Cruel! . . . Is it nothing to you that you leave me here alone?"[35] Rather than listen to Psyche and try to comfort her, Orual focuses on her own pain. Her faux love of Psyche parallels the very descriptions of holy love she uses when talking about the gods that she accuses of being evil. Reflecting upon the myths surrounding the god of the mountain, son of Ungit, she remarks that "some say the loving and the devouring are all the same thing."[36] Orual is both hypocritical and inconstant, and in this, she is profoundly human in her blindness.

Orual longs not to love Psyche but to consume her, to control her, to possess her. Psyche is her source of temporal happiness and meaning, and she will kill or be killed rather than lose this. These toxic motives become very clear when Psyche and Orual meet again and the truth is revealed: Psyche has not been tortured or consumed—she has been transformed by Cupid, the god of the mountain, into a real demigoddess, glorified and made whole. Orual seethes with jealousy and anger over her sister's happiness. She cannot imagine her Psyche being happy if Orual is not in her life. Her manipulative strategies become increasingly more destructive until she takes a dagger and cuts her own arm to show Psyche the pain she is willing to endure in order to, as she phrases it, save her sister. She then threatens to kill Psyche and commit suicide if Psyche refuses to leave the palace of the god and return home with her.

Although Orual's motivation is clearly self-interest rather than love of the other, she lacks self-awareness and truly believes that she loves her sister. She is delusional, blinded by her own selfishness and pain. Interestingly, this novel was written four years before Lewis's *The Four Loves*, an analysis of the four types of love as defined by the Greek words *storge*, *philia*, *eros*, and *agape*. In defining these loves, Lewis also defines what love is not. In a very famous passage, he explains that human love will always entail some sort of loss and pain because we bare ourselves when trusting another, and the other, in their humanity, can never fully and unconditionally love us with the agape love of God. Love is both risk and, ultimately, sacrifice: "To love at all is to be vulnerable. Love anything and your heart will be wrung and possibly broken. If you want to make sure of keeping it intact you must give it to no one, not even an animal. Wrap it carefully round with hobbies and little luxuries; avoid all entanglements. Lock it up safe in the casket or coffin of your selfishness. But in that casket, safe, dark, motionless, airless, it will change. It will not be broken; it will become unbreakable, impenetrable, irredeemable. To love is to be vulnerable."[37] The "casket or coffin of your selfishness" is a place where one resides out of fear and often looks like an absence of human connection. In Orual's case, it becomes an obsession that turns from love to hatred inside of her. When Psyche tells Orual about her beautiful husband who has given her a lavish palace and visits her only at night, Orual's heart becomes acidic, festering in jealousy and resentment that turns into hatred: "Something began to grow colder and hard inside me."[38] Rather than make herself truly vulnerable and accept the loss of her sister, unconditionally rejoicing in Psyche's happiness, she chooses to see truth as delusion. While she sees Psyche "bathed in life and beauty and well-being . . . from the top of her head to her naked feet," she chooses to ignore goodness, beauty, and truth and replace it with hatred, ugliness, and falsehood.[39] Because she cannot control or possess her sister, she dismisses Psyche's happiness as insanity and illusion.

To avoid true vulnerability, Orual chooses a false narrative, an all-too-common human tendency. Although Psyche reaches true happiness and fulfillment in the arms of the god, Orual uses all the energy she can to block this love, even threatening murder and suicide as a last attempt to control. In *The Four Loves*, Lewis makes a distinction between "Gift-love" and "Need-love," explaining that God's love is the ultimate Gift-love in which "there is no hunger that needs to be filled, only plenteousness that desires to give."[40] Psyche experiences Gift-love in her relationship with Cupid. Paradoxically, she must give completely of herself to receive a very selfless, unconditional love. Orual's love, or perversion of love, is a form of Need-love that is recognizable to all human beings: "Need-love cries to God from our poverty."[41] While Orual claims that the great god Ungit and her son, Psyche's lover, "devour" in order to "love," she is the one who devours. She believes that "to be eaten and married to the god might not be so different," yet she is the one consuming out of her own hunger.[42] After Psyche confides to her sister that she has always had a "longing for home," a home that she has now found, Orual responds, "I only see that you never loved me."[43] Rather than acknowledging her own grievous shortcomings, she projects the blame on Psyche, telling her that she is "cruel" and has a "heart of stone."[44]

Orual's bitterness and desire to control lead to a very diseased idea of love, and, at some points, her story causes readers to wince as we recognize ourselves. It is often much easier to create a false narrative, to project blame, and to deny reality than realize our own weaknesses. This novel is gripping, beautiful, and painful reading. It calls for spiritual surgery. As Orual writes her testament against the gods, Lewis asks us to reflect upon the wretchedness of the human condition— our own wretchedness. It is a wretchedness that is both pitiful and despicable. Orual has created the gods in her own image, projecting her own brokenness upon them in order to serve her narrative of victimization. She has to believe that the gods are cruel and vindictive in order to retain her belief that Psyche could only be happy and saved while with her. When Orual sees the great palace where Psyche resides, she sees it with her spirit, and her lie to herself and others about its existence is a denial of the hunger of her very soul. At one point, Psyche asks, "Have you no wonder?"[45] Orual lacks the eyes of a child, eyes of curiosity, wonder, and faith. It is much harder for her to see herself than it is for the child in O'Connor's story, for a child's rich imagination keeps her in a state of wonder, curiosity, and longing. It also continually reminds the child of her utter dependence upon God. In speaking with her sister about the real world that has satiated Psyche's desires, Orual admits, "If this is true, I've been wrong all my life. Everything has to be begun over again."[46] And this, of course, is a sacrifice that Orual cannot make. Although the gift of this life is offered to her, she says, "I don't want it. I hate it, I hate it!" instead finding refuge in the false belief that "I ruled myself."[47]

After spending her life trying to rule herself, Orual eventually becomes the queen of Glome, and she does so with kindness and grace. The greatness within her prevents her wretchedness from destroying her. But the deepest greatness within her is her capacity to finally see and listen to the gods. Although she has long prepared to present her case against the gods, she has no choice but to be silent when she meets them face-to-face. As a queen, she wears a veil to cover her ugliness, but this veil is also a symbol of the self-deception that has controlled her life. She eventually realizes, "My anger protected me for only a short time; anger wearies itself out and truth comes in."[48] But this can only happen after the gods, "those divine surgeons," had "tied me down and were at work."[49] As Orual's story ends, it also begins. It seems that the final answer to Orual's longing is that the vision that transcends her own pain and her misconstrued logic is reality. Orual cries out to the gods, begging for answers to questions about her loneliness, her ugliness, and her loss of Psyche. But the frenzied narration becomes calm when she realizes that "the complaint is the answer."[50] She can finally see her complex rhetorical flourishes as mere babbling, her anger as woundedness. She knows that in this moment, she "was being unmade."[51] The answer she was looking for could not be uttered in words because words are too abstract, too practical, too disconnected from the real. The answer to all her longing, pain, and misplaced anger is in the face of the gods, who ultimately give her a face, an identity. Orual, like all human beings, needed to spend time alone, contemplating her own wretchedness so that she realized her utter dependence on the gods (God) for redemption and eyes to see the real way of love, self-sacrifice. Once recognizing this in ourselves, we can see that so much of our human frailty lies in the attempt to avoid facing our own wretchedness. Seeing this in ourselves and others can lead us to feeling a deep sense of what Graham Greene calls "pity" for the state of broken image bearers.[52] This, once again, is a step toward the path of empathetic love.

THE AGE OF ADZ

But this is a rocky path, especially as humans continue to cling to false ideas of love that are more rooted in self-preservation or individual glory than sacrifice. Each of these works of art reminds us of the constant pendulum swing between reality and fantasy, truth and delusion, cynicism and romanticism. But each also reminds us that the imagination can be informed through interactions with prophetic art, enabling us to see our common humanity more clearly. Sufjan Stevens's experimental 2010 album *The Age of Adz* is another reminder that love is too easily confused with consumption or a form of narcissism. Unlike his many previous folk-focused albums, this one revisits the noisy experimental electronica of 2001's *Enjoy Your Rabbit*. But *The Age of Adz* combines Stevens's folk flourishes with chaotic rhythms, tinny autotune, and so many other tricks of the glossy rock star trade. In the making of this album, indie-folk darling Stevens both mocks himself and examines himself. It's no surprise that Flannery O'Connor is one of his biggest literary influences. The eccentric, unpredictable sonic offerings are bookended by two short folk pieces in which we can hear Stevens's delicate voice loud and clear, charting a path from chaos to clarity. The album's first song, "Futile Devices," posits that words are empty when trying to explain love or clearly describe the human condition. After describing words as "futile devices," Stevens launches into an album containing some of the most cryptic lyrics of his highly esoteric catalog.[53] The words are in the background as the music itself expresses the "tangled" knot of human existence in a way that transcends words.[54]

Like Orual in *Till We Have Faces*, Stevens, the central character of his own autobiographical album, recognizes that words are not always connected to meaning—perhaps not ever fully connected to it. There is no clear vocabulary of the soul, especially if the mind coaxes the soul to lie to itself. And on Stevens's somewhat shocking album, he deconstructs the Romantic idea of the artist as prophet, even asking if his sense of personal calling is a delusion of grandeur. As he entangles his narrative of spiritual wrestling with highlights from the life of mentally ill folk artist Royal Robertson, he asks whether the desire to create is evidence for transcendent meaning or a coping mechanism for existential despair in a possibly godless universe. This is a raw, intimate portrait of a man searching for the capacity to connect with another human being. As we know, the arts can feed our imagination in the way of contemplation, compassion, and empathy—but they can also serve as a distraction, perhaps especially for the artist. As Stevens deconstructs his own ego, he recognizes that his prophetic role must be based on humility rather than grandeur. If it is not, then all he (and we) ends up with are layers of chaotic delusion that look deep and meaningful.

Stevens's album takes on an impossibly large, abstract collection of questions about God, life, and relationships. He wades through the wretchedness of his own self-deceit, yet he begins this journey with deceptively nice words about how hard it is to speak "love" to his partner: "And I would say I love you / But saying it out loud is hard / So I won't say it at all / And I won't stay very long."[55] These words are, as the song title tells us, "futile devices." He does, however, attempt to describe the existential experience of love: "But you are life I needed all along."[56] After this gentle proclamation, the album leaves the familiarity of folk confession and plunges into the broken psyche of Stevens, the artist. He admits that it is all "too much," yet "I want it all, I want it all for myself."[57] Although the words he has used on past albums emphasizing his devout Christian faith connect the present act of creating to the reality of eternity, he now questions that belief: "When it dies, when it dies / It rots / This is the Age of Adz / Eternal living."[58] The album is steeped in cynical irony as Stevens considers that perhaps "eternal living" is a dream produced by the "Age of Adz," and the reality *could* be that we, and all the things we create, simply "rot."[59]

The album's title has a double meaning that sheds some light on the many tensions in the story that Stevens is telling. An "adze" is an instrument used for cutting and shaping wood, and the same adze could also take its own creation apart. As an artist creates, she is assembling a structure, a story, a picture of reality; but art can also be used as a tool to tear this structure down and examine it. An "adze" in the hands of an artist can both construct and deconstruct, and in this album, Stevens is deconstructing his use of words to express truth and meaning. His tangled sense of self and reality is exposed, raw, and painful, and he cries out at one point, "I want to be well." As Pascal so often wrote, we are creatures that love to be distracted from the very root of our sickness or to be distracted from the recognition that the sickness exists at all.[60] In thinking of Stevens's treatment of the human condition on this album, it is helpful to highlight the second symbolic use of the term *adze* in the title of the song and album. Stevens's shortening the word to "adz" is a significant play on words so that the song and album title looks like the "Age of Ads." As Stevens explores the hidden places within his psyche, he works to disentangle the images of pop-star America from the reality of his role as a creator.

Zadie Smith's focus on the "originating trauma" in the stories of contemporary Western fiction relates to the perplexing trauma that is described—or better yet, sounded out—in Stevens's album: "Why are these writers burned, what is the originating trauma exactly? Two things seem prominent: fear of death and advertising. The two, of course, are intimately connected. There is no death in advertising, as an industry it is the league of anti-death, and this generation has seen advertising grow to inhabit the very fabric of their lives. Meanwhile death reveals itself as the nasty sting they never imagined at the end of the tale."[61] Although Stevens's world is inundated with images of a material future, an attainable, mythological eternity, he is aware that this is a false construct. This understanding of reality based on ads that lie about the dark undercurrent of life and death must be deconstructed. So the "Age of Adz" is chopped down and reshaped, as if with an adze. In his video for "Too Much," we see images of Stevens wearing a Nike T-shirt, tangled up in fluorescent ropes and aluminum foil pieces, dancing as if he is leading an aerobics class.[62] He is larger than life, but the images make no sense; they are all gloss and no substance. They are "too much," but his self-image is "riding on that."[63] And the entire album critiques this need for distraction, this fear of facing the real self and the real human condition. All the glossy lies must be deconstructed if one is to see himself and others honestly. Only when a clearing is made, a space for the light of reality, can true empathy connect one human being to another. But this often seems impossible.

In the album's final song, "Impossible Soul," Stevens takes us on an existential odyssey through the deepest deceptions, finally revealing themselves with painful, self-deprecating truth. This intentionally messy composition is twenty-five minutes long, and its movements are extreme, poignant, confusing, and even despairing. "Impossible Soul" is full of chants, tinny autotune choruses, and lots of seemingly happy pop. But the celebration is an illusion, another distraction to cover up the inconstancy of Stevens's "impossible soul" as he sings to his partner, reminding her that "it's a long life" with "only one last chance."[64] And because they only have one chance, he asks her to dance, to share distraction with him, to pretend that the word *love* is real. But the last four minutes of this noisy, messy, falsely jubilant self-parody wind down to a few final unexpected minutes of bare folk chords. The autotune has been scrapped and the real Sufjan emerges. His greatest moment on the album is a simple confession of his wretchedness as a "selfish man" who wants "nothing less than pleasure" when he asks his partner to spend the night.[65] This is a confession not of love of other but of self-love. Empathy and compassion are absent, and the chaos of the album is the work it takes to deconstruct the many false facades that the artist has erected in the name of love and art.

The speaker's lover is a victim of his consumption—but then again, so is he. Like Orual in *Till We Have Faces*, he initially believes in his own definition of love, something that leads to pleasure and self-protection. But their love is not really love at all but a sort of practical narcissism. *The Age of Adz* is a journey of a sick soul limping along while believing its own false narrative. According to writer/priest Thomas Merton, the "beginning of love" only occurs when we submit our will to the will of the other, letting "those we love be perfectly themselves" rather than attempting to "twist them to fit our image."[66] In recognizing the dangerous, deceptively safe haven of our own worship of self, we can begin to see and confess our own particular patterns of wretchedness. Only then are we being honest about the desperate, yet glorious, reality of the human condition. As Stevens examines even his supposedly prophetic impulses, he reveals the "impossible soul" that is so familiar to us all, the constant back and forth between truth and deception. This is a portrait of the imagination gone wrong, erecting idolatrous towers inside the self. But as we take this journey with Stevens, the embattled artist, we see the great and painful sacrifices it takes to reveal our own motives. After identifying these and resisting them, we can move forward in love and empathy, even more informed about the battle that is within both ourselves and our neighbors.

Better Call Saul

Stevens's album illustrates the ways that the sins of self-love and pride can erode the relationship with the self and prevent love and empathy for the other. This perpetual erosion of self and disconnect to the neighbor is also a large theme in Vince Gilligan's hilarious, harrowing portrait of lovable con man Saul Goodman in the television series *Better Call Saul*. Like Orual and Stevens, Saul constructs false narratives that guide his relationships. But unlike Orual and Stevens, he is fully aware that he is doing it. His story is less about delusion than it is about intentional falsifications. But even this has its hidden deceptions as the con artist realizes that relationships cannot survive without the oxygen of humility, honesty, and empathetic love. Gilligan's beautiful and notorious *Breaking Bad*, a series that examines the ways that pride destroys relationships, is perhaps the most well-crafted television series to have ever been made and an admittedly very rough ride. The character of Saul Goodman, amoral con man lawyer for a seedy underground network of methamphetamine dealers, is a character whom many would initially rather forget. In *Breaking Bad*, Saul is known for his garish suits, equally garish commercials, and purely pragmatic approach to making as much money as possible. The show's central characters, high school chemistry teacher / meth cook Walter White and his former student / current dealer sidekick Jesse Pinkman, reach out to Goodman when they need a lawyer who knows their business and intentions. At one point, Jesse explains to his (then) naive former teacher, "You don't need a criminal lawyer; you need a *criminal* lawyer."[67] And Saul Goodman is that man, his last name as ironic as we expect it to be. Saul is a shell of a man, as slimy and self-interested as they come. He seems irredeemable.

Even the actor playing Saul Goodman, Bob Odenkirk, was hesitant when he heard the series proposal because "I don't like Saul."[68] But watching *Better Call Saul*, the prequel to *Breaking Bad*, makes the viewer feel both convicted and sad, not two responses that one expects when watching the life story of such a reprehensible character. The show reminds viewers, once again, of the complexity of the human condition and the tragic plight of all human beings when they ignore the *imago Dei* in themselves and others. We learn early on that Saul Goodman is not the main character's real name (surprise, surprise). The series' sad-sack antihero is a man named James McGill, "Jimmy." He has been a fast-talking con man / scam artist most of his life, so much so that he picked up the nickname "Slippin' Jimmy."[69] Jimmy/Saul's glory and wretchedness are often concurrently on display, battling it out for the claim to his identity. As seedy as he is, Jimmy is also very smart and very charming, perhaps a more likable Eddie Haskell.

Jimmy's story is defined largely by his relationship with his older brother, Chuck, a successful lawyer whose mental illness has forced him to be homebound as he fears the toxic impact of electricity on his body. Jimmy visits Chuck every day, shuffling through his dark house in order to place groceries and ice in a cooler. He even drives across town regularly to buy Chuck's favorite newspaper, only available at one newsstand. Jimmy loves Chuck, and we learn that, to some degree, he has always wanted to be Chuck—or at least wanted to win Chuck's approval. Jimmy chooses to believe that Chuck is telling the truth, that his brother's illness is purely physical rather than mental—even as Chuck has confined himself inside a house with no electricity, asking any visitors to place cell phones in his mailbox and touch a metal rod to "ground themselves" before entering the home.[70] Jimmy is like a loyal puppy dog, often straying off the path and getting into trouble but coming back to the one he loves, begging for approval. But Chuck does not approve. We see a flashback of Chuck's former life as an attorney, using his position and skills to get Jimmy released from jail when Jimmy commits an obscene petty crime. Jimmy's crimes are seemingly harmless, and almost all of them are spiteful acts to disempower the status quo rich. As crooked as he was, there was still a faint glimmer of Robin Hood justice. Well, not always. Jimmy was also always sneaky, even stealing money from the cash register of his kind yet gullible father's convenience shop. As much as he continually got into trouble, he was always accepted with open arms back into the family. His waywardness made him even more lovable, it seems.

Although Chuck is brilliant and successful, his jealousy of and resentment toward Jimmy grows exponentially—so much so that when Jimmy secretly passes the bar exam and becomes a lawyer, Chuck does everything that he can to block Jimmy's success. In one heartbreaking scene, Jimmy confronts his brother after he finds out that it is Chuck who has been willfully working against him, preventing him from gaining reputable employment. A broken Jimmy begs Chuck to tell him why he does it, why he would block opportunities for his own brother. Chuck's cowardice turns to steely cold anger when he looks at Jimmy with dead eyes, full of contempt: "You are not a real lawyer. University of American Samoa . . . an online course? What a joke! I worked my ass off to get where I am, and you make these shortcuts—and you think that suddenly you're my peer? You do what I do because you are funny, and you make people laugh. I committed my life to this! You don't slide into it like a cheap pair of slippers and then reap all of the rewards."[71] Chuck's resentment is acidic and devastating. He continues by telling Jimmy that "the law is sacred."[72] Chuck hides his pride and jealousy behind loyalty to some abstract concept of morality, the "sacred" law.[73] He tells Jimmy that "if you abuse that power, people get hurt." Chuck's self-deception is as thick as his hate.[74] Jimmy, clearly hurt, asks, "I thought you were proud of me?" and Chuck responds, "I was—when you straightened up and got a job in the mailroom."[75] Jimmy winces at the pain of this condescension, responding, "So that's it—keep old Jimmy down in the mailroom because he's not good enough to be a lawyer."[76] And Jimmy is right. He sees clearly through his brother's coded words. The final blow comes when Chuck lets Jimmy know that he has absolutely no faith in his brother's possibility for redemption: "I know you. I know what you were. What you are. And people don't change. You're slipping Jimmy. Slipping Jimmy with a law degree is like a chimp with a machine gun."[77] Chuck's brutal comments ignore the deep goodness in Jimmy: his faithfulness as a brother, his kindness to his elderly clients, his incredible perseverance to secretly pass the bar exam. Throughout the series, Chuck's jealousy of and cruelty toward his brother only work to make Jimmy become more human in our eyes. We pity him and search for glimpses of his goodness, an exercise that inches, ultimately, toward the development of empathy.

Of course, Chuck is correct on many fronts—Jimmy is a brilliant con man, and he does drag many others, including his unflappably stable girlfriend, Kim, down with him. But Chuck's motivations are far more personal than this. In this regard, the series provides a modern-day allusion to the prodigal son parable, in which Chuck is the older brother and Jimmy is the prodigal. Chuck has always done things the right way: he obeyed his parents, he married a very beautiful and accomplished woman, he went to a reputable law school, and he built one of the most lucrative, prestigious law firms in the Southwest. Jimmy, on the other hand, always cut corners, spun stories, and squandered the kindness and love of his parents. His law degree came from an online course given by the American College of Samoa, and in the series' present day, he cons his way into attracting business by staging a publicity stunt in which he heroically rescues a worker falling off the edge of a billboard. He also attracts the worst company and clients, including cartel associates and dirty cops. But he does so with quick wit, charm, and humor. When one of the cops arresting his client tells him that, in his white suit, he looks like Matlock, without a beat, Jimmy responds, "You are wrong. I look like a young Paul Newman dressed as Matlock."[78]

Regardless of his wit and accomplishments, Jimmy has a deep sense of shame, and he feels more at home in humble settings with broken people. To some degree, he still sees himself through his brother's eyes: as a loser who does not deserve more than the dregs. Even when he lands a lucrative job in a high-powered firm, he feels like a misfit. The firm supplies him with a lush apartment and a luxury car, yet he sneaks back into his one-room office/apartment in the back of a nail salon. It's the only place he can really sleep. And he breathes a sigh of relief once he has (purposefully) been fired from the job and can surrender his corporate car for the rusty two-tone clunker that he loves. These are the things that comfort him because he does not feel worthy of anything else. Jimmy knows he is a prodigal, yet Chuck does not realize the damage that he does as the "older brother."

In the parable from Luke 15, Jesus tells his disciples that when the prodigal comes home after a life of debauchery and waste, his father is overjoyed, running to him with open arms. Yet his brother, the "good" son, stands back, seething with anger over the attention his younger brother receives. He tells his father, "Look! All these years I've been slaving for you and never disobeyed your orders. Yet you never gave me even a young goat so I could celebrate with my friends. But when this son of yours who has squandered your property with prostitutes comes home, you kill the fattened calf for him!"[79] The father in the parable explains to the eldest son that he is deeply loved and that everything the family owns is also his. But he also expresses his deep joy, a reason to "celebrate and be glad, because this brother of yours was dead and is alive again; he was lost and is found."[80] We do not hear the brother's final response in the parable—but his father's love for him is clear. He is not favoring one son over another but finding joy in regaining a lost son. In the world of *Better Call Saul*, Chuck never allows the hardness of his heart to break for his often-lost brother. Unlike the parable, there are hints that their childhood was dysfunctional and that Jimmy was truly treated as a favorite, a toxicity that could certainly explain the division between the brothers.

Chuck's near deification of the law is a type of performance-based legalism somewhat paralleling the works-based morality of the older brother in the parable. He is clinging to his own idea of goodness, and Jimmy is a deviant who can never be redeemed or measure up to Chuck's standard. Jimmy is finally able to outsmart Chuck and undermine one of his brother's court cases, ruining Chuck's self-image and reputation. Although what Jimmy does is highly unethical, he does it for the sake of his girlfriend, Kim, in order to give her what was rightfully hers. The murky morality of this situation is typical for the story lines of *Better Call Saul,* and as we follow along, we wrestle with what is truly right or wrong in a relational context.

After Jimmy betrays his brother, they have one final interaction—and the words spoken to Jimmy by Chuck inevitably push him head-first into amoral quicksand. At the beginning of the scene, Jimmy tells Chuck that he has regrets for what he has just done. Chuck's response is completely emotionless as he describes how he sees Jimmy:

> Don't bother. What's the point? You are just going to keep hurting people.
>
> Jimmy—this is what you do. You hurt people over and over and over and over and then there's this show of remorse. If you are not going to change your behavior, and you won't, why not just skip the whole exercise?[81]

Chuck's diagnosis of Jimmy is dehumanizing and cruel. He sees no hope in or for his brother. Chuck is manipulative and abusive, a master at gaslighting who positions himself as the victim. He knows that Jimmy sees himself through Chuck's eyes, and he refuses even a trace of validation. The final words spoken from Chuck to Jimmy are the ultimate death blow to Jimmy's sense of self, value, and purpose: "I don't want to hurt your feelings. But the truth is, you've never mattered all that much to me."[82] Because Jimmy sees himself in the eyes and esteem of his brother, this kills him. Jimmy soon dies, and Saul Goodman is born.

Saul is the epitome of all the things that Chuck hates. He lacks a moral compass, he has poor taste, and his wretchedness is worn as a badge of honor. The dysfunctional family dynamics in *Better Call Saul* are seeds that eventually grow Jimmy into Saul, a poignant example of the ways in which an outside force can impact the existential pendulum swing between "great" and "wretched" inside a troubled man.[83] In Saul's case, both abuse and lack of approval coax him toward clinging to wretchedness, and he ultimately defines himself by it. Unlike O'Connor's story, Lewis's novel, and Stevens's album, there is not an obviously redemptive ending here. But the power of this series is its depiction of Jimmy's beautiful humanity even after he heaps dirt and grime upon himself and all that come near him. Contrary to what Jean-Paul Sartre teaches, Jimmy/Saul's value is not determined by his poor choices. He behaves despicably but is still worthy of love. While watching this series, viewers once again see the to-and-fro-ing of an inherent, pitiable human condition—and they also see the tragedy of a man whose lack of childhood support and empathy leads him to self-destruct.

A RAISIN IN THE SUN

Like Jimmy, Walter Lee Younger in Lorraine Hansberry's play *A Raisin in the Sun* is psychologically and emotionally damaged from the abuse he has endured. Unlike Jimmy, this abuse is not familial but systemic, and for the working-class Black Younger family, this means that it is even more inescapable. Hansberry's seminal play about injustice and familial trauma illustrates the ways in which, in order to understand the perceived wretchedness of another, we also need to look at their position in society. Walter Lee Younger has the same human tendencies as Orual, Saul, and others, but his path is even rockier because of the color of his skin. Hansberry is asking her readers, many of whom have never experienced the impact of systemic injustice, to see Walter Lee as a full, complex, redeemable human being. He is a difficult character, but like every human being, he is worthy of compassion and empathy.

Walter Lee Younger lives in a tiny Chicago apartment with his wife, Ruth; younger sister, Beneatha; mother, Lena; and young son, Travis. He is a proud man—so proud that it causes him pain every morning when he sees his child using the living room couch as a bed.[84] Walter's father has died, and he is supposedly now the head of this intergenerational family, yet he acts more like his son than he does his deceased father. The play opens with Walter's wife having to go to great lengths to wake him up for work. In fact, he is harder to wake up than young Travis, and Ruth is responsible for forcing both of them into the day. Hansberry's play exposes both the wretchedness and greatness within Walter, but she particularly emphasizes how his socialization in a systemically racist society has triggered some wretched, yet understandable, responses.

Walter is a chauffeur for a wealthy white family, and he can barely make ends meet for his own family. For this, he feels great shame and wants to prove to himself that, even as he is disempowered by a white supremacist infrastructure, he is still a man. Walter is a hard worker, but he also has some con man tendencies, not unlike Jimmy's. He's always looking for a get-rich-quick scheme, and he goes so far as investing the family's inheritance in one such scheme without even telling his mother. Like so much African American literature, Hansberry's play exposes the dark underside of the American dream in a country where, as Martin Luther King Jr. posits, there are "two Americas."[85] Although Walter hates the white supremacist class system that, to some extent, defines his sense of identity, he realizes that he must play by its rules in order to succeed and be seen as a man who can provide for his family. He plays by these rules for so long that he eventually internalizes them, a common response to racialized trauma. In order to get by, Walter must assimilate. His sister, Beneatha, attempts to resist assimilation by dating a Nigerian man and spending time studying about Africa. But her boyfriend mocks her because her very hairstyle, a straightening perm, is evidence of the ways that she has internalized white standards of beauty and social acceptance.

Both Beneatha and Walter struggle to define their identities in a society where they are born with what W. E. B. Du Bois calls a "double consciousness."[86] They are not at home in their country of origin, yet they are not accepted as fully human in their country of birth. And the ways in which they are taught to see their own value is through the eyes of white America, always subject to the white gaze. Walter sees wealth and comfort as the hallmarks of the American dream; they are two of the country's founding values and the tools he must use to validate himself. If he learns the clever games of white supremacist materialism, then they can benefit him and his family. This all comes to a head when he is given another opportunity to make lots of money. His mother's dream of owning a house is near fulfillment as the family's offer on a suburban home with a white picket fence has been accepted. But soon after they begin packing to leave, a white man named Mr. Linder comes to their apartment to try to convince them to not move into the neighborhood. He is willing to offer them a large sum of money to buy them out and keep the neighborhood white. Lena, Beneatha, and Ruth strongly reject the bribe, recognizing that to accept it would also be accepting a white supremacist narrative that claims that Black Americans are not fit to live in white society. Accepting this offer would deny both their dignity and their full humanity.

Walter, however, is more concerned with the practical than the ethical, and he is willing to sell this dignity for the sake of preserving what he sees as his manhood. Beneatha angrily challenges him, yelling, "Where is the bottom?" and claiming that he is not a "man, but a rat."[87] Walter is dehumanizing himself and taking the family with him, yet he shows no concern for this. His mother gently asks him, "Baby, how you going to feel on the inside?"[88] In his response, we see the war that is within Walter Younger, the resistance of greatness, of *imago Dei* recognition, for the sake of a man-made identity bought from racists. As he pauses to answer his mother, Hansberry writes that "the word 'man' has penetrated his consciousness."[89] Walter's speech, baring the ugliness of his intended deed, is explosive, devastating: "Fine. . . . Going to feel fine! . . . I'm going to look that son-of-a-bitch in the eyes and say. . . . That's your neighborhood out there! You got the right to keep it like you want! You got the right to have it like you want! . . . And you people just put the money in my hand and you won't have to live next to this bunch of stinking niggers! . . . And maybe, maybe I'll just get down on my Black knees . . . Captain, Mistuh, Bossman . . . Great White Father . . . just gi' ussen de money. . . . And I'll feel fine! Fine! FINE!"[90] Walter drops to his knees, affecting the dialect so often used in minstrel shows to mock Black Americans. He knows he is a sellout, and he yells louder and louder in order to convince himself that he is "fine" with it. Walter is aware of his internalization of white supremacy, and this awareness leads to his salvation from it. Only in recognizing this particular form of wretchedness can he escape it.

When Walter's family questions his actions, he says, "I didn't make this world! It was give to me this way!"[91] He is right. He is a Black man living in a country that originally defined his only worth by treating him as a commodity. According to that mindset, the Black man is only as good as the amount of money he can bring in. Walter attempts to reappropriate this, making it work for himself for the sake of his "manhood." Instead, it chips away at his humanity. When he decides to accept Linder's money, his mother sits, rocking, and moans, "Yes—death done come in this here house."[92] Although the family will receive lots of money, it is a trade-off for her son's spiritual death and the death of the family's dignity. Walter will be paid to embrace his wretchedness, turning a blind eye to its damage. Beneatha is understandably enraged and claims that there is "nothing left to love" in her brother.[93]

It is at this moment in the play that we see the redemptive power of empathy. And as the play's readers and viewers witness it, they also create space for it in themselves. Walter's mother recognizes that there is always deep greatness in a human being, and even if they have been socialized to ignore it, it cannot be fully destroyed. She tells Beneatha, "There is always something left to love."[94] She then challenges her to see Walter as he really is: "Have you cried for that boy today? I don't mean for yourself and for the family cause we lost the money. I mean for him: what he been through and what it done to him. Child, when do you think is the time to love somebody most? . . . It's when he's at his lowest and can't believe in hisself 'cause the world done whipped him so? When you start measuring somebody, measure him right, child, measure him right. Make sure you done taken into account what hills and valleys he come through before he got to wherever he is."[95] Lena asks her daughter to think about what it would be like to be a man in Walter's shoes, beaten down by a society that thinks of him as nothing more than a servant. Walter's desperate grab for money is a complex reflection of both his wretchedness and his greatness. He desperately wants to provide for his family, but he has inherited the myth that money is the only thing that can give him his humanity in a racist world.

As despicable as Walter's initial decision is, it's so very understandable. When someone has been treated like an animal for so long, they must adapt and even behave along the lines of their very abusive treatment. But his mother's tender, bold empathy saves Walter. Just as he is about to receive the money, Lena places Travis in front of him. He will have to look at his child as he sells his dignity for a "manhood" defined by white supremacy. As he looks at Travis's face, the face of his own future, he cannot do it. He resists the easy temptation, and the greatness, his true manhood, emerges. He is saved by his mother's empathy, and as we witness this, our own empathy for Walter grows.

Each of these stories focuses on a central character's struggle to navigate a lifelong desire to be loved and recognized while, at the same time, being constantly confronted with their tendencies toward wretchedness. The fickle child in O'Connor's story provides a blueprint of the inconstancy of the human condition, especially for those who cling to faith while battling their own pride. Both Orual and Stevens's artist have fooled themselves into believing that their self-love is a love of the other. Jimmy/Saul is an endearing con man, desperately wanting acceptance from his brother but unable to accept himself. Instead, he clings to his "slippery" badness rather than his equally enduring goodness. Walter is a man who wants to provide for a family that he loves, but his identity has been stripped away by a racist society that defines him only by what they see as his badness. All of these characters are both wretched and glorious, and their experience of life and a desire to love and be loved are anything but simple. As we follow their journeys, we are reminded that human beings are incredibly complicated, chaotic, and complex, and we feel the exhaustion of just being human. As we see ourselves on the screen, in the song, or on the page, we realize that all humans are this complicated, this depraved, this beautiful, this worthy of love. The more we expand our understanding of the human condition, the more we expand our desire to empathize and, hopefully, turn this desire into an embodied reality.

Chapter Three

STORIES AS
SELF-REFLECTION

Convicting Narratives

King David's conscience was seared. After committing adultery with Bathsheba, he then put her husband, Uriah, on the front line to be killed in battle. Second Samuel shows us that the very man "after [God's] own heart" no longer had eyes to see his sin or ears to hear the pain he caused others.[1] But then the prophet Nathan came to visit him to tell him a story that moved him deeply, reigniting the hidden empathy and sense of justice within him. David's lack of self-reflection constricted his capacity for imaginative empathy so much that he could not see past himself. As he heard the prophet's story of a poor man whose dearly loved lamb was taken away by a rich man who had many of his own lambs to spare, the king "burned with anger" and exclaimed, "As surely as the Lord lives, the man who did this must die!"[2] David's blindness to his own sins is astounding, even frightening. He was unable to read himself or discern truth from the metaphorical narrative that paralleled his own life. Nathan eventually tells him that he, in fact, is the cruel, selfish man in the story and that he must repent. Only then does David admit, "I have sinned against the Lord."[3]

Narrative has the power to captivate our minds, to prick our consciences, to help us see ourselves more clearly. We cannot love and understand the other *as* ourselves if we do not have love and understanding for ourselves. Sometimes self-love looks like painful honesty that leads to conviction. Without this self-reflective honesty, we cannot see ourselves clearly, so any significant changes will be superficial.

The path to spiritual transformation is a painful one, and as both Flannery O'Connor and Blaise Pascal show us, we have normalized hiding from ourselves. We are so afraid to sit alone in a room—to take genuine inventory of our inner worlds—that we need to be shaken up, disturbed, and confronted by an outside source. These apocalyptic awakenings are disruptive as they challenge our apathy and denial, but they are the means to rehumanization from dehumanization.

One of the most disturbing aspects of reading 1 and 2 Samuel is how quickly David develops a callous over a once-soft heart. In his pride, he loses sight of his wretchedness until God sends a prophet to enable him to see it. The means to this disclosure is the telling of a story. We see a similar pattern in Shakespeare's most famous play, *Hamlet*. As the story opens, Prince Hamlet has just lost his father, King Hamlet, to mysterious circumstances. To make matters even worse, his mother has married his uncle, Claudius, shortly after the king's death. Prince Hamlet is rightfully angry with his mother's hasty marriage, but his focus soon veers to his uncle, the newly crowned King Claudius, when he is visited by his dead father's ghost. The ghost of King Hamlet tells his son that his death was not natural or accidental; he was murdered by the same brother who is now the king and Hamlet's stepfather. Hamlet is outraged but also dubious. He does not know if he can trust this ghost because "the devil hath power t' assume a pleasing shape."[4] He then has an ingenious idea based on his understanding of the convicting powers of art. He stages a play called "The Mousetrap" for all in the castle court to see, and the plot is based on the murder story that he was told by his ghost father.[5] He knows that if Claudius sees the murder on stage and is truly guilty, then he will react in such a way to expose his guilt. Hamlet's famous line, "The play's the thing wherein I'll catch the conscience of the King," is correct.[6] His uncle watches the play, sees the staged murder, and runs out of the theater in a moment of shame and conviction. Great stories that reflect the truth of our condition and even expose our specific behavioral patterns can be powerful agents for self-reflection that lead to change.

Reading, watching, and listening to stories can enable us to see both our own wretchedness and our own glory more clearly. Ironically, we spend a good deal of our lives trying to hide our wretchedness from others, from ourselves, and even from God. The fact that we can often see, feel, suffer, and acknowledge our own self-deception is a gift. Christ acknowledges the gift of having eyes to see wretchedness when, in Mark, he is accused of eating with "sinners"; he responds, "It is not the healthy who need a doctor, but the sick."[7] Unlike the Pharisees, these "sinners" knew the depth of their need and, in humility, sought a cure. Paradoxically, this sort of humble honesty about our distorted inner life is the first step toward a transformative self-love. We must be able to see how we hurt ourselves and others before we can actively change and begin to love both ourselves and others.

Any story telling the hopeful truth about our own spiritual narrative must show both wretchedness and greatness in a trajectory from dehumanization to rehumanization. As we witness both the internal wrestling and the process of conversion or sanctification in the lives of fictional protagonists, we are prompted to examine our own lives. These stories can function similarly to the prophet Nathan's story, enabling us to see the reality of our own patterns of depravity and the concrete hope for redemption. The films *The Tree of Life* and *The Addiction* and the short story collection *Life after God* all prophetically illustrate the movement from chaos to peace in their protagonists. Each personal transformation is the result of a supernatural outside source and/or unexpected, painful circumstances pressing down on the protagonist's fragile sense of self and reality. As we watch these outside sources propel protagonists toward their internal change, we are coaxed into a space of uncomfortable spiritual self-analysis because of the story, itself an outside source. These stories of self-reflection, spiritual encounter, and final transformation help readers adapt a posture of empathy as we see the ways in which the close analysis of self can lead to change. If this can happen for the problematic characters on the page and screen, it can happen for us. And if it can happen for us, it can happen for our neighbors. Each of these stories of confession and redemption focuses on the glorious process of self-awareness that leads to confession and change. And as we bear witness to this process through fiction, we are redirected to bestow grace upon our fellow human beings, seeking to empathize as they wrestle toward transformation.

THE TREE OF LIFE

Director Terrence Malick's well-known arthouse film *The Tree of Life* not only employs traditional narrative forms to expose human wretchedness; it relies on disorienting abstraction, shock, exaggeration, and distortion to confront viewers with their own depravity, making the invisible visible. This film demands viewer participation. It does not *work* if we sit back and passively await entertainment or an easily unearthed message. While attentively following its perplexing narrative, we must do a lot of our own work. As with all deeply spiritual, complex works of art, there are many questions left unanswered. Unlike many comfortable mainstream movie narratives, these films resist popular, big-bucks formulas. The growth of the soul is never formulaic.

The Tree of Life begins with a series of whimsical images from a young girl's early life: cows in a field, a child holding a baby lamb, a field full of sunflowers. But these comforting images are, at the same time, melancholy, as a somber dirge plays in the background, accompanied by a voice-over of a woman reflecting upon the childhood teaching she received from the nuns that led her school: "The nuns taught us there are two ways through life—the way of nature and the way of grace."[8] The voice continues, explaining that "grace doesn't try to please itself. Accepts being slighted, forgotten, disliked. Accepts insults and injuries."[9] Throughout the movie, we see examples of the "way of grace" as Christlike sacrificial love but also, at times, unhealthy submission.[10] The actions of "grace" as Malick defines them provide a sharp contrast to the way of nature: "Nature only wants to please itself. Get others to please it too. Likes to lord it over them. To have its own way. It finds reasons to be unhappy when all the world is shining around it. And love is smiling through all things."[11] The way of nature is the survival of the fittest, the drive to succeed at all costs, even if it harms others on the way. This dichotomy is an artistic reflection of Pascal's description of the human condition: the great battling the wretched, the *imago Dei* battling depravity, the spirit battling the flesh.

The woman in the film's introductory voice-over is Mrs. O'Brien, wife to Mr. O'Brien and mother to three boys, including the film's chief protagonist, Jack. The O'Briens are a devout Catholic family living in a suburban Waco, Texas, neighborhood in 1956. Malick's main narrative focuses on both the past and present of Jack's spiritual coming-of-age story that we experience along with him through flashbacks, shots from the present day, and enigmatic scenes from an ethereal future outside of time. The film contains both macro- and micronarratives as we watch the daily life events of the O'Brien family unfold while contained within a larger story: the creation of the world, God's work in the world, and the end of time.

As Jack is born and grows up, we see him move from childhood innocence to preadult experience, and his two guides, his mother and father, are polar spiritual forces at war within him. Mr. O'Brien is an ambitious businessman who defines his manhood by how successful he is in the material world and how much he can mold his young sons into successful men in his own image. He ultimately follows the "way of nature" as he ignores the needs of his family, the created beauty around him, and his own prideful arrogance.[12] Mr. O'Brien's children are nervous around him, as he could snap at any minute if his boys gravitate from the scripts he has written for their lives. When their father leaves his wife and sons for a few weeks on a business trip to Asia, the family collectively breathes a sigh of relief. Mrs. O'Brien becomes a child again, chasing her boys around the house and squealing in response to the pranks they delightfully play upon her.

Mrs. O'Brien's approach to the world looks more like the "way of grace."[13] She is captivated by the life, beauty, and freshness of the world around her as well as the inner lives of her own children. In one strange, beautiful sequence, young Jack sees his mother floating in the air, twirling around, her skirt blowing in the breeze. She is a nymph, a fairy, lighter than air yet a well of deep love and empathy. Here Malick is showing us a child's view of his mother: she is magical, otherworldly, and ever-present. But Jack's experience of reality is not always so full of joy, peace, and simplicity. Like any child, Jack develops his central ideas about God through his relationships with his parents. The more he endures the unpredictable wrath of his domineering, perfectionist father, the more he begins to ask questions about the goodness of God. Jack and his brother are always scolded for putting their elbows on the dinner table—but their father freely puts his elbows on the table. Jack is angry with this hypocrisy; he is also angry that his father flirts with women, "insults people," and never gets caught or rebuked. At one point, Jack asks God, "Why does he hurt us? Our father?"[14] When Jack witnesses another boy his age drowning in a pool, he relates the line of reasoning about his father's hypocrisy to the character of God. He asks God if the boy was "bad," and he cries out to God, "Where were you? You let a boy die! You let anything happen."[15] The most painful question that Jack asks God as he is consumed with grief over the seemingly nonsensical loss of his friend is "Why should I be good if you aren't?"[16] As the film continues, we see Jack's increasing skepticism as he questions God, viewing him through the broken lens of his father's behavior while also asking age-old questions about suffering and the problem of evil.

Although Jack's mother is a portrait of grace, her grace is only human and sometimes seems more like fear, cowardice, or conformity to midcentury understandings of gender roles. In one scene, we see Mr. O'Brien react violently at the dinner table to Jack's mildly sarcastic comment. Mrs. O'Brien comforts the boy but does little to protect him. In a voice-over prayer from the adult Jack, we learn that Mrs. O'Brien was his spiritual guide: "You spoke to me through her."[17] Like the nameless child from O'Connor's "A Temple of the Holy Ghost," Jack is a profoundly spiritually sensitive child. As a man, he remembers in prayer that "you spoke with me through the sky, the trees. Before I knew I loved you, believed in you. When did you first touch my heart?"[18] At the same time that he is attuned with the profound glory of God all around him, he is also doubtful, constantly wrestling with grace and nature; he is a picture of what Francis Schaeffer calls a "glorious ruin."[19] As he questions God's role in the world, he begins to resent his grace-filled mother for not protecting him from his father and finally lashes out at her.

It is easy to see the mother/father and grace/nature dichotomy that the film initially presents as just that, a set of binaries that define each character completely. But Malick's narrative is far too complex (and too informed by the biblical narrative) for this. As a child, Jack refers to this seemingly simplistic set of binaries when, in a voice-over, he whispers, "Father. Mother. Always you wrestle inside me. Always you will."[20] Yet the figures of "father" and "mother" are not merely symbolic cardboard cutouts. They are also both glorious ruins moving toward transformation. Mrs. O'Brien's internal wrestling frames the entire film. After the innocent, almost idyllic opening scenes of the child Mrs. O'Brien, we see the adult mother receiving a message that her son has been killed. All details are left out, as the focus is on her suffering with her own grief and her understanding of God. We hear her screams echo over shots of the neighborhood, and then in a haunting voice-over, we hear her questions and final petition directed to God: "Was

I false to you? Lord, why? Where were you? Did you know? Who are we to you? Answer me."[21]

As Mrs. O'Brien cries out these words in her spirit, the narrative that has been somewhat linear thus far collapses into abstraction. We suddenly see rushing water, glimmering shots of the sky, and other decontextualized images of nature and life; we are disoriented, perhaps even frustrated. But as we watch expansive, glorious shots of the planets and heavenly bodies as well as detailed shots of water, land, birds, animals, and human cells evolving, we finally realize that this is the creation of the universe. The music pulsating over these images, from Zbigniew Preisner's "Requiem for a Friend," is somber and powerful, full of joy, strength, and sadness. Although we are witnessing the formation of magnificent life-forms, we are also listening to a portion of a requiem, a song for the dead. The portion of Preisner's piece that we hear is titled "Lacrimosa," Latin for "tears," and it derives its name from "Our Lady of Sorrows," a traditional portion of the Roman Catholic Requiem Mass.

In this sequence of the film, the macronarrative of creation and the micronarrative of an individual human life converge. Mrs. O'Brien's weeping is likened to that of the Virgin Mother, and we are reminded that life has been given via pain and suffering (of childbirth, of the sacrifice of Christ) and that weeping is deeply human and deeply sacred. This very beautiful yet perplexing sequence of images and sounds is a story—*the* story. This is even more poignant if we reflect upon the film's opening epigraph that appears on a silent, black screen before the film begins: "Where were you when I laid the foundations of the earth? . . . When the morning stars sang together, and all the sons of God shouted for joy?"[22] These lines from Job are some of God's answers to Job when he asks questions, similar to those from Mrs. O'Brien, about his sudden, mysterious, and devastating suffering. Mrs. O'Brien's glory—her grace-filled childlike sense of wonder and endearing love—is not what leads to her transformation. It is her recognition of wretchedness, not so much her depravity but her understanding that she is completely powerless, vulnerable, and fragile. As she cries out to God in both anger and confusion, she speaks her own pain and begins to see the way forward: beauty, grace, mystery. The power of the creation is the same power that can rehumanize the parts of her that have died in her son's death. And as we watch her almost passive transformation, the moments when she is stunned into silence and wonder, we are also speechless. Our passivity, along with hers, can become active—the paradox of submission unto life.

Mrs. O'Brien's questions for God are like Jack's questions for God: they both ask why God has not protected them from pain and suffering. To some degree, this is every human being's set of questions for God. A lack of knowledge and inability to understand the knowledge that we think we have are also parts of human wretchedness. The use of disorienting, abstract images in this sequence intentionally forces us out of passivity. We must participate, contemplate, and even meditate on what we are seeing and hearing to try to make sense of it. In this sense, art that is not formulaic and simplistic helps us appreciate mystery and trains us to be attentive to the things of the Spirit. Film scholar Joseph Kickasola argues that "abstract images are particularly valuable for expressing the transcendent, in that they subvert our categorical, sense-making cognitive patterns and force us to re-conceive time and space in more open terms. In a metaphysical context, we would say these terms are cosmic, eternal."[23] This subversion of our "categorical, sense-making cognitive patterns" can feel frustrating and even threatening if we are used to having what Theodor Adorno sees as "standardized" formulas presented to us through art.[24] These depictions of reality tell us what is real rather than alluding to something real beyond our human categories. Films like *The Tree of Life* push us into an uncomfortable yet rewarding space where we can reconceptualize both our humanity and our relationship to God. Both things occur because we are participating in the story before us on the screen, practicing empathy and a sense of community with both the characters and the film director.

Although Malick's narrative is nonlinear and often abstract, there is also much that is concrete and recognizable. During the funeral of the middle O'Brien child, the priest attempts to comfort the family by saying, "He's in God's hands now."[25] But we faintly hear Mrs. O'Brien's inner voice respond, "He was in God's hands all along."[26] These simple words offer little comfort because the mystery is too big, too incomprehensible. In this grief-filled moment, pat phrases feel cruel. After the funeral, one of Mrs. O'Brien's friends resorts to a sort of cruelty, or at least callousness, when she paraphrases the words of Job 1:21, "The Lord gives and he takes away."[27] Although these words could ultimately become a comfort if contextualized to highlight the good-ness of God, she instead follows the verse recitation by saying, "Well, you still have the other two."[28] Later in the film, the same questions are raised when using yet another reference to Job. In a flashback scene, the priest asks the congregation, "Is there nothing which is deathless, nothing which does not pass away?" and the camera pans to a stained-glass image of Christ.[29] The priest's convicting words also target the weaknesses of both Mr. and Mrs. O'Brien: "We must find that which is greater than fortune, fate. Nothing can bring us peace but that. Do you trust in God? Are your friends and children your security?"[30] Just as the sermon foreshadows the wrestling of Mrs. O'Brien's soul upon the death of her son, it also serves to highlight Mr. O'Brien's dan-gerous lack of wrestling. His dog-eat-dog ideology of worldly success leads to spiritual corrosion. Rather than reflecting upon the content of this very convicting, relevant sermon, he instead conducts business outside of the church, using any moment to network. Once in the car, he tells his children, "If you want to succeed, you can't be too good."[31]

Jack follows his father's advice and becomes the self-appointed black sheep of the family. He screams at his mother, steals a woman's slip, and plays painful pranks on his seemingly angelic little brother. Malick traces Jack's relationship with human depravity from the moment when, as a toddler, he first throws a fit and yells "mine!" when a sibling tries to take his toy.[32] Like the child narrator of "A Temple of the Holy Ghost," elementary-age Jack kneels by the side of his bed, reciting rote, passionless prayers. But over the sound of those prayers, we hear a whispered voice-over, the hushed nuance of Jack's true inner prayer: "Where do you live? Are you watching me? I want to know what you are. I want to see what you see."[33] As much as Jack's young heart and mind desire knowledge of God, he also knows that he is more like his father than his mother. He almost has a compulsion to do harm, to sin, and in a paraphrase of Romans 7, he states, "I don't do what I want to do. I do what I hate."[34]

Jack's world abruptly changes when his father loses his job. But the major change for the O'Brien children is not the impending move to another city for work but the spiritual awakening of their father. The same man who tells his sons, "Your mother's naive; it takes fierce will to get ahead in this world," loses the fire behind that will when he is laid off.[35] His entire identity has been based on a masculine construct of power and success. And in subscribing to this worldly ideology, he missed the glory all around him. Like Coleridge in "This Lime-Tree Bower," he can only see the ample, lush beauty of creation and his fellow human beings when he stops focusing on himself. In one of the most beautiful moments of the film, he confesses his own wretchedness, which, paradoxically, allows him to see glory around him and become more glorious himself: "I wanted to be loved because I was great. A big man. I'm nothing. Look. The glory around us. Trees. Birds. . . . I dishonored it all and did not notice the glory. I am a foolish man."[36] Not long after this dramatic and redemptive perception change, Mr. O'Brien embraces Jack and tells him, "You're all I have. You're all I want to have."[37]

After this moment of unexpected reconciliation, the film moves forward in time and then, once again, outside of time. We first see a vibrant city scene and the adult Jack in his confining office space. Soon Jack is in a desert space, a no-man's-land, wandering toward what seems to be nothingness. He finds a doorframe in the middle of this open space, hesitates, and then walks through as the "Agnus Dei" is sung, proclaiming the ultimate message of reconciliation: "Behold the Lamb of God, who has come to take away the sins of the world."[38] We hear Jack's voice asking to be led: "Keep us. Guide us. To the end of time."[39] As the adult Jack staggers through the desert, he soon comes to a beach and a vast ocean. This desert landscape is both Jack's inner world and his future outside of time. As in the poem by the same name, this is a wasteland that is empty and dry—but there is a source of water on the edge of the desert, a safe source of life if one trusts and follows transcendent guidance. Once Jack reaches the edge of the water, he sees his childhood self, his mother, his father, and even his deceased brother.

They embrace one another, and soon after, adult Jack falls to his knees, overcome with the glory surrounding him. He submits, and we know that the "lines of spiritual motion" are at work.[40] This final scene highlights the real plot of the story, the spiritual transformations of Jack, his father, and his mother. The scene fades out and we see Mrs. O'Brien in a room in this same otherworldly space, her head cradled by two female angelic figures. She raises her open hands in an act of praise and submission, saying, "I give him to you. I give you my son."[41] As the scene closes, we hear the gentle yet full choral strands: "Amen, amen, amen."[42] Perhaps the film itself is a prayer, and these final words meaning "so be it" reflect the desires of our glorious, ruined hearts and minds.

The last images of the film take us back in time, where we see a cityscape, an elevator going up, a bridge over water, and a field of sunflowers. The heavenly, hope-filled images toward the end of this film echo the mysterious claim that "I am making everything new."[43] Yet the film does not end on these scenes of new, eternal beginnings. It ends within time, focusing on the sunflowers that opened the film, reminding us of the cycle of life and death, the feeling of both seasonal newness and seemingly endless repetition. There are grounding scenes of natural life interjected (seemingly randomly) throughout the film, breaking any sort of linear narrative. We see flashes of the wasteland desert of the soul, the rushing water of new life, trees blown by the wind of the spirit. They are both beautiful and, at times, chilling in their mystery.

Malick's film demands a sort of devotion, a determined patience. When it was released, many moviegoers reportedly walked out of theaters in the middle of the unexpected fifteen-minute creation sequence.[44] The inclusion of big-name actors such as Brad Pitt and Sean Penn was a lure to the general public, and some expected a typical, linear film formula. Yet this film reads us as much as we read it, and it demands hard, even frightening, work on our part. *The Tree of Life* pinpoints the most tender, painful questions about our understanding of God and the presence of suffering, and it asks us to sit in the tension with hope for ultimate reconciliation. As Roy Anker explains, the film answers the questions about the mystery of suffering with reminders about the mystery of beauty.[45] And neither of these are answers that we can fully, rationally understand. Self-transformation comes in the act of submitting to the mystery, and empathy comes from recognizing the presence of both of these mysteries in every human being.

THE ADDICTION

Abel Ferrara's 1995 cult vampire film, *The Addiction*, is also a narrative of redemptive, surprising self-transformation, but its focus is heavily on the ruined part of the human condition, so much so that it could be called grotesque in the O'Connor sense of the term. Of course, O'Connor claims that she prefers to use the term *literal* to describe her seemingly exaggerated characters because she is simply putting the wretched tendencies of the human condition under a microscope.[46] *The Addiction* is an unexpectedly theological analysis of the ways in which human wretchedness can consume us, negatively empowering us to consume others. The most surprising aspect of Ferrara's film is its hope for resurrection. "Knowing our wretchedness without knowing God leads to despair," says Pascal, and so many films that tell the truth about evil sit in that despair.[47] But this film's attention to the complexity of the human condition, its potential for both evil and good, is convicting in its relatability. It takes us into the darkest parts of ourselves, reminding us that the darkness cannot overpower the light. It also illustrates that our neighbors who have plunged into the darkness are never fully away from the potential for light. Empathy itself is a form of grace and light, and a film like this increases our empathy as it increases our understanding of the presence of light even in the seemingly darkest souls.

In *The Addiction*, Abel Ferrara retells the old story of a vampire's ability to seduce and consume in order to tell the even older story of seduction in the garden that led to original sin. In doing this, he creates a powerful narrative trajectory from dehumanization to rehumanization as one of the worst sinners ultimately submits to the mystery of redemption. Like *The Tree of Life*, the film relies on a kind of abstraction to force us into a space of contemplation. Like Catholic author Flannery O'Connor, lapsed Catholic filmmaker Ferrara and screenwriter Nicholas St. John, a devout Catholic, use artful, grotesque shock intended for initial disorientation and eventual conviction. Yet this abstraction is not ethereal and beautiful; it is the abstract, impenetrable reality of evil as seen in the grotesque, bloodsucking behavior of a young woman who is bitten by the very sin that takes root in her and eventually controls her.

In this grim morality tale, graduate student Kathleen develops an addiction to blood after she is seduced and bitten by a Casanova, a female vampire. As her addiction grows, she objectifies and then consumes her friends, colleagues, and random strangers in order to satisfy her increasingly insatiable need for blood. After first being bitten, Kathleen goes to a hospital for help—but nothing can be done. Although there is no official diagnosis, we know that the disease, although physically manifest, is spiritually rooted. The scenes of her first night's suffering are painful to watch: a feverish Kathleen writhes in her bed almost as if she is having a seizure—crying, mumbling, rocking. As the infection spreads, viewers are repulsed and frightened by her pain. The film only works if we, the audience, participate in the narrative, seeing our own desires for sinister feeding manifest on the screen. As this propels us into self-examination, we see ourselves in Kathleen, and we recognize the sacredness even in the darkness, thus reminding us that all human beings have the capacity for both evil and good.

In the days after the first hellish night, Kathleen's pain becomes normalized, and she manages to go to her doctoral classes, wearing sunglasses to prevent the light from affecting her. In one of the several graduate school classroom scenes within the film, Kathleen's professor, who frequently speaks of Sartre and Nietzsche, focuses on the Calvinist understanding of total depravity, including the hidden, dark impulses within every human and how this relates to the doctrine of predestination. He states that "the unsaved don't recognize sin in their lives; they are unconscious of it. They don't have pangs of conscience because they don't realize evil exists."[48] Kathleen's professor continues, explaining that in Calvinist theology, it is considered a work of grace to be able to see your own sin and even to suffer from it in order to reach a state of "metanoia."[49] If the sinner is dead to the knowledge of their own sin, it is impossible to turn to God; they must first become desperate and needy, which leads to confession of sin. As Kathleen sits in the classroom under the objective teachings of this doctrine, we are reminded that she both knows of and, currently, loves her evil; her addiction is making her less cognizant that her predatory behavior is evil, for it has become a need that defines and consumes her.

Early in her struggle with bloodlust, Kathleen still has a sense of identity and a conscience, wanting to cause her victims the least pain possible. She uses needles to get blood from her victims, then shoots up like a garden-variety addict. But as her desires overtake her, she abandons the conscience that is her core self. In this sense, the evil that she does has become her good, as it is her only sustenance. Pascal explains that this "addiction" is a danger for every human being, that "true nature having been lost, everything becomes natural. In the same way, the true good having been lost, everything becomes their true good."[50] He then explains the disorienting and nullifying powers of addiction to sin and once again claims, like Calvin does, that humans cannot know God until they first know their own wretchedness. Their recognition of wretchedness is an indicator of the image of God within them: "The greatness of man is great in that he knows himself to be wretched. A tree does not know itself to be wretched."[51]

The ongoing war between the imprinted image of God (goodness) and depravity (evil) within a human being is a movement toward the reception of grace in an internal struggle of the will. Again, this internal struggle holds a mirror to the audience members, both those of us aware of our own sin addictions and those who, like Kathleen, have normalized them to the point of invisibility. This inner theological battle is alluded to in a familiar genre convention that Ferrara incorporates, in a slightly altered manner, into the film. Bram Stoker's *Dracula* introduced the notion that "a vampire cannot enter a dwelling unless it is first invited by one of the inhabitants. In other words, a vampire cannot influence a human without that person's consent."[52] But in *The Addiction*, the contest of will is made more overt; when Kathleen is first approached by the vampire seductress, Casanova, she tells her to "look me in the eyes and tell me to go away."[53] Rather than needing an invitation to come in, Ferrara's vampires ask for a struggle of wills, and it takes a greater inner will (of character, not physical power) to forcefully say no to the coercive vampire. As the film progresses and Kathleen becomes more aggressive in her attacks, she couples her invitations for freedom with a violence of will that is palpable in her voice and jagged body motions. At one point, she yells at one of her victims to "look sin in the face and tell it to go away."[54] She is confessing her loss of humanity, the fact that she has been consumed completely by consumption. She speaks a truth—but she is so frightening that almost all of her chosen human sources of sustenance are unable to resist her will with theirs.

As Kathleen's bloody desires consume her, she abandons Calvin's central ideas about spiritual submission and, instead, embraces the Nietzschean idea that might makes right. Kathleen's transformation is both intellectual and spiritual—but the intellectual is purely secondary once the spiritual corrosion has occurred. The devolution of the central character is most obvious in her bodily suffering, the suffering of an addict that forces viewers to squirm in their seats as they watch her feed her own self-destruction. She becomes an embodiment of the very texts she reads; the war of the soul and mind takes its toll on the body, and this war is only put to rest through the power of a final incarnation. The more Kathleen feeds upon the powerlessness of her victims, the more her humanity is lost. In this, Ferrara reminds us that when we seek power through consumption, we ultimately become a slave to our desires. Complete freedom is a myth, merely a seductive hell. As Tyler Durden explains in *Fight Club*, "The things you own end up owning you."[55] Durden is talking about identity-defining consumerism, a different type of consumption than vampirism, but both are crippling addictions, a means to disempower others in order to empower ourselves. And both ultimately "own" us.

Psychiatrist and theologian Gerald May claims that although we see acute manifestations of addiction in some individuals, "the psychological, neurological, and spiritual dynamics of full-fledged addiction are actively at work in every human being."[56] May sees "addiction" through a Judeo-Christian theological lens as a normal feature of the fallen human condition, something that is exacerbated when one stifles the soul's desire for God, thus attaching to objects or people in obsessive ways. The horror of Ferrara's film reflects this in its multidimensionality, its spiritual implications transcending the garish fatalism of a one-dimensional slasher flick. As Kathleen attaches more completely to her addiction, she is defined by her actions because she now has lost sight of her soul, only believing in the reality of her actions. As she dehumanizes others, exerting her "impact on other egos," she becomes more dehumanized.[57] Her rehumanization, like ours, can only occur by recognizing and naming her addictions. While watching Kathleen feed off others to serve her own deluded needs, we can clearly see the metaphor for our own sickness. This sickness, shared with the film's protagonist, the viewer, and all human beings, is the enemy of empathy and love.

After an interaction with her mentor in vampirism, Peina, Kathleen realizes that "it makes no difference what I do—whether I draw blood or not. It's the violence of my will against theirs."[58] Her defining will-to-power, an insatiable desire for blood, soon becomes her absolute will, and she has become nothing more than her need for short-term fulfillment. In one cruel scene, Kathleen pretends to be ill on the street, and when a stranger comes to her aid, leaning over to pick her up, she preys upon this moment of vulnerability and charity. Empathy is seen as weakness, both because self-sacrifice is a type of vulnerability and because this compassion, what Nietzsche calls "pity," is so foreign to the mental and spiritual framework of one addicted to self-serving power: "The weak and the botched shall perish; first principle of our charity. And one should help them to it."[59] In a truly satanic turn of character, Kathleen benefits personally from the vulnerability and compassion of the other. The film is a modern morality play, and Kathleen is the everywoman, both victimized and empowered (in a Nietzschean sense) by original sin, the cancer that is continually metastasizing.

In her last exertion of power, Kathleen invites a large group of friends, professors, and academic administrators, many of whom have been victims of her addiction, to her graduation party. The celebration soon becomes an orgiastic bloodbath as Kathleen and her dark protégés turn on the unsuspecting guests in order to feast on them. This is the most overtly and obscenely grotesque horror scene in the film; contorted vampiric figures swarm over the living and dead, scrounging for sustenance. As multiple vampires prey upon one figure, they seem to lose distinct human form and come together, oppressed and oppressors, as heaving collections of animal flesh, matted hair, and blood. The vampires rely on their purely natural instincts for survival via the power of the will. Ironically, this extreme focus on individual will transforms individuals into a mass collection of bodies devoid of individuality. The dehumanizers become the most dehumanized as the hellish scene exposes not freedom but animalistic chaos. The scene is significant, as it shows the collective result of unacknowledged sin addictions. It is as overpowering as it is grotesque, yet Kathleen's continual hunger brings her to the point of debilitating satiation, a vivid depiction of the fatal end result of feeding off others: Kathleen is isolated, miserable, and close to dead.

Perhaps the most horrific image in the film is of the engorged body of Kathleen after the bloody bacchanalia. She is drunk on blood, swollen, bloated—so full that she is weak. Outside of the venue, she falls to her knees, covered in blood, then convulses on the ground in the fetal position. She is reduced to the position of a newly born child, helpless and bloody. Lili Taylor, the actor who plays Kathleen, explains that the feast scene is "the typical bottoming out of the addict's way of life."[60] She sees Kathleen's destruction/redemption as an "unconscious process" in which she "went so far down that there was nowhere else to go than to fall to her knees, so to speak."[61] Before Kathleen can truly grow and be redeemed, Kathleen must break or "bottom out," as Taylor says.[62] Only in this moment does she face the acknowledgment of the very wretchedness that leads to her salvation. She becomes like a little child who can no longer lead but must be led, nurtured, and supported. Once seemingly all-powerful, she collapses in the street, helpless and covered in blood, now one of the "least of these."[63] Her livelihood is subject to the passersby on the street—not their blood but their empathy. They stoop down to cradle her, honoring her humanity as sacred and worthy of help.

At the end of the film, the ideas of strength and power are further redefined as Kathleen wakes up in a stark white hospital room bed below a crucifix, her once-bloody figure now sparkling clean. Casanova mysteriously appears, trying to lure Kathleen back into her previous state of raw, worldly power, but Kathleen resists the temptation. Casanova disappears just as mysteriously as she appears, and Kathleen then asks for a priest to come and administer extreme unction while she quietly prays, "God, forgive me."[64] Interestingly, we do not see her drink the communion wine, the blood of Christ, but she consumes wafers transubstantiated into Christ's body.[65] Kathleen's ultimate surrender is a salvific act of will brought upon through bodily and spiritual suffering. Now that she has seen her own wretchedness, she can reach the state of metanoia. The selfishness that had consumed Kathleen as she consumed others was the opposite of self-love. When she was finally forced to surrender, falling on her knees, broken and bloated, she began the process of rehumanization. The vampiric woman who had been avoiding mirrors finally sees herself reflected back honestly and knows that she must change or experience full spiritual death. Ferrara's portrait of brutal transformation is grotesque, exaggerated, larger than life. But it is also what O'Connor calls "literal" in its visible depiction of the invisible spiritual war inside of all human beings when they ignore their tendencies toward isolation, cruelty, and selfishness for the sake of power.[66] To begin to know and love the self, one must face these tendencies and surrender them, creating space for spiritual growth, which includes the internal struggle of the other. Empathy can only follow honest surrender. And as we watch this film, squirming in our seats, we see that all human beings are deserving of empathy not because of what they do but because of what they were created to be.

LIFE AFTER GOD

The Tree of Life and *The Addiction* garner our participation through the use of abstraction or the grotesque. The characters are larger than life in their capacity for sin and grace, yet we still see ourselves in them enough to empathize with their plights and rejoice in their transformation. The spiritual reanimation and transformation that takes place in Douglas Coupland's 1994 short story collection, *Life after God*, are even more immediately recognizable than those in *The Tree of Life* and *The Addiction*. *Life after God* veers away from abstraction and the parabolic grotesque, placing a familiar contemporary, commodified Western cityscape in the forefront of its stories. Coupland's characters look much like most of his readers, middle-class inhabitants of Western countries who have been nurtured on consumerism. We see ourselves and our neighbors as we discover a home in the similarities, perhaps finding more connections than differences. But this identification still takes active participation. Coupland's writing style is so fluid, casual, and enjoyable that it is often easy to breeze right through, not initially recognizing the poignancy of the mirror that he holds up to his readers. We need to pause, reread, and reflect as we read. Coupland's characters, like most of us, are comfortable in their day-to-day lives; they experience no world-altering events that come crashing down upon them. Yet they are slowly learning that the suburban comfort that promised a golden future is ultimately unfulfilling. This is a common thread within much contemporary popular fiction, perfectly described by Tyler Durden in Chuck Palahniuk's 1996 novel *Fight Club*: "We're the middle children of history, man. No purpose or place. We have no Great War. No Great Depression. Our Great War's a spiritual war . . . our Great Depression is our lives. We've all been raised on television to believe that one day we'd all be millionaires, and movie gods, and rock stars. But we won't. And we're slowly learning that fact. And we're very, very pissed off."[67] Unlike the protagonist of *Fight Club*, *Life after God*'s central characters are not "pissed off" but empty. And the narrator in each of these stories, a young suburbanite named Scout, is blessed to recognize his own emptiness. While his contemporaries are numb to their indescribable lack, trying desperately to heal the mysterious wound through their addictive behaviors, he is searching, "scouting" for something—or someone—substantive.

In the very middle of the story collection, the words "You are the First Generation Raised Without Religion" appear in the shape of a cross.[68] This image is on an introductory page to a story called "In the Desert," a postmodern *Pilgrim's Progress* of sorts in which a young, nameless protagonist (who we later learn is Scout) drives through the open and empty Mojave Desert carrying a secret and shameful burden in the trunk of his car. As he drives, he focuses only on the "nothingness" that surrounds him and wonders if "feeling nothing is the inevitable end result of believing in nothing."[69] The setting of this story is an unusual one for Coupland, whose writing almost always focuses on the indigenous people of suburbia, a land of artificial milk and honey and well-manicured lawns, the very settings in which Vancouverite Douglas Coupland grew up. Although "In the Desert" is not set in the suburbs, it is like a spiritual map of the inner world of the suburbanites featured in the other stories contained within *Life after God* (and his fifteen novels). It is also not unlike the desert that Jack wanders through in *The Tree of Life*, as both expose spiritual emptiness yet lead their protagonists to relational reconciliation. The placement of this desert story in the middle of the collection exposes the internal wasteland of Coupland's affluent protagonists, products of the same middle-class, secular environment; these privileged members of society are spoiled for choice and continually feel the pangs of loss for having no guidance to make these choices. Beneath this veneer of material comfort and silence lies a deep discomfort and emptiness, a desire to find meaning beyond the world of supermarket checkout lines, mall shops, and pop icons.

Each story in this collection traces the religious impulse in the lives of "secular" children, now adults, who grew up living a "life after God."[70] In doing this, Coupland is continually humanizing characters who would otherwise be easily labeled and dismissed: Stacy, the glamorous, pretty alcoholic; Donnie, the self-destructive hustler; Kristi, the seemingly normal housewife who is addicted to normalcy and irony. As we see a character such as Cathy, a metalhead runaway in "My Hotel Year," talk about the "magical world underneath the surface of the water" and pothead Todd in "1,000 Years: Life after God" talk about the "pure spot" inside of us all, we come to realize that they, like all of us, are seeking some experience of transcendence even if they do not have the theological vocabulary to describe it.[71] The collection's final story, "1,000 Years: Life after God," finally provides answers for these seeking wanderers. This story is set in lush West Vancouver, where we again encounter Scout, the book's narrator, and the friends that he refers to as "my fellow fetuses." They are leisurely floating in a pool the temperature of blood or perhaps amniotic fluid.[72] Scout tells us that as they float in the pool, they are unable to differentiate between their own bodies and the pool's water; the controlled temperature and lighting have lulled them into an artificial comfort as they are relaxed by the sound of the buzzing pool filter that cleans the water. As Scout and his friends float in this secure, sterile, and pleasant environment, they listen to cliché love songs, the music of manufactured emotion and commercial replication. Although these songs repeatedly sing about "love" based on formulaic pop conventions, Scout admits that he and his friends do not believe their message.[73] There is an interesting connection here between satiation, comfort, and a lack of true relational connection. These young people have been so formed by their own comfort that they do not have the capacity for self-sacrificial love. Love is only about fuzzy feelings, another layer of comfort and pleasure. There is no space or even comprehension of the kind of love born out of empathy. Coupland tells us that they are the children of an earthly "paradise" that has no grounding in transcendent truth, and this false paradise persuades them into believing it is so safe, real, and sufficient that it "rendered any discussion of transcendental ideas pointless so now all they have is this 'earthly salvation on the edge of heaven.'"[74]

These children of privilege, experiencing "life after God," have developed no overt yearnings for a reality beyond their parents' making.[75] Scout contemplates this comfortable yet unsatisfying trade-off, wondering what they have gained in the absence of faith in anything beyond themselves: "I think the price we paid for our golden life was an inability to believe in love; instead we gained an irony that scorched everything it touched. And I wonder if this irony is the price we paid for the loss of God."[76] Scout directly links the inability to love with a golden life that discourages him and his friends from even conceiving of the possibility of a source of authentic love outside of the saccharin-tinged artificiality of pop-song romance. Instead of inheriting a sense of wonder, a desire to seek for the source of any such "love," they have inherited a numbing, defensive irony that "[scorches] everything it touched" and becomes "the price we paid for the loss of God."[77] Both material saturation and defensive irony are enemies of love that is born from empathy.

The focus of irony as a double-edged sword is a central concern of *Life after God*. In these stories, the protective shell of irony distances its users from any unaffected acceptance of either spirituality or human relationships. Coupland's teenage ironists appear terrified of belief, trust, and commitment, as they have no vision of reality past the contingent world of their suburban dreamscape. Scout feels the damaging effects of his own use of irony as a reflexive defense mechanism. It has replaced and prevented any sort of reliance on faith, either relational or spiritual, for this generation "raised without religion."[78] There is an inherent connection between the absence of belief in God and the presence of an irony that "scorches" everything and everyone.[79] Just as Sartre has pointed out, if there is no God, then there is no human community based on a shared likeness and spirituality. And in Coupland's fictional world, a belief in God's absence is the norm. Because of this, each character forms a shell of protection, the insulated coating of irony that constantly deflects, mocks, and creates distance. This is the relational violence of "life after God," an inability to communicate, love, or show empathy.[80] If God is dead, so are love and empathy.

In his poignant essay "E Unibus Pluram: Television and U.S. Fiction," David Foster Wallace voices a cautionary view of irony that echoes both Scout's and Coupland's own trepidations: "Irony, entertaining as it is, serves an almost exclusively negative function. It's critical and destructive, a ground-clearing. . . . But irony's singularly unuseful when it comes to constructing anything to replace the hypocrisies it debunks."[81] After irony's "ground-clearing," the only "reality" left to fill the vacuum is irony itself.[82] Although it exposes what is perceived as hypocrisy and conformity, it ultimately becomes its own absolute, a norm that, according to Wallace, "tyrannizes us."[83] Coupland himself argues that the cynicism inherent in an ironic worldview is "lazy thinking posing as depth and coolness."[84] This type of thinking encourages both artificiality and a lack of substance, as "there's no nutrition in cynicism."[85]

When we meet the adult Scout, however, we find that he is both a corporate player and a sojourner searching for something real and enduring beyond a fortuitous capitalist dreamtime. He has moved past irony and mourns his lack of a religious upbringing and admits that he, like everyone else, has "religious impulses," something that he confesses thinking about every day.[86] Rather than cynically dismissing this longing for faith, he embraces it wholeheartedly, confessing that "sometimes I think it is the only thing I should be thinking about."[87] This conviction intensifies as Scout reflects on the somewhat glamorous environs of postreligious suburbia, recognizing the desperation in the adult eyes of lifelong friends. The protective shell of ironic adolescence has worn thin as they have moved beyond the cynicism of their halcyon days to disconnected moments of burnt-out fear and empty exhaustion.

One of Scout's childhood friends, now divorced "Malibu Barbie" Stacey, fuels her desperation with alcohol as she and Scout lament schoolmate Mark's recent discovery that he has AIDS.[88] Irony and cynicism cannot protect them from the deep pain and mystery of life as they hit rock bottom, but they have not been given the tools to know how to cope through love, authentic relationships, or beliefs. The bubble of their glossy yet empty suburban childhoods has finally burst, and there is nothing for them to cling to.

As we meet another of Scout's friends, "normal" housewife Julie, Coupland emphasizes that the lost children of suburbia do not necessarily have to develop fatal diseases or bottomless addictions to finally face their emptiness and dissatisfaction with the lost paradise of their youth.[89] Julie has two kids and a "nice-guy" husband with a sensible and secure job and lives in a neighborhood that is "about as suburban as suburban gets."[90] But she ultimately expresses a desire for something more than the "comforting virtual world of suburbia": "You know—I'm trying to escape from ironic hell: cynicism into faith; randomness into clarity; worry into devotion."[91] Coupland's placement of religious language in the mouths of supposedly postreligious suburbanites is telling. Irony's Teflon coating has protected Julie from the fear of commitment and sincerity, but she is trapped within the flames of its deathly protection. But as Julie looks at her immediate cultural and familial surroundings, she finds no alternatives to a faithless, ironic existence. She claims that she tries "to be sincere about life and then I turn on a TV and I see a game show host and I have to throw up my hands and give up."[92] These fake replications of manufactured sincerity, the ecstatic game show hosts and saccharin-induced pop songs of her world, force her back into ironic hell. She must distinguish herself from the feigned sincerity of "cheesy celebrities," emphasizing this distinction with a self-aware irony that prevents absorption into the system.[93] Although Julie appears to be happy, normal, and satisfied, she recognizes that her relationships lack a sort of selfless devotion that makes a truly human connection. She is unable to trust, and this lack of vulnerability gives rise to a protective cynicism. Her sincerity about her own insincerity is a longing for human connection, empathy, and acceptance.

The story is written in a confessional mode as Scout continually tells his readers that what he is saying is hard for him, emphasizing that, like Julie, he is a child born of irony and cynicism. Yet he has finally arrived at a point where "sincerity ceases to feel pornographic" because of an insistent need that "burns inside us to share with others what we are feeling."[94] These confessions are the beginnings of a submission, a transformation, as he longs to look at himself honestly and acknowledge his need for relationships both human and transcendent. Scout is the everyman, burned by the cynicism of a post-God affluent world, yet his deeper spiritual longings, the longings that are present in all human beings, even if dormant, animate his humanity.

Desperate for an authentic connection with some transcendent other, Scout decides to leave his corporate job and trash his antidepressants. After a business trip to New York, he catches an Amtrak train to Washington, DC, to watch the presidential inauguration rather than take his scheduled return flight to Vancouver. Having finally done something sporadic and real, differentiating himself from the mere cogs in the corporate system, he comments that "I was beginning to feel like a person inside a story for the first time in years."[95] Ironically, Coupland uses the experience of attending a presidential inauguration, a ceremony that could be seen as the pinnacle of system enforcement, to liberate Scout from the realm of the artificial. As he feeds off the communal vibes, he notes that "suddenly I realized that I was feeling—well, that I was actually *feeling*. My old personality was, after months of pills and pleasant nothingness, returning."[96] Having tasted the real, Scout returns home, unable to force himself back into the corporate world and the job he refers to as "the evil empire."[97] He explains to his colleague and friend Kirsty that now he can "see life differently," and he can't push this discovery under the rug and become a robot programmed by companies or pills again.[98] He also explains that he went to the inauguration because there was "something there I needed to see—evidence of a person or a thing larger than a human being."[99] This ambiguous comment sounds as if Scout recounts what he has seen almost as the divine right of presidential inauguration, that there is some large and benevolent controlling force behind the ceremony and its attendants. His desire to be in a crowd alone but sharing a central focus with others reveals a desire for shared, human community based on some sort of connecting force beyond the self.

Scout's quest for something larger than both himself and a closed, deceptive capitalist system continues as he leaves the city for the forest, searching for "purity" and "sanctity."[100] In the wilderness, Scout finds both freedom and sacred silence while "preparing [his] story."[101] Having abandoned the protection of irony and pills and the delusions of his artificial Eden, he anticipates that "this is the end of some aspect of my life, but also a beginning—the beginning of some unknown secret that will reveal itself to me soon. All I need to do is ask and pray."[102] Scout prepares his confession alongside the revitalizing natural world, a vision much closer to the biblical Eden than to the false paradise of suburban youth. Still in his business suit, Scout huddles next to a soaked tent, drinking running water from a deep pool. This water, unlike the tepid, stagnant water of the man-made pool in the story's opening, appears to be the living water of his new life. Just as the warm, amniotic pool water was an incubator for him and his "fellow fetuses," this water promises a cleansing and renewing second birth.[103]

Toasted by the intense sun, Scout peels off his clothes and immerses himself in the water. The last few pages of *Life after God* read almost like a psalm, the heartfelt reflections of a despairing, wandering man who has found his way home. Scout suddenly hears an amazing, unifying sound that overpowers yet connects everything: "And the water from the stream above me roars. Oh, does it roar! Like the voice that knows only one message, one truth—never-ending, like the clapping of hands and the cheers of the citizens upon the coronation of the king, the crowds of the inauguration, cheering for hope and for that one voice that will speak to them."[104] This jubilant exclamation focuses on revelation rather than tension; Scout is overpowered by a sense of unity, truthfulness, and reality in nature. But strangely, his most immediate point of reference for the unity contained within nature's clapping hands is the clapping hands of the inauguration. The focus on transcendent unity within nature and the sound of clapping hands seems to echo the powerful, joy-filled words of Isaiah 55: "You will go out in joy and be led forth in peace; the mountain and hills will burst into song before you, and all the trees of the field will clap their hands."[105] The clapping of hands in the natural world provides a picture of reality charged with the life of God.

Scout's thirst has never been quenched by the chlorinated pool water of a comfortable middle-class life; he thirsts for something real and clean. The unsatisfactory futility of Scout's labor in the world's current system yields no meaningful rewards, only money to buy more things. After praying, waiting, and experiencing the thundering voice through nature, Scout finally confesses his deepest understanding of truth, a confession so far from irony that its sincerity is tender yet startling and raw: "Now here is my secret: I tell you with an openness of heart that I doubt I shall ever achieve again, so I pray that you are in a quiet room as you hear these words. My secret is that I need God—that I am sick and can no longer make it alone. I need God to help me to give, because I no longer seem capable of giving; to help me be kind, as I no longer seem capable of kindness; to help me to love, as I seem beyond able to love."[106] This is the revelation that Scout previously prayed for, the climactic point of his story—the truth that molds his collection of experiences into a story. According to this revelatory assessment, Scout's previous life as a fully autonomous individual, seemingly *beyond God*, was crippling. In this moving coda, Coupland is making a direct connection between the reality of God and the possibility of kindness and love. Without being connected to the source of love and kindness, human beings are unable to be loving and kind. Although all the collection's characters desired relationships, their relationships ultimately failed because the lack of God is also the lack of selflessness that must be present if empathy and love are to be born. According to Scout's wilderness revelation, a culture beyond God is also beyond love, kindness, and generosity.

Scout must actively admit his weakness, shed his ironic coating, and expose the raw nerve of a desperately needy existence. As he reflects upon this painful yet exhilarating confession, he walks deeper into the "rushing water."[107] The roar and clapping of hands grow louder and louder, and Scout allows himself to finally be holistically absorbed into a new understanding of reality that transcends all others and reflects a pattern of truth, wholeness, and purity. The clapping hands "heal" and "hold"; they are "the hands we desire because they are better than desire."[108] Perhaps these hands are not just the joyous euphony of nature's response to God but also an image of the molding force of the Creator. Scout's final words connect God's hands with the hands of those created in his image: "These hands—the hands that care, the hands that mold; the hands that touch the lips, the lips that speak the words—the words that tell us we are whole."[109] The emphasis on hands and lips is central to the connection between the self and God. The creating hands of God have touched the lips of Scout, the storyteller, and his ability to speak with his mouth and act with his hands reflects a creative nature that demonstrates a possible image of God's reality. Scout is finally whole, part of a larger story, entirely dependent upon the divine narrator who is beyond the constricting lines of irony. Only in being a participant in this larger story is he able to forge connections with other human beings, to love, to forgive, to show kindness. As readers, we empathize with Scout's longing for God, just as Scout recognizes that without a connection to the ultimate source of empathy, he can have no love, forgiveness, or kindness for other human beings.

Just as Coupland's Scout needs to feel connected to a larger story in order to know how to love, so do we. As we watch microstories *The Tree of Life* or *The Addiction* and read *Life after God*, our attention pivots toward the macrostory of creation, the fall, and redemption. Each of these very different narratives ends in a transformation that can only come from submitting to the author of the great story. And in this submission, a quest for power, self-preservation, or irony is shed to make space for the other. As we watch and read about these acts of submission, we self-reflect, and our own postures of life and worship are challenged. Each of these stories reflects the paradoxical truth that to really live and commune with others, you must die to self. And in this death, this submission, a space for empathy is created.

Chapter Four

WHO IS OUR NEIGHBOR?

Hear Me, Christian Neighbors

In a powerful scene from Dave Eggers's 2006 novel, *What Is the What*, Sudanese refugee Valentino Achak Deng is in his Atlanta apartment, struggling both physically and mentally, desperate after being bound and gagged by robbers. New to the United States and not very streetwise, Valentino is both kind and naive enough to open the door to help a woman in need; he is subsequently hit over the head by her partner in crime, a man wearing powder blue that he thereafter refers to as "Powder."[1] As the two intruders walk back and forth past a helpless Valentino, stealing the very few items he owns (all of them donations), he is silently weeping. But he is also aware that there is an evangelical Christian couple living in the apartment below him, and in his mind, he cries out to them for help: "In a furious burst, I kick and kick again, flailing my body like a fish run aground. Hear me, Christian neighbors! Hear your brother just above!! Nothing again. No one is listening. No one is waiting to hear the kicking of the man above. It is unexpected. You have no ears for someone like me."[2] While reading the real story of Valentino's brief captivity, readers are also reminded of their own deafness to the needs of refugees with stories like his. Valentino cannot cry out loud, but there is still hope that his Christian neighbors will somehow know that he is in need. Tragically, they "have no ears for someone like me."[3] Eggers's wording here alludes to the many instances in Scripture, both Old and New Testaments, in which prophetic voices rebuke groups or individuals who "have eyes but do not see, who have ears but do not hear."[4]

Since his arrival in Atlanta, Valentino has been invisible to and out of earshot of his Christian neighbors, who have shown him little hospitality. They do not know his tragic life story of being a child escaping a civil war. Eggers's placement of these direct, desperate, and convicting cries at the beginning of the novel, framing the long (over five hundred pages) narrative, implies that we are all the "Christian neighbors," that we carry the privilege of not knowing the pain and injustice in the room directly below (or above or beside) us unless we have ears to hear and eyes to see. As the robbery continues, Valentino's inner cries become more desperate: "Hear me Atlanta! I am grinning and tears are flowing down my temples because I know that someone . . . will come to the door."[5] He refuses to give up hope. He knows that he cannot survive without the help of another willing and listening human being: "Open the door and let me stand again! If I have my hands I can stand. If I have my hands I can free my mouth and tell you what happened here."[6] Not only does Valentino need to have his hands free to act and defend himself, but he also needs to have his mouth unbound so he can tell his story.

The act of telling one's story is a powerful means of rehumanization after dehumanization has occurred. To be able to speak "what has happened here" and have another actively listen is life-giving and transformative for both the speaker and the listener. Yet Eggers begins *What Is the What* with the image of Valentino bound and gagged, unable to communicate or be heard. The listeners that he so desperately needs are also, either willfully or unknowingly, bound because of their blindness and deafness to his needs and his story. Valentino is one of the so-called Lost Boys of Sudan, and the trauma and cruel obstacles that he experienced as a young child are unimaginable for most Americans, especially those who are white and middle class. Valentino's cry for help from his Christian neighbors is the cry of a neighbor in need—a neighbor who is invisible unless we make an intentional effort to look, listen, and learn from his story.

EYES TO SEE AND EARS TO HEAR

This picture of a neglected neighbor recalls Christ's parabolic imperative: we must be attentive to the needs of our neighbors, no matter how different they appear to be from us. The Good Samaritan sacrificed his time, comfort, and safety to someone who was not only foreign to him but also a potential oppressor. But Western, middle-class comfort can easily dissuade us from seeking the stories of those beyond our immediate socioeconomic, national, religious, or racial proximities. In fact, their differences should prompt even more understanding and attentiveness on our part as we realize the limitations of our own knowledge and experience. We do not know what we do not know. Many white, middle-class Americans could live their entire lives without considering the needs, the lament, the mourning of someone like Valentino Deng. Yet Christ continually reminds us that we must have ears to hear the prophetic declarations of the truth of his divinity as well as all that he teaches, which includes the commandment to love our neighbors as ourselves. Christ's wording echoes the phrasing of the Old Testament prophets, including Isaiah and Zechariah. This lengthy section from Zechariah 7 is helpful as we consider Valentino's plea to his spiritually and morally deaf "Christian neighbors": "This is what the Lord Almighty said: 'Administer true justice; show mercy and compassion to one another. Do not oppress the widow or the fatherless, the foreigner or the poor. Do not plot evil against each other.' But they refused to pay attention; stubbornly they turned their backs and covered their ears. They made their hearts as hard as flint and would not listen to the law or to the words that the Lord Almighty had sent by his Spirit through the earlier prophets. So the Lord Almighty was very angry."[7] According to the words of the Lord here, in order to show justice, mercy, and compassion, we must "pay attention" rather than become like those who "turned their backs and covered their ears."[8] This lack of attention and inability to listen is a sign of hard-heartedness—and this seems to be the frequent disposition of the comfortable human heart.

The arts provide diverse opportunities to become more attentive: to open our eyes and unblock our ears. This is especially true when considering the stories of those whom we do not usually encounter in day-to-day life or those whom we tend to label, demonize, or dismiss. Author Marilynne Robinson explains that "community, at least community larger than the immediate family, consists very largely of imaginative love for people we know or whom we know very slightly."[9] The human imagination, like the human heart, veers toward similarity rather than difference. Intentionality is key in overcoming this natural tug toward familiarity and comfort. The beautiful thing is that the more intentional we are in becoming familiar with the other, the more we learn about the diverse beauty of the image of God. Our true familial connections transcend blood and culture—but to love the other as we love ourselves, it is essential to also note and respect differences, even those that make us uncomfortable. Jewish philosopher Martin Buber claims that "all real life is meeting . . . all actual life is encounter."[10] And although we might not each have an opportunity for an in-person encounter with the life experience of Valentino Achak Deng, the act of reading about Valentino's life is an act of love that may create space for a life-changing encounter. As Buber also notes, any time we allow ourselves to have a *real* encounter with another human being, it is impossible not to be changed ourselves. In reading stories like Valentino Deng's, our imaginations can be expanded to become attentive to their life experiences, and in turn, our hearts and minds become more open to loving our neighbors.

Dave Eggers's partially fictionalized "autobiography" of Deng is an easily accessible invitation to his "Christian neighbors."[11] These encounters, in which one may engage different communities and individuals whose suffering and humanity are so often overlooked or even denied, are made possible via the arts. Like *What Is the What*, the powerful Sundance series *Rectify* invites us into the strange, beautiful story of someone whose voice and life experience are often overlooked or blatantly ignored. The peculiar protagonist of *Rectify* is Daniel Holden, a man recently released from death row. Both refugees and convicts are image bearers whose stories are easy to disregard from a space of sheltered, suburban comfort. Likewise, the cry of the African American community, still experiencing systemic oppression, is too often silenced by those afraid to listen. Angie Thomas's dynamic young adult novel *The Hate U Give* invites its readers to witness the devastation of police brutality through the eyes of teenage protagonist Starr Carter. *Unbelievable*, a popular 2019 limited series on Netflix, focuses on empowering the timid voice of Marie Adler, a rape survivor, yet another oft-silenced group. The protagonists within each of these stories are a representation of a "neighbor" whose story has so often been lost, ignored, or suppressed. As we read or watch these books or series, it becomes evident that listening to the stories of our oppressed neighbors is a reflexive activity. Just as their storytelling expands their humanity, our contemplatively listening expands our humanity.

Like the Samaritan in the famous parable, Christ asks us to stop, look, and listen in order to address the needs of our neighbors with open arms, even if those in power choose to walk by and ignore their humanity. And like the priests in the Good Samaritan parable, "Christian neighbors" are sometimes the first to walk past their voiceless, abused neighbors.[12] These powerful character studies provide us the opportunity to truly mourn with those who mourn as we participate in their suffering by witnessing it with eyes and ears that are open to believe, love, and lament. Rather than objectifying their protagonists, these writers and filmmakers weave tender narratives that slowly, gently, yet unwaveringly allow us to experience life events of injustice, abuse, and pain vicariously through them. As we sacrifice time and emotional energy to listen, watch, and participate in these stories, we practice empathy. This softens our hearts, widens our scope of vision, and unplugs our closed ears to listen to the cries of our neighbors.

WHAT IS THE WHAT

On the final page of *What Is the What*, the book's narrator, Valentino, speaks directly to his readers for the first time, explaining the impact that telling his story has on him: "Whatever I do, however I find a way to live, I will retell these stories. I have spoken to every person I have encountered these last difficult days . . . because to do anything else would be something less than human. . . . It gives me strength, almost unbelievable strength to know that *you* are there."[13] Valentino's impassioned confession indicates that the retelling of his harrowing story empowers him, allowing him to regain and expand his own humanity. *What Is the What* is a story about storytelling, continually reminding its readers that listening to stories makes us more human while instructing us in the most empathetic ways to listen. This is most clear when the narrator finally and directly addresses his readers at the end of the novel, emphasizing the fact that telling his story helps him begin to feel whole after years of abuse and neglect. Eggers's narrative retelling of Lost Boy Valentino Achak Deng's brutal childhood journey from Sudan to Kenya and, eventually, to America is a primer on how to listen to / read stories hospitably.

What Is the What is a series of flashbacks framed by a present-day narrative, and the present-day voice of Valentino is the most powerful element of the story. As readers encounter Valentino's voice in the novel, we connect his past to his present, and this allows us to understand the many factors that have made him the man he has become. At one and the same time, we see him as an abused child, a heroic survivor, an ambitious immigrant, a devoted Catholic, a doubter, and, ultimately, a human being, both like and unlike us. As we read and listen, he becomes more human in our eyes, no longer a newspaper headline or evening news blip but a complex, glorious image bearer. While witnessing the ways that Valentino is shunned and silenced, we also learn the devastating impact of a lack of empathy: "When I first came to this country, I would tell silent stories. I would tell them to people who had wronged me. If someone cut in front of me in line, ignored me, bumped or pushed me, I would glare at them, staring, silently hissing a story to them. You do not understand, I would tell them. You would not add to my suffering if you knew what I have seen. The stories emanate from me all the time when I am waking and breathing, and I want everyone to hear them."[14] Although Valentino recounts multiple ways in which he was dehumanized during the Sudanese Civil War and resettlement in a Kenyan refugee camp, the story frequently focuses on the ways in which he is treated in present-day America as a one-dimensional annoying foreigner rather than a complex human being. Valentino renarrates many instances in Atlanta when he is abused or ignored—by those robbing him, by the police investigating the robbery, by the attendee at the hospital where he receives treatment after the robbery. They are unable to hear or see the urgency of his need and refuse to acknowledge the veracity of his story. As they mistreat or silence him, he is continually triggered, slipping into the details of his past. At the same time, he tells his story in his own mind to those unable to listen, reciting the very facts that they could know if they only took a moment to ask and listen. This gives Valentino a sense of retaining his own humanity as they continue to dehumanize him. It also reminds us that listening to the story of another helps preserve their dignity, something that was so often taken from Valentino and many like him.

The novel's jolting opening scene, the robbery, reflects the very vulnerability of the invitation Valentino extends to us, his readers. As

Valentino welcomes a stranger in his home, his hospitality and trust are met with hostility and cruelty. He is a good neighbor, even as he is perceived and treated as an outsider, a foreigner—yet his faithfulness by way of a kind invitation leads to abuse rather than community. Valentino feels the most violated by these thieves when they go through his nightstand drawers, rummaging through his memories (photos, letters, etc.). As invited listeners into his story, will we come in and listen—or will we rob and abuse, rustling through Valentino's memories while using the story to fulfill our own agendas, ignoring the humanity of its narrator? Loving intentionality and our own empathetic submission are the keys to resisting a kind of voyeurism or trauma tourism so that we can truly listen, learn, and, hopefully, begin to love more deeply. As Valentino recalls painful memories of abuse from his past that correspond with the actions of his present-day encounter with a thief, he tells us that "the man before me, Powder, would never know anything of this kind. He would not be interested."[15] The anonymous intruder is devoid of empathy, and this stems from both an inability to listen and a deficit of imagination. He does not see Valentino as a broken, beautiful human (like himself) but an opportunity for self-advancement. Valentino is not a person but an "it" to Powder, who refuses to enter a relationship with him. He is a means to an end, silenced and objectified. Martin Buber argues that "relation is reciprocity," which includes the act of inquiring and listening.[16] But Powder is simply sidelining Valentino rather than encountering him for his own sake. Concerningly, Powder's lack of interest in Valentino's story parallels the lack of interest from the Christian neighbors. In this, Eggers instructs us in the right way to listen, not as a means to an objectifying end but in a relational, reciprocal fashion.

When Valentino's captors leave the apartment to transport some of what they have stolen, they leave a young boy, possibly their son, to watch over him. The child sits still, glaring into the television set, and in his mind, Valentino begins to call him "TV Boy" while allowing his imagination to wander into the boy's story.[17] In doing this, he imaginatively identifies with the boy because of their shared emotional orphaning, and this becomes a trigger point for his own memory. Inside his mind, he says to the boy, "It was not so long ago that I was like you. . . . Perhaps you, too, are a child of war. In some way I assume you are. They come in different shapes and guises."[18] In doing this, Valentino models the act of participating in another's story for his readers, even if it takes a very large imaginative leap. Although this child guard knows nothing of Valentino's story or his particular suffering, Valentino recognizes that TV Boy, too, is a victim of abuse far beyond his own understanding. He connects his own experience of trauma with the very foreign, yet shared, suffering of this child. Hearing another's story is not enough—one must find a connection and dwell within it. Only then is empathy born.

This connection with TV Boy is a trigger that reminds readers that Valentino's story is both individual and collective, that his inability to exorcise his own haunting, in turn, enables him to retell the stories even of those who were lost in death. Throughout the novel, he gives voice to those whose lives were lost throughout his journey as he retells the stories of his childhood. In doing this, he extends empathy and ascribes both humanity and dignity to his childhood friends who did not complete the treacherous journey across the continent. As with TV Boy, he makes it his responsibility to dwell within their stories of loss in order to empathize and give them a voice: "Every boy had a story like this, with many places they thought they might stay, many people who helped them but who disappeared, many fires and battles and betrayals."[19] The powerful tale of Monynhial, a boy who never spoke but continued walking as his eyes sunk deeper into his head, is perhaps his most harrowing memory. Monynhial left the line of boys, too exhausted to continue, and dug a hole into which he crawled. According to Valentino, "on the third day he decided to die in the hole, because it was warm in there and there were no sounds inside."[20] No one actually observed this, and although the story of Monynhial's moment of death is a purely imagined part of the narrative, Deng says, "None of the boys who walked with me saw Monynhial perish in this hole but we all know this story to be true. It is very easy for a boy to die in Sudan."[21] Valentino expresses here that the truth of fiction can become an emotional stand-in for lost facts. Even—and especially—in the absence of observable facts, fiction has the ability to ascribe dignity and provide a memorial. This imagined ending is a result of Valentino's childhood capacity for attentive empathy, and the story he tells enables us to empathize with this silent, solemn young boy as he meets his death. Through this imagined narrative, the unfamiliar becomes familiar and this lost child is given a story, identity, and final dignity. As a boy in Sudan, Achak Deng was given the name "Valentino" by a priest, christening him after a saint who healed a woman's blindness and was eventually martyred for it.[22] Eggers positions this information in the middle of the novel, emphasizing Valentino's prophetic role as a storyteller. He is told by the priest that "I think you will have the power to make people see."[23] Valentino's prophetic gift is shared via Eggers's gift of crafting fiction to disclose multiple truths—about trauma, about the urgency and need for storytelling, about learning how to hear and see our neighbors with love and empathy.

The intertwining of both fact and fiction is essential to the novel's capacity to elicit our empathy. Although this novel's narrative structure appears conventional, it takes a radical step to show us how to truly connect and dwell within Valentino Deng's story. Like Valentino himself, author Dave Eggers must fictionalize some of the forgotten or lost parts of the story's narrative in order to present readers with the emotional, moral, and spiritual truth of these young men's shared suffering. As Pablo Picasso very famously said, "Art is a lie that makes us realize truth," and the fictional portions of this narrative enable a fuller picture that can inhabit and grow within our imaginations.[24] Some critics asked why Dave Eggers would fictionalize such a powerful story, implying that perhaps this is the appropriation of Deng's story for Eggers's own purposes. But this question ignores the fact that Deng asked Eggers to tell his story, spent months relaying the events of his life to Eggers, and trusted him with the decision concerning how the story could be most effectively told. On an obvious level, the story must be fictionalized for gaps to be filled in; Valentino was only six years old when forced to flee from his home. The novel moving from fact into the realm of fiction also enables a more inclusive truthfulness, as Valentino can then be the mouthpiece for the collective tales of those who traveled alongside him and lost their lives.

But the most telling argument for turning fact into fiction lies in Eggers's own role as a listener, a participant in the story. It is not his story—but he has hosted it and embodied it in a way that not only enables Valentino's voice to be heard but also encourages the reader to take on the story and dwell within it rather than stand outside, staring and pointing in curiosity. Eggers is a devout listener. And there are other figures in the novel who have ears to hear Valentino

Deng—including the founder of the Lost Boys Foundation, Mary Williams, and Valentino's sponsor, Phil Mays. After his initial connection with Phil, Valentino is invited to have dinner with the Mays family every Tuesday night. And after each of these dinners, the two men sit on the floor of the pink upstairs playroom in Mays's house, where Valentino recounts his story to Phil, the first man who would sit and listen. They talk for hours, and Phil is silenced under the weight of hearing Valentino's tales of brutality and cruelty. As the men rise to leave, they always embrace. When Valentino says goodbye to Phil after their first meeting, he turns back around to see his sponsor crumpled and weeping behind the steering wheel of his sleek sports car, the stories penetrating his very soul. Included within the novel are several vivid descriptions of active listening such as this one—and Eggers, the author, developed an acute sense of this gift in order to tell this deeply traumatic story in a way that humanizes rather than objectifies.

In her study on trauma narratives, *Unclaimed Experience*, Cathy Caruth emphasizes the significance of "the way in which one's own trauma is tied up with the trauma of another, the way in which trauma may lead, therefore, to the encounter with another, through the very possibility and surprise of listening to another's wound."[25] Like Buber, Caruth emphasizes the importance of a life-giving encounter, but this encounter is perhaps most transformative when both the speaker and the listener recognize their shared wounding. This is especially interesting to consider knowing that Eggers was orphaned as a teenager by the death of his parents and had to take on the very adult role of caring for his younger brother. Like and unlike Valentino, he has experienced the perceived loss of childhood at an early age. But Eggers does not bleed onto the page. This is not his story. Eggers's relationship with Deng in the writing of this book is an exemplary picture of the ways in which human beings can discover their common humanity amid differences that so often create barriers. And Eggers's capacity to relay Deng's human familiarity speaks to any readers who have experienced suffering, felt isolated, or questioned their faith. At the same time, he does not reduce Valentino or his story to just these things. He is both very different and very familiar. Like all human beings, the beauty we see here is in both the unity and the diversity of the human experience. Eggers does not attempt to colonize Deng's story for his own purposes but creates space for the telling and invites readers to reciprocate, to form a relationship with Deng and his story. *What Is the What* is a perspective-changing, thus life-changing, novel, and Eggers's sustained, respectful attention to Deng's story informs readers' imaginations as they see Deng's life in full-bodied color rather than the condensed, flattened black and white of news headlines.

RECTIFY

Daniel Holden, the fictional central character of Ray McKinnon's sleeper Sundance Channel series, *Rectify*, is also likely to be seen in the news headlines, reduced to the status of undeserving other but in a very different context from that of Valentino Deng. The series takes us into a state prison, as well as the prison of an individual broken mind, so that we may mourn and rejoice as we encounter both dehumanization and rehumanization. This intense exploration of an ex-con's internal world helps us "remember those in prison as if you were together with them in prison" and remind ourselves that prisoners, society's failed outsiders, can also be "the least of these."[26] McKinnon provides an often heartrending opportunity for us to explore the mind and world of the mysterious Holden so that we can see both his pain and the humanity that is so often mischaracterized or ignored. In doing this, he reminds us that although imprisoned, prisoners are not animals but human beings made in God's image. Regardless of their behavior or mental disposition, they never lose their status as image bearers.

In thinking of the series' tender portrait of Holden, his family, and his community, it is helpful to revisit the whiskey priest's powerful words from *The Power and the Glory*: "When you visualized a man or a woman carefully, you could always begin to feel pity . . . that was a quality God's image carried with it . . . when you saw the lines at the corners of the eyes, the shape of the mouth, how the hair grew, it was impossible to hate. Hate was just a failure of imagination."[27] As viewers carefully follow Daniel Holden's experiences, interactions, and struggles, we begin to see "the lines at the corners of the eyes, the shape of the mouth," the beauty and glory of an image bearer who has been misunderstood, falsely accused, and abused.[28] This quiet series leads us through the steps to begin to visualize "carefully" so that it is "impossible to hate."[29] The more we know, the more we can imagine ourselves in Daniel's mind, his shoes, his circumstances. Daniel also has a need to tell his story—but the trauma of his carceral experiences has rendered him unable to know that this action would empower him. It's too painful to even consider. Although recently set free, he is imprisoned by his memories and emotions, so much so that he must relearn how to connect with others. Daniel's character is a powerful reminder that trauma does not erase someone's story or make them less human, so we need to be patient with them as they work to reclaim their story. Watching *Rectify*, following Daniel's slow movements toward recognizing and understanding his own story, can teach us a kind of quiet, loving patience that leads to empathy.

Daniel Holden has been on death row for almost twenty years for supposedly raping and killing his (then) teenage girlfriend, Hayley. Although most of the small town of Paulie, Georgia, has chosen to remember Daniel in the most inhumane ways, his sister, Amantha, has faith in both his innocence and his humanity. In the series' opening scene, thirty-seven-year-old Daniel leaves his home behind bars for the first time since he was seventeen years old. A recent DNA test has proven that Daniel is not guilty of the rape, so he is released (but not exonerated). As Daniel's eager mother, Janet, and long-suffering, faithful sister drive to meet him upon his exit, we see Daniel's final interactions with a seemingly kind officer. The officer offers him a drink, respectfully turns his back when Daniel is changing from prison to civilian clothes, and even gently ties his tie for him. Daniel looks slightly stunned, confused; he is not used to being treated as a human being. These tender, kind moments are striking in such a dehumanizing prison context. After spending most of his prison time in isolation, parts of Daniel are broken, including a natural capacity to accept kindness and interact normally with other human beings. When Daniel exits the prison into the arms of his sister and mother, he is stiff, robotic, until he begins to weep. After his first evening home with his family, Daniel's much younger half brother, Jared, says to his mother, "He didn't hardly say anything tonight."[30] Janet quietly responds, "He doesn't know how to, honey."[31] As the days slowly pass by (the entire first season covers a total of six days), Daniel's communication does not become more natural—but we see that in the real world of Paulie, he is both like a child and a foreigner. He delights in the wonders of the convenience mart: the hot dogs on rollers slowly moving by like a Ferris wheel, the ridiculous size of a Big Gulp. He rolls on the grass outside, relishing the sensory experiences of freedom.

After being in a cell for so long, the miniature wonders of Paulie, Georgia, feel as strange, new, and awe-inspiring as a trip to the Grand Canyon. One of the show's writers and directors, Scott Teems, points out that the world of Paulie's residents is very small, both physically and philosophically. He contrasts this to Daniel's world, which "could not have been smaller on a literal level," yet, ironically, "is far more expansive than any of the characters on the show because they don't ever leave their little town."[32] Daniel has to "leave the town in his mind," Teems continues. "He has to go somewhere else in his mind in order to find a way to 'survive.'"[33] Daniel is a voracious reader with a vivid imagination, and this means of escape does not just disappear when he leaves prison. It becomes both healthy and destructive as he struggles to adjust to life in the small town that cannot contain him. Just as viewers are reading Daniel through watching a show, Daniel is reading the world through his books. As more of his humanity is revealed to us, he is reading and engaging with stories in order to feel more human himself. Unable to claim and confront his own story, he relies on these surrogate stories to teach him how to live outside of the prison walls. And as he reads, he becomes more empathetic to the plight even of those who have neglected or harmed him.

Like Valentino's story, Daniel's story is told with a continual interjection of flashbacks in order to help us understand the traumatic history that has led to the eccentric, endearingly odd man he has become and is becoming. In different memories, Daniel's mind travels back to the first time he was raped in a prison shower, moments of torment from the sadist in the cell next to him, and the grief and horror of watching his only friend being led to his execution. These "repetitions," compulsive memories of his past traumas, are daily reminders of a man who has so often been defined as other, criminal, abnormal.[34] Daniel's face carries the weight of his unresolved trauma; he often looks distant and forlorn, out of place. His speech is deeply affected, its cadence unusual and uncomfortable. At the same time, he is a proper Southern gentleman who is truly gentle, incredibly witty, and deeply empathetic to the suffering of others. He is both earnest and, often, sarcastic in his painful honesty.

Although deeply kind, Daniel sometimes experiences unpredictable explosions of anger, not an uncommon reaction from a triggered victim of extreme trauma. Teems explains that Daniel is like a person "walking around with no skin on . . . like when you are in a dark room and walk outside into the bright light . . . a sensory overload."[35] After spending more than half of his life confined and alone with the impact of ongoing mental and physical abuse, he is easily overstimulated, both by reminders of his past and the raw data of everyday experience. At one point when Daniel visits his sister, expecting her to open the door, he instead finds his lawyer and her boyfriend, Jon. He is stunned and deeply disrupted: "I'm shocked to find you here. I'm not used to contemplating all the variables one might encounter. If you don't have the years of experiences, there isn't the repetition of everyday living to make things mundane. Mundane is calming and soothing. Mundane isn't out of the ordinary. And when everything is out of the ordinary, it can be too much sometimes."[36] Daniel longs for the gifts of the "mundane." But nothing is mundane, even in small-town Paulie, Georgia, where he has lived only behind bars and inside his head for nineteen years.

As noted before, Teems emphasizes that Daniel's mind is far more expansive in its worldview than that of his fellow Paulie residents. Part of this is because of Daniel's love of literature and his ongoing process of feeding his intellect and heart with the works of Flannery O'Connor, Thomas Aquinas, and others. His heart and imagination have not atrophied while he is in prison. They have, in fact, expanded, as he exercises both his intellect and his capacity for compassion while residing in imaginary worlds or contemplating the complex secrets of humans in the real world.

As much as reading has fed his mind and soul, Daniel's continual isolation has led to more concerning forms of escaping from reality. He drifts in and out of his real-life present, and at times, he is unable to separate real memory from false memory, recollection from hallucination. The true past experiences that he has repressed commingle with what seem to be hallucinations. Like a waking dream, he repeatedly envisions meeting his executed friend, Kerwin, in a cow field or even reuniting in the same jail cell. We know from the series that Kerwin and Daniel only spoke through the grate between their two cells, seeing each other's faces for the first time when Kerwin was being led to his death. Yet Daniel continually sees and revisits him during his sleep and during his waking hallucinations. There are times when even the viewer of the series is unsure if Daniel's present experience is a dream, a hallucination, a flashback, or present-day reality. These surreal sequences within an otherwise naturalist/realist show include an excursion with a seemingly unhinged older man who leads Daniel into a cow field that contains a beheaded statue of a woman, a place that Daniel revisits in his visions. Although broken, the statue is devastatingly beautiful, so much so that Daniel says, "It's the beauty that hurts you most."[37] In this moment, we become even more aware of all the beauty of mundane life that Daniel has missed and must be mourning. Toward the end of his encounter with this older, nameless man, he wrestles with him, a scene that intentionally evokes the mystery and strangeness of Jacob wrestling with the angel. Daniel's breaks from present reality become more and more concerning to him, and we see him weep because he cannot even remember whether or not he killed his former girlfriend.

Because of this confusion between real life and fantasy, Daniel is a mystery even to himself. And to the residents of Paulie, Daniel's behavior is odd, at best, and threatening, at worst. They have not seen his suffering and understood the turmoil inside of him, nor have they wanted to. Daniel's own stepbrother, Teddy, an insecure yet seemingly confident good old boy, is one of the most disapproving of the town's residents. Teddy has a pretty face that wears a perpetual smirk; he would have been a big fish in his small-town high school pond, yet his normality begins to unravel when Daniel comes onto the scene. Teddy is immediately jealous because of the empathetic attention his pretty, sweet Christian wife, Tawny, shows Daniel. He doubts Daniel's innocence and continually shoots verbal barbs in his direction or behind his back to let everyone know this. For the first two seasons of the show, Teddy is a nearly despicable character, as, more than anyone, he represents the callousness of the small Southern town's constituency. But as Teddy eventually endures suffering himself, some of it of Daniel's making, his humanity becomes more apparent.

Scott Teems includes the initially unlikable Teddy in a powerful description of the show that a friend shared with him: "Our show sees its characters as God sees them."[38] "We see our characters not just for who they are but for who they could become," Teems elaborates. "We see them with grace."[39] A character like Teddy needs a lot of grace even though he is initially unable to extend it himself. Teems explains that we all want to be seen with grace and that this is the "gift for a show that wants its characters to grow and become better versions of themselves."[40] Teems explains that he loved writing Teddy's character because he most closely related to Teddy as the character who embodies what he himself could have become. Teddy's small world resembles the world that nurtured Teems, but Teems, like Teddy, was challenged enough to finally transcend its boundaries. This notion that the show sees the characters as "God sees them" is another key to why this series helps us grow our capacity for empathy.[41] The show's writers see the characters they crafted through eyes of love, focusing honestly on their sin yet also on their beauty and potential.

The creators of *Rectify* also highlight "how God sees" characters who have committed horrible crimes and been redeemed, depicting their growth into undeniably glorious human beings.[42] The most moving picture of this is in the character of Kerwin, Daniel's fellow convict, occupying the cell next door. Unlike Daniel, there is no question whether Kerwin is guilty of the crime he has been charged with: the murder of a child. While participating in a gang initiation ritual, Kerwin shot at a car with an opposing gang member in it; he had no idea that a little girl was also in the car. Kerwin is a murderer consumed with guilt for his crime. The one hope he has remaining on this earth is the hope for Daniel's eventual freedom. At one point, he tells Daniel that he thanks God for their friendship and, in particular, the hope he has for Daniel's life outside bars: "It gave me something to live for."[43] When Kerwin is preparing for his execution, he talks with Daniel about the belief that he will soon see the little girl he has killed, and he wonders what he will tell her. Daniel says, "Let her know who you are now. Who you have become."[44] Kerwin responds by telling Daniel that he cannot even remember who he is, to which his friend responds, "You are a beautiful person. That's all you need to remember."[45] Kerwin is indeed a beautiful person, and we see this in his deep empathy and care for Daniel and the joy of a life he shares with a friend whose face he never sees. His character is a powerful example of the famous quote from Bryan Stevenson's *Just Mercy: A Story of Justice and Redemption*: "Each of us is more than the worst thing we have ever done."[46] The security and comfort provided by Daniel and Kerwin's friendship are eventually shattered as Kerwin is escorted from his cell on death row to the execution chamber.

Daniel is so grieved and heartbroken that he cannot watch as Kerwin is led past his cell, but Kerwin begs him to show himself: "Look at me. Look at me, brother." Daniel finally has the strength to move toward the bars and see Kerwin's face, which is full of love for him. He tells Daniel, "I know you did not do it!" to which Daniel responds, "How do you know?"[47] Kerwin's final words to Daniel are beautiful and deeply affirming: "Because I know you. Because I know you. Because I know you."[48] This scene is painfully poignant, a reminder that all human beings have an intrinsic desire to be both known and loved, even when the knowing includes knowledge of our sins. Daniel's empathy for his friend is exemplary, as he does not ignore the sin but sees that Kerwin is still worthy of love and redemption. Kerwin's faith in and empathy for Daniel is equally powerful and impacts him so much that Daniel often either dreams of Kerwin or has hallucinatory visions of meeting him again when both of their cell doors are open and they can occupy the same space, laughing, talking, just being human. One of Daniel's dreams of Kerwin is especially vivid as Kerwin yells excitedly to his friend, "Wake up and live! Life is a gift!"[49] Daniel tells Kerwin, "You are my best friend, Kerwin. My only friend, really. I don't think I can do this. It's too complicated out here."[50] As light spills out of the dream cell, Kerwin assures his friend that he can do it, that there is hope for him. And after Daniel has been set free, he takes a trip to meet Kerwin's mother and brother, to tell them what an honorable man his friend was.

Although Daniel can see the honor in Kerwin, he still struggles to see it in himself. He believes in the beauty and importance of Kerwin's story but not in his own. In the series' last season, Daniel is living in a halfway house in Nashville, and the director of his program tries to get him to push past the wall of silence and shame that so limits his relationships. Daniel finally admits that he is "so lonely, so deeply lonely" and that Kerwin had originally protected him from that.[51] But according to Daniel, the many years he spent alone after Kerwin's death seemed to damage him to the point of no return: "You go so deep into yourself you lose yourself. You crumble and have no ego. Lose any sense of self. How profound that loss is, the psychic glue that binds your whole notion of existence. I think therefore I am. I think too much, therefore I am not. If I am not, then I am nothing. If I am nothing, then I am dead. If I am dead, then why am I so . . . lonely?"[52]

After several troubling months with his family, Daniel's time in the halfway house finally pushes him in the direction of life. He fears that the family that had so wished to see their broken son and brother made whole again will be disappointed, "no matter the surgeons who attend to me."[53] But while in Nashville, Daniel is surrounded by a community of support, and he finally relays his past traumas to those outside of his family, including a psychiatrist. In the safe context of the halfway house and his relationship with his new girlfriend, Chloe, he feels strong enough to finally face and share his own story. His roommate, a middle-aged Black ex-con called "Pickle," verbalizes the sense of family accountability that the men in the home have for one another: "To some degree, we've got to be our brother's keeper."[54] In this context, Daniel is finally able to face his shame and enter the grieving process for all the life he has lost and the many ways he is broken.

Although the show ends with some hope for Daniel's new stage in life, it does not have a Hollywood resolution in which everything broken and lost is magically repaired and restored. In the last episode, Amantha says, "Nothing can rectify what happened. Nothing can bring back Hannah or my dad or my eighteen-year-old brother."[55] And she is right. The losses experienced can never be fully reversed, but we do see Daniel on the path to greater self-acceptance and healing. In paraphrasing ideas from Flannery O'Connor's *Mystery and Manners*, series writer Scott Teems explains that the way the story is told is the story's meaning. If a viewer can easily extract the meaning out of the story, then it is not a good story. It is reductionist or sentimental; it's not true to the complexity of the lived experience. Teems explains that the writers had to "go to some dark places" in writing these characters:

> And that is the beauty of drama—you are allowed to experience vicariously these darker and heavier emotions and lighter emotions—the breadth of emotion that we usually don't get to experience in our day to day lives. If we are lucky, fortunate, we don't experience the darker stuff very much. But when you can experience that vicariously you can then have empathy for

people who are going through those things and you can hopefully grow as a person. That is really the ultimate gift of drama and what this show was all about was trying to create empathy within those that watch the show and make the world a better place. As trite as that sounds, I really do believe that it is true.[56]

In going to both the dark and light places, the show's creators give their viewers the gift of embracing empathy while watching these lives become more fully human on screen. In watching Daniel's story, we are made more aware of what Psalm 79:11 calls the "groans of the prisoners" and perhaps more compelled to take Christ's words to heart: "I was in prison and you came to visit me. . . . Truly I tell you, whatever you did for one of the least of these brothers of mine, you did for me."[57] Daniel and Kerwin, an innocent prisoner and a guilty one, are both deserving of love, and their need to tell their own stories must be met with empathy if they are to be valued and understood.

THE HATE U GIVE

Daniel Holden, a white man, has endured subhuman treatment and been denied empathy because he was imprisoned and labeled a criminal. But as we know from both history and recent news headlines, including the death of George Floyd, some Americans are treated as criminals simply because of the color of their skin. Angie Thomas's novel *The Hate U Give* is a powerful narrative about this form of injustice toward Black Americans. Reading it is an act of love that reflects a desire to cross a bridge in order to grow in empathy and join in lament with the Black community. The majority of white America has historically struggled with "mourn[ing] with those who mourn" when it comes to the Black community's ongoing struggle with racial profiling and other related injustices.[58] Martin Luther King Jr. famously said that there are "two Americas," one for the white, dominant culture and one for a large portion of Black Americans that "has a daily ugliness about it that transforms the buoyancy of hope into the fatigue of despair."[59] Because the impact of historical and contemporary racism is often invisible to white Americans, there is a general resistance to believe the Black community, to lament, and to mourn with them. This is a difficult bridge to cross, and without great, focused, and informed intentionality, it is very difficult for a white American to empathize with this aspect of the Black American experience. In turn, it is easy to distrust, ignore, and even infantilize Black brothers and sisters who speak out about their oppression. Thomas's poignant novel *The Hate U Give* gives the majority access to seeing the world through the eyes of a Black high school student whose family and community have been devastated by injustice and violence.

In the Gospels, we see that Christ was deeply concerned with injustice, so often giving his direct attention to those whose voices had been stifled by the status quo while suffering abuse from both community and religious leaders. He knew their human sins, but he also knew their wounded humanity. This is the Christ of the oppressed, the liberator who hears the cries of the many who are disempowered victims of injustice. Because of this, when *The Hate U Give*'s young protagonist, Starr Carter, sees Officer 115 on the news wearing a cross around his neck, she remarks, "We must worship a different Jesus."[60] For Starr, it is devastating and confusing to see a white Christian not hear or see her community's injustice and suffering, especially as the Christ she believes in is not only *the* great empathizer but also a victim of injustice. Officer Brian Cruise, or "115" as Starr usually calls him, has just shot and killed one of her childhood best friends, Khalil. Starr was the only witness to his death. Thomas's sobering young adult novel asks the very hard question that Americans, especially white American Christians, need to be asking ourselves: How can we worship the same God, believe we are all created in his image, yet ignore the cries of the Black community's pain under the weight of systemic injustice?

Like Valentino Deng, Starr wonders where the empathy from her white Christian neighbors is for her recently killed friend, her community, and herself. The novel continually asks questions like this, challenging its readers to inform themselves through listening to heartbreaking stories of oppression and inequity. As we follow Starr's role as a witness, the novel helps us see and feel what it is like to be a Black teenager in contemporary America. Angie Thomas asks her readers if we, too, will become witnesses instead of averting our eyes from suffering and injustice. The novel is an invitation to empathize with the Black community.

Sixteen-year-old Starr both loves and hates her life in Garden Heights, a primarily Black neighborhood where everyone knows everyone else and where her father's store, Carter's Grocery, is one of the centers of the community. Starr's father, Maverick, has spent his entire life in Garden Heights, where he used to run with the King Lords, a local gang. As much as his past life still invites danger, he loves the community and its people and does not want to live elsewhere. Starr's mother, Lisa, was also born in the Heights, but she has been on the outside and longs to get out for good. Starr explains that the local high school is "where you go to get jumped, high, pregnant, or killed. We don't go there."[61] When Starr was in elementary school, she witnessed one of her best friends, Natasha, get shot and killed in a gang initiation gone wrong. Since that life-altering event, Starr's mother has insisted that Starr and little brother, Sekani, as well as their half brother, Seven, all attend a predominantly white college prep school called Williamson, a safe forty-five-minute drive from Garden Heights.

Although most readers can empathize with the difficulty and awkwardness of wanting to be accepted by their peers in high school, Starr's situation is even more difficult to negotiate. She lives in two worlds, reminiscent of King's "two Americas," and she finds that she must be "Starr #1" in her home, Garden Heights, and "Starr #2" in posh, white Williamson.[62] Thomas's emphasis on the daily sense of being overwhelmed, misunderstood, and exhausted as a Black student in a predominantly white institution will ring true to many of her novel's Black readers and be a wake-up call to many of her white readers. In drifting from the streets of Garden Heights to the squeaky-clean halls of suburban Williamson, Starr must learn to always be on her guard, to code switch in order to negotiate her Blackness in a sea of whiteness. On the wall of Starr's childhood home hangs a painting of Black Jesus right next to a photo of Malcolm X holding a shotgun. The family reads the Bible and the Black Panther's Ten Point Program together and learns to recite portions of both.[63] She is steeped in the history of Black suffering and the Black struggle at home, but in the alternate world of Williamson, Starr's best friend, Hailey, unfollows her on Tumblr because she refuses to look at a posted photo of the brutally disfigured Emmett Till in a casket. When white Americans are faced with the brutal reality of Black trauma, responses like Hailey's are not uncommon. This knee-jerk, protective action is a desire to not face the pain from which one might have benefited or been complicit. When Starr code switches or tones down talking about the impact of racism in order to fit in and make her white peers comfortable, she must edit, translate, or even stifle parts of her story. This pressure to modify Starr's story and to shut out the pain of the truth of history are both barriers to empathy.

Hailey is only comfortable with Starr's being Black when she is willing to conform to the speech, history, and habits of Williamson. In other words, she only loves Starr when Starr is unlike other Black people, when she looks a bit different (in a fetishized, exotic way) but is still white inside. In George Tillman's excellent film production of *The Hate U Give*, Starr says that she needs to avoid using slang while at Williamson because "slang makes them cool but makes me ghetto."[64] This is the struggle of many Black people in white spaces, and Thomas's story makes these issues, often invisible to white readers, become visible to all of her readers. Her brilliant description of Starr's struggle to find an identity while living in two worlds, having to hide a portion of herself in both, is an invitation for readers, especially white readers, to see the world through the eyes of someone like Starr. And that someone is a description of millions of our Black neighbors.

The novel opens with misfit Starr attending a Garden Heights party with her street-smart friend, Kenya. It is awkward for her because, although she lives in Garden Heights, she does not attend school there, and these parties are not part of her social world. Like many high school parties, there is alcohol, petty jealousy, and a room full of kids attempting to look and be cool. Starr is not one of them. She looks dumpy and plain in her hoodie and sweats, obviously not prepared to one-up the competition. During this boring (for Starr) revelry, she runs into one of her childhood best friends, Khalil, and the meeting is magical in the way that any reminder of childhood innocence and first love can be. She and Khalil have lost touch—yet they immediately fall into familiar rhythms talking about their childhood love of Harry Potter and the embarrassing photos of their toddler bath times together. Starr lights up, finally delighted to be at this party. But soon after, a gunshot is heard and reality breaks through. Everyone scatters.

Starr feels safe with Khalil, and he offers to drive her home. They laugh, they flirt, and Starr regrets having lost touch with Khalil, her first crush and her former best friend. As the two drive away from the party, Starr playfully makes fun of Khalil for rapping along to Tupac Shakur, a hip-hop artist from her father's generation. Khalil does not give in to the mockery. Instead, he proudly educates Starr on the brilliance and relevance of Tupac's description of hood life. Tupac was part of a group named Thug Life with an album of the same name—and he also had a tattoo on his arm of this phrase. Khalil explains that T-H-U-G-L-I-F-E is an acronym for the phrase "The hate you give little infants fucks everyone."[65] Starr is surprised, confused, and intrigued. Khalil believes that this name, the lifelong motto of Tupac's artistic vision, is an apt description of life in Garden Heights and life for Black Americans in general. Just as Khalil teaches Starr, he also teaches the novel's readers. In the pages that follow, readers begin to see how children growing up under the far-reaching tentacles of racist policies and ideologies are impacted in ways that devastate the entire community. In witnessing this, we can see the complexity of the very issues that are often so oversimplified for the sake of ideological or political gain. *The Hate U Give* enables readers to see the prophetic wisdom of Cornel West's famous line, "Justice is what love looks like in public."[66] Starr and her Garden Heights friends have not been loved by the systems that determine so much of their day-to-day lives. As she exposes the compounded impact of centuries of injustice to the Black community, Thomas asks us to empathize with a young man and woman who are wounded victims of this lack of freedom and equality.

Starr does not fully understand Khalil's points about Tupac's motto and the life that she, as a Black girl, has lived, but the two friends continue to joke, listen to music, and just enjoy each other. This all changes when they see blue lights flashing behind their car and hear a voice coming through a loudspeaker, commanding them to pull over. Officer Brian Cruise, badge number 115, walks up to the car door and asks Khalil for his license and registration. The issue is a busted taillight, but the longer the officer withholds this information, the longer Khalil grows agitated and angry. Starr recalls when her father gave her "the talk" about how to act if apprehended by the police.[67] In this moment, Thomas highlights one of the many key differences between the "two Americas": at a young age, Black Americans are given an instructive and protective talk about how to interact with the police. The talk that Starr received was many years ago—but she remembers it all and anxiously begs Khalil to place his hands on the steering wheel. He does so briefly, but then his anger gets the better of him and he mouths off to the officer. Starr panics, realizing that Khalil, who was raised in a very broken, chaotic home, must have not been given "the talk." Officer Cruise then asks Khalil to get out of the car and put his hands up while he leans against the vehicle. Khalil follows orders—but then he ducks down to ask Starr if she is OK while, at the same time, picking up a hairbrush from inside the car.

The next thing Star hears is the three shots of the officer's gun, the result of a defense reflex that ends up killing Khalil. Starr screams, and Officer 115 holds the gun on her as well. She exits the car, sobbing, and bends down to cradle Khalil's lifeless body. After the murder, "115" claims self-defense, thinking that the hairbrush was a gun. This pivotal tragedy at the heart of the story echoes the plot narrative of so many stories that we hear on the news, that we read on the internet, that we transform into hashtags.

Starr cannot take her eyes off the body of her friend: "They leave Khalil's body in the street like it's an exhibit."[68] His body is left uncovered, and Starr cannot bear to see her friend so exposed. In the weeks to come, his life and reputation are also exposed in front of the court of public opinion. Although he was unarmed and innocent, he is seen as guilty because there were rumors that he belonged to a gang and sold drugs. But this was not the Khalil that Starr knew, and she becomes outraged that he is seen as the criminal rather than the victim in this scenario. Khalil was tried, convicted, and killed in a matter of seconds, directly in front of her eyes. "To be accused was to be convicted," says Frederick Douglass when speaking of the lives of the enslaved who worked for his master.[69] The word and judgment of a white man, of the person wielding power and upholding the system, held much more weight than the truth. Angie Thomas's decision to make Khalil's murder the instigating event of the novel's action is also a decision to ask the sobering question of whether things are really that much better.

As the novel continues and we contemplate this question, readers are asked to silence the critical, nonbelieving voices crowding our minds in order to actively listen to Starr's very young, very bewildered, and very traumatized voice. Because she is a child, both likable and relatively innocent, we are further disarmed when reading about her suffering. The days following the shooting are foggy for Starr as she is haunted by nightmares; intrusive memories of holding her bloody, dying friend; and guilt for not speaking openly about what she witnessed. When she does speak with the police, she is retraumatized. And this happens again, days later, when she must speak to the district attorney about what is referred to dismissingly as "the incident."[70] As she recalls that fatal night, she can still see the life draining out of Khalil as he dies in her arms. The trauma trapped within her body forces its way up, and she gags. Maverick rushes to bring a trash can over so that she can bend and violently "cry and puke" and continue to "cry and puke."[71]

Starr is a very sympathetic, earnest character, so much so that even her dishonesty when confronted about Khalil's death is understandable yet painful to watch, deepening our space for imaginative empathy. Her proximity to the death of one assumed to be a criminal would further alienate her from her white peers at Williamson. Like any teenager, she longs to be seen as normal, to become a vibrant part of the school's in-crowd. Because of this, Starr hides the fact that she witnessed Khalil's death, even denying that she knew him. As the news of Khalil's death becomes widely publicized, a large group of Williamson students ditches school to go to the protests. Many, including her supposed friend, Hailey, are eager to go, not for Khalil's sake, but in order to miss class. Starr becomes increasingly angry at Hailey and the other students using the death of a Black man as an excuse to skip school. These protestors are opportunists riding on their privilege yet unaware of its toxicity. After school, Starr is with her friends Maya and Hailey watching television when the story of the shooting comes on the news. Because Khalil's name is associated with drugs and gang activity, the officer is seen as a victim, even though he is the murderer. Officer 115's father speaks to the reporters, defending the goodness of his son, who is a family man and churchgoer. Meanwhile, Khalil is still dead, silent, without a voice. The sting of this becomes too much for Starr, and she realizes that seeing this biased, dehumanizing spin "kills a part of me."[72] Just as Starr recognizes the depth of her pain, Hailey's face falls, and she expresses sadness for the officer: "His life matters too, you know."[73] This is a step too far for Starr; the betrayal signals an end to the friendship.

Thomas artfully reminds readers that responding to the heart-cry slogan "Black Lives Matter" with the knee-jerk response "All Lives

Matter" is another barrier to developing empathy for members of the Black community. This is a cry that needs to be attentively and humbly received by those who claim to love Christ. In the case within the novel, Khalil's life has been taken away through no fault of his own, yet the attention is diverted to the life of one still living, still denying his responsibility for Khalil's death. Like anyone in the Garden Heights community, Starr has seen firsthand the present impact of the historical reality that, in America, white lives have often been valued far more than Black lives. This is seen in the redlining laws that created a neighborhood like Garden Heights, in the lack of resources for the Garden Heights public school, in the fear of Blackness that killed Khalil.

Hailey's response shows a lack of self-awareness, a lack of awareness of history, a lack of awareness of Starr's reality and her feelings. It is the opposite of empathy, yet it is perhaps reflective of some of our own natural tendencies. It is so much easier and seems much more natural to empathize with those who look and live most like us to the detriment of those who have the greatest need. The film version of *The Hate U Give* interjects another, tense conversation that reflects some of these same truths. Starr explains the reasons behind the anger she has in response to Hailey's comments about the news story, and she emphasizes that she, like Khalil, is Black. When Hailey responds, "You're different, Starr," the subtext is very clear: Starr is one of the good ones, not a typical Black person.[74] Starr then makes it even more clear: "You mean I am a nonthreatening Black girl."[75] Hailey does not back down but admits that this was what she meant and plunges more deeply into the wound by saying, "Your friend wasn't."[76] Again, Hailey's complete inability to see both her own privilege and her own inherited racism prevents her from having empathy, from seeing Starr as a beautiful Black image bearer rather than just a more domesticated white person who happens to have Black skin.

In the film version of the novel, Starr's wealthy white boyfriend, Chris, also makes comments that expose a lack of self-awareness and an inherited racial understanding of reality, something that must be acknowledged and deconstructed if one is to move toward empathy. Chris is gentle and kind; he does not have the same "mean girl" energy that Hailey does. He truly cares for Starr, and he tries to show this by saying, "White, Black. We're all the same. . . . I don't see color. I see people exactly as they are."[77] But Chris is living in a society where the norm is whiteness, and to say, "I don't see color," a form of what sociologists call "color-blind racism," actually denies the distorted lens through which he, and white Americans in general, has been taught to see his Black neighbors. As therapist Resmaa Menakem explains, "This everyday form of white-body supremacy is in the air we breathe, the water we drink, and the culture we share. We literally cannot avoid it. It is part of the operating system and the organizing structure of American culture. It's always functioning in the background, often invisibly, in our institutions, our relationships, our interactions."[78] The background "operating system" of whiteness makes itself invisible, and the person who has not deconstructed their whiteness fully cannot see the suffering of their Black neighbors.[79] If "white-body supremacy is in the air we breathe," we must work hard to label it as not normal, to resist so that we are able to begin listening, the first step toward true empathy.[80] Chris's intentions are good, but he is blind to the damage they cause. Starr responds, making the invisible visible: "If you don't see Blackness, you don't see me."[81] Starr is asking Chris to see her, including her very Blackness that is both beautiful and abused. Angie Thomas is asking her readers to do the same thing when reading Starr's story. And in this intentional act of sacred listening and focusing on the beauty of designed difference, space is created for imaginative empathy.

Thomas focuses much attention on Khalil's backstory, emphasizing the ways that a biased media and a largely racist community want to label him as nothing more than a criminal. This is another example of the story of an oppressed person being distorted, ignored, and heavily edited for the sake of a larger agenda. Khalil did commit crimes—but they did not define him or make his life less valuable. Even before his fatal final moment with Starr, he was full of desperation. Although the local media knew and broadcasts that Khalil sold drugs for the King Lords, a dangerous local gang, they did not know the reasons he did it. His image flashes on the television along with the mention of drugs and gang involvement, creating an "other" caricature that many white viewers, such as Hailey, can easily hold in their minds. But this was not the real Khalil, a young man who was selling drugs as a last-chance measure in order to pay for his beloved grandmother's cancer treatment. He had no father at home, and his mother was an addict, unfit to care for him. His grandmother was his life and love. He did not join the gang, but he agreed to run drugs for them in order to raise money for medical bills. He did not own a gun or engage in violence, and he was not the caricature of fearful Blackness that was featured on the news. Thomas attempts to, and succeeds in, showing us the humanity not only of innocent Starr but of one who has engaged in criminal behavior. Both are worthy of empathy and love.

Khalil was an image bearer, yet he lived on the underside of the "American dream," in the often misunderstood or forgotten side of King's "two Americas." In *Between the World and Me*, Ta-Nehisi Coates explains the ways in which the "dream" is a nightmare for a young Black man in his America: "I have seen that dream all my life. It is perfect houses with nice lawns. It is Memorial Day cookouts, block associations, and driveways. The Dream is tree houses and the Cub Scouts. And for so long I have wanted to escape into the Dream, to fold my country over my head like a blanket. But this has never been an option, because the Dream rests on our backs, the bedding made from our bodies."[82] The comfort of American suburbia, the privilege that prompts Williamson students to "protest" for the sake of skipping school, the mythology that white Americans can be color-blind—all of these are the result of a dream that has been made possible by the disempowerment, abuse, and death of Black Americans.

Thomas's novel humanizes those who are often vilified in the national cultural conversation. As we watch a fictional reenactment of one of the slayings of Black men so often seen on the news, the novel asks us not to turn off the channel but, instead, to turn the page—to keep going. And in turning the page, we learn who Khalil actually was and who Starr currently is in the aftermath of a trauma that no child should endure. Once Starr's eyes are opened to the injustice that killed her friend, she cannot push down the rage, and she finds her voice and learns how to tell her story. She joins the community Black Lives Matter protest, and her voice speaks, yells, weeps for Khalil and for all of the other unarmed Black Americans who have been needlessly killed and then ignored by the system. She recognizes that the fight can be despairing: "No matter what we say. No matter how loud we shout. They refuse to hear us."[83] But she will not take this refusal as an answer. She will shout, write, post, march, and educate until her white neighbors can hear and see her.

Just as Starr finds her strength to speak up for Khalil and for herself, Thomas's novel is a powerful appeal to her readers to "speak up for those who cannot speak for themselves," including those whose lives have been lost to the invisible stronghold of white supremacy.[84] She challenges her readers to truly "mourn with those who mourn," and she reminds us that the first step is listening to and believing the stories of those mourning. In doing this, we can "carry each other's burdens," an act of love informed by empathy.[85]

UNBELIEVABLE

Marie Adler, central protagonist of the Netflix limited series *Unbelievable*, also understands the pain of not being seen and heard as well as not being trusted. Although she has tried to speak for herself and tell her story, the reality of her pain is still invisible to those around her. She has spent most of her young life being treated like an unsolvable problem rather than an exploited human being deserving of empathy. Because of this, she struggles to trust anyone. Her story of sexual assault, followed by the secondary abuse of silencing, is important to engage as we consider what it means to grow our capacity for empathy. Watching Marie's treatment at the hands of many appointed to help her, we see the end result of having one's story stifled or distorted. Like Valentino, Daniel, Starr, and Khalil, Marie's story needs to be told, and the more we look directly in the eyes of this pained young woman, the more her sacred being takes shape in our minds.

In the first meeting with her court-appointed therapist, Marie says, "No matter how much someone [says] they care about you, they don't."[86] Marie has good reason to believe this. A young adult who has been moved from foster home to foster home, both of Marie's birth parents and many of her foster parents have abused her. She knows that she has been unwanted all of her life. The details of her records make even the hard-boiled detectives first hearing her story cringe: in one foster home, she was forced to survive on dog food. Marie's history of continual dehumanization culminates into two cases of assault: the hours-long vicious rape by an anonymous, masked intruder and then the aggressive questioning and lack of trust from the male detectives who are assigned to the case.

Like Valentino's story, Marie's story is a true one. And like Valentino, the lack of empathy from others in her life deepens the impact of Marie's abuse. The importance of engaging stories like these is in deepening our understanding of those who have been silenced so that we can grow in patience and attentiveness. Marie Adler's story as detailed in *Unbelievable* also reflects the experience of many victims of sexual assault. Unlike so many police procedurals, *Unbelievable* highlights Marie's unique personhood by spending just as much time focusing on the mental and emotional impact on Marie, the central assault victim, as it does on solving the crime. In this sense, the series is particularly helpful in feeding our imaginations with the lived experience behind the newspaper headlines, enabling us to see the victim as more than just a victim. To this end, the first episode of the series is shot solely from Marie's perspective. We learn that in the middle of the night, a man breaks into her apartment, a single unit in a transitional group home for foster children. This masked intruder ties her up with the shoelaces from her own tennis shoes, rapes her repeatedly, and takes photos of her. Marie is left bound and gagged, and once she is able to free herself, she calls her ex-boyfriend and then her most recent foster mother, Judith, for help.

When the police come to Marie's apartment, she is calm yet fragile, and she struggles to remember details. She does not cry or show obvious signs of distress (to an untrained eye). Immediately after this scene, she is taken to the hospital to have every part of her body swabbed, poked, inspected, and retraumatized. Significantly, the entire first episode, and most scenes throughout the series featuring Marie, are filmed in a very bleak, almost colorless light. There is a sense of life being stripped out of reality and replaced with a cold, clinical gray/blue. This is especially obvious when Marie is in the police precinct, under the unforgiving fluorescent lighting of Detective Robert Parker's office. It is painfully noticeable that all of the police officers that come to the scene of the crime and all of the detectives in the local precinct are male. As Marie sits on the other side of Parker's desk, she looks small and afraid, childlike. She is, after all, just eighteen years old. And in her life, authority figures have, more frequently than not, been untrustworthy predators. Detective Parker shows little compassion or empathy; he merely collects data in a clinical fashion. There is no gentleness in his manner or acknowledgment that the human being sitting in front of him *is* a human being, and that this human being has been violated.

In front of Parker, Marie must relay the crime's dreadful timeline and details for the third time since it occurred. She gets confused, she misses some things, and she is clearly flustered. Marie shows little emotion in her face, but as she redescribes the trauma that she has endured, the show's viewers see the terrifying flashbacks that are uncontrollably interjecting themselves into her present train of thought. Viewers see that, like Valentino, Daniel, and Starr, so much of Marie's present self is hindered by the constant, disruptive memories of the ways that she has been violated. Like most trauma victims, Marie was unable to be fully present in her conscious mind as the traumatic event was occurring. This is a means of protection as the psychological pain of the moment is a weight too great to bear. The impact of acute trauma is still absorbed, however, by both the body and the unconscious mind. It can manifest in both physical and psychological symptoms, most notably what Freud referred to as "repetitions," unwelcome flashbacks that violently intrude everyday waking thoughts and/or the world of dreams.[87] This emphasis is significant because to an untrained observer, she seems to not be impacted by her trauma. And this is the way many survivors present themselves to the world by whom they are misunderstood and misjudged. If we are to have empathy for someone like Marie, we need to understand the way the mind works to protect itself in cases like hers. Although she seems calm, perhaps even undisturbed, her inner world is on fire, constantly bombarded by intruders.

In his best-selling book *The Body Keeps the Score*, Bessel A. van der Kolk explains that "Traumatized people chronically feel unsafe inside their bodies: The past is alive in the form of gnawing interior discomfort. Their bodies are constantly bombarded by visceral warning signs, and, in an attempt to control these processes, they often become expert at ignoring their gut feelings and in numbing awareness of what is played out inside."[88] As Marie recounts the details of her account, she experiences almost unbearable flashbacks, "visceral warning signs" that make her want to shut down, retreat, go numb. While listening to the detective, Marie tries to remember the same image in her room that she focused on during the rape: a carefree photo of her enjoying life at the beach. This is a symbol of both freedom and safety, serenity and life. During the interview, she drifts away for what seems like minutes at a time, and the viewers drift with her, remembering the powerful, comforting crashing of the waves. She is unable to be actively present in the moment.

Unbelievable masterfully emphasizes that this is not Marie's flaw but the way that she attempts to make herself safe and restore her battered humanity. Detective Parker, however, does not have eyes to see Marie's momentary dissociation. He only sees a fidgety, child-like young woman taking too much of his time while she stumbles through answering routine questions. He is flippant and businesslike when he tells her that now, after verbally recalling the event to strangers, she must write it all down. As she hesitates, he clearly views her with suspicion rather than compassion. Perhaps Detective Parker is like many of us when encountering victims of trauma: uncomfortable, hurried, even cynical. It is no surprise that Parker eventually uses Marie's statement as a weapon against her. In an act of deep betrayal, Marie's former foster mother calls Detective Parker and, in a roundabout way, heavily implies that Marie has fabricated the story of her rape. He believes this, and he once again asks Marie to come down to the station, where he, along with several other male detectives, proceeds to interrogate her. As a result of their manipulation, she breaks down, losing any sense of clarity and composure. She is threatened with jail time for false reporting and becomes so frightened and intimidated that she finally confesses to lying about the assault. She leaves—defeated, ashamed, and unheard.

Marie's story, one of the many true stories of sexual assault, prompts its viewers to ask how we may be better neighbors to someone like Marie, a young woman who has been a victim of neglect, cruelty, and violence for most of her life. It is very easy to look away from or reject a person whose stories don't always match up, who appears distracted, confused, and distant. And in Marie's case, she even lies in order to escape further interrogation. The false admission that she made up the rape account causes her friends and counselors in her current home, a transitional foster care center, to reject her. Once her story makes it on the news, she is asked to work in the stockroom of her minimum-wage retail job because they don't want her on the floor. She is also issued a citation and charged with false reporting, taking up too much of the city's time and resources. She eventually loses her space at the group home. Marie's lie about not being raped leads to dire, isolating consequences, but when she is asked by a therapist what she would do differently if she could choose again, she says that she would lie earlier on. Almost all of Marie's actions that seem to not make sense actually do; they share the internal logic of self-protection. Marie does not have the support or the tools to withstand the pressure of public opinion, interrogation, or false accusations. More than anything, she needs someone to listen. She desperately needs the empathy that only comes from trust, submission, and patience for her convoluted recollections and feelings.

When Marie is forced to visit a court-appointed therapist, viewers have more direct access to her crumbling internal world. At first, she is angry to be forced to see a counselor and, in protest, she sits in silence for most of the session. Although a trained counselor, her therapist is also a good, empathetic neighbor who forces nothing upon Marie. She merely creates a safe space for Marie to do whatever she wants, even if it is sitting in silence. After Marie's recent experiences with cold interrogation, any more intrusive questioning would add to her abuse. But the kindness of silence is a comforting gift. When Marie finally can't stand the silence anymore, she asks her therapist if she is curious about Marie's story. Her therapist still demands nothing from her patient—but she offers these words:

> Here's what I think: No one makes up something like that unless there is an element of truth to it. Whether you were raped that night or invented a story of being raped that night, I think the truth is you've been violated. You are carrying burdens that were dumped on you by people who didn't love you as well as you deserved to be loved. And that's what I'm curious about: How I may help you carry those burdens a little more lightly, or maybe even lay some of them down? But this is your time. And we have a few minutes. If there is something you want to tell me about that night I would love to listen.[89]

Marie's therapist only speaks after listening. And her act of listening is full of openness and empathy that grows as she watches Marie, seeing how uncomfortable she is in her own body. In response to Marie's pain, she does not try to change the subject or romanticize the tragedy. Instead, she responds directly with truth and compassion, stating that she believes Marie, which in turn, encourages Marie to see herself as someone worth being believed.

These acts of empathy are empowering, as is the genuine offer to "carry these burdens."[90] The gentle words of the therapist tell Marie that she is known and still accepted, that her abuse is not her fault, and that she deserves more. Marie's therapist also gives her, a young woman who has never had much control over her circumstances, control of the encounter. Marie may speak if she wants to—and her words, her story, her being—are all valuable. Marie has been labeled as a criminal, and after a while, she internalizes this moniker. She has also learned that, in general, her words are not valued, and she would not be believed. Because of this, it hurts less to lie and face the repercussions than it does to tell the truth and not be believed. Marie's lie is simply another layer of protection against abuse. Although most of us are not trained therapists, we can glean much wisdom from the therapist's response as we see how it transforms Marie's demeanor and capacity to communicate.

Marie's therapist is not the only good neighbor modeling empathy for the show's viewers. In the second episode of *Unbelievable*, we meet two female detectives in Colorado on the trail of a serial rapist. They know nothing of Marie Adler's case, as it occurred miles away in Washington State and was quickly dismissed. As we watch detectives Karen Duvall and Grace Rasmussen speak with rape victims, including an elderly dormitory house mother and a fragile young woman named Amber, we witness two human beings who prioritize the humanity of rape victims even before the data that must be collected. Their interactions are calm, gentle, and honoring; they ask permission before they do anything else. As the two detectives interact with each other, we learn that Duvall is a devout Christian, wife, and mother of two. She has the words "Here I am, send me" from Isaiah 6:8 on her dashboard, and as she drives Amber to the hospital after the rape, she explains to her that the verse is a reminder of her particular calling.[91] The work that she does is sacred. The partner that she acquires for this case, Grace Rasmussen, is brash and profane, an outspoken atheist who even mocks her colleague's beliefs. Yet when encountering victims of rape, she is fiercely protective of their privacy, emotional well-being, and personhood. Both women are not only devoted to solving the crimes and preventing any more abuse but are also dedicated to helping their dehumanized victims become rehumanized. They are doing redemptive, even holy, work. As we watch their work, the way that they actively listen to victims and often sacrifice their own agendas and quotas, we see the way that empathy can help transform the one on the receiving end as well as the one offering it.

In speaking about the impact of trauma, Bessel A. van der Kolk explains that "the greatest sources of our suffering are the lies we tell to ourselves."[92] And as we see in *Unbelievable*, these lies are often a means of protection and/or the internalization of the false narratives one has absorbed because of toxic situations, individuals, or environments. Marie believes that she cannot win, that the system that ignores the abuse she suffered is bigger than her, a forgotten individual. She is also shaped by the lies that have been violently forced upon her through various forms of assault, including rape. These lies tell her that she is an object, has little value, is not worth being heard. And the lies that she herself will tell are safer because she can control them. Marie knows that other people are unpredictable and have an incredible capacity to hurt her; they are not safe. In talking with her therapist, she describes the plot of *Zombieland* in chilling detail that reflects the danger and sadness of her own situation: "In order to survive, you have to assume everyone else is an enemy. Even if they say they have your back and say they are going to protect you. They won't. They won't. You're on your own."[93] Her paralyzing lack of trust is understandable, even as it causes her to feel monstrous. The deterioration of Marie's mental health is predictable because "being able to feel safe with other people is probably the single most important aspect of mental health; safe connections are fundamental to meaningful and satisfying lives."[94] This lack of safety in Marie's life causes her to withdraw deeper into herself. Yet her therapist and the two female detectives just trying to do right are the neighbors who finally see and hear her. In watching this show, viewers see and learn about the lived experience of a rape victim and survivor of lifelong trauma, reminding us to not silence their fragile voices with our doubt, suspicion, or inability to listen and believe.

Each of these stories reminds us that, although we are our brothers' keepers, it is very easy to ignore this responsibility. The main characters in each story have been either literally or figuratively bound and gagged, silenced. Their stories have been dismissed, ignored, or twisted. Reading or watching these stories gives us a gift of seeing the world through their eyes in order to better see our own responses or lack thereof. Empathy comes after listening and watching, and these works all provide us with the imaginative proximity to do so. These personal encounters have the power to prompt us to "speak up for those who cannot speak for themselves, for the rights of all who are destitute."[95] Like the Samaritan passing by the beaten man on the road, our empathy must prompt us to stop, linger, reach out, and act upon the shared responsibility of being image bearers.

Chapter Five

STRUCTURED FOR EMPATHY

A SHOCKING, SHARED EXPERIENCE

The first pages of Toni Morrison's Pulitzer Prize–winning novel, *Beloved*, are quite unforgiving for the casual reader. She is not gently invited into the novel's world; instead, she is forcefully shoved into the chaotic, disorienting reality that protagonist Sethe and her daughter, Denver, inhabit. Sethe is an escaped slave, both literally and figuratively haunted by a past that bleeds into the present. The book opens with the lines "124 WAS SPITEFUL. Full of baby's venom."[1] The jarring juxtaposition of the words "baby" and "venom" are an unfiltered introduction to the perverse inhumanity at the heart of the novel's world. *Beloved* is based loosely on a news-clip story of the harrowing details of Margaret Garner's life. In an act of fierce love and protection, Garner cut the throat of her infant daughter to prevent her from being stolen back by Garner's former master, a man who repeatedly raped and abused her. In the retelling of this event as Sethe's story, Morrison explores the interior world of a woman whose story, for the most part, has been erased from history. The novel also serves as a memorial to the "sixty million and more" who remain nameless yet whose blood still cries out from the ground, often unheard.

The narrative structure of Morrison's novel matches its violent, disruptive content. Just as a deeply traumatized Sethe experiences the nonlinearity of a world haunted by what she calls "rememories," so do readers.[2] Together with Sethe, we must work to renarrate broken pieces of a fractured past, hoping toward wholeness. *Beloved* is a powerful example of art that demands a very intentional, deepened level of participation from the reader. As we participate more deeply in

Sethe's story, trying to piece it together, we understand more about her desire to be loved and known and are, hopefully, compelled to desire these things for her as well. This novel is not a piece of art that can be read lightly for entertainment; engaging with both its form and its ideas takes serious, focused work. In the introduction to the novel, Morrison explains why she tries to make her readers lose their footing as they enter the novel's world: "There would be no lobby into this house, and there would be no 'introduction' into it or the novel. I wanted to reader to be kidnapped, thrown ruthlessly into an alien environment as the first step into a shared experience with the book's population—just as the characters were snatched from one place to another, from any place to another, without preparation or defense."[3] This "shared experience" is jolting, alien—but if the reader is patient, attentive, and hospitable, she soon sees that sharing Sethe's fractured perspective is a gift that can help grow imaginative empathy.

A CRISIS OF REPRESENTATION

Works of art like *Beloved* that have an especially experimental, atypical, and difficult narrative form present a unique opportunity for reader engagement. One of the main reasons that this is particularly helpful is apparent when revisiting Picasso's statement, "Art is a lie that makes us realize truth."[4] These unconventional works of art resist familiar, prescribed artistic formulas that tend to win over the masses. When art is produced according to a formula, even a good and complex formula, it usually presents a picture of reality that will never be fully real. The experimental works of art in this chapter rely on diverse forms that challenge the traditional mimetic view that art holds up a mirror to reality, reflecting and imitating it. Although they attempt to point us to some truth, they do not provide a traditionally tidy, realistic snapshot of a false reality. Instead, they are influenced by the early twentieth-century aesthetic shift known as the "crisis of representation" that led to artistic experimentation and the development of an avant-garde genre of art.

After Friedrich Nietzsche proclaimed the death of God and Freud discovered the fluid wonders of the unconscious mind, the traditional artistic form that claimed to reflect an ordered, objective reality seemed disingenuous. Without the acknowledged existence of a God that provided a shared, objective truth, individual perception was championed as the truest truth. No matter how much one attempts to paint a realistic picture of a tree, that image is always, to some degree, a lie because an artist (or writer) can only paint her perception of the tree. This rupture in the art world was even more extreme when attempting to re-present the human form. The days of painting ideal beauty or constructing paragraphs that belonged to a linear, ordered narrative were gone. We can see this shift quite clearly when looking at Picasso's early realist works next to his later, more abstract works. This is also apparent when comparing the linear narrative structures from Victorian novels written by Dickens and Austen with the stream of consciousness writing of James Joyce and Virginia Woolf as well as the fragmented poetry of T. S. Eliot. These artists shifted their focus from an objective understanding of reality to the subjective, splintered inner reality of the modern subject, and in their artistic offerings, content matched form, appearing fragmented, nonlinear, and without a discernable moral. Art was still seen as a "lie," even if it was more honest about its subjectivity, but this lie does point to some truths about the human experience, including highlighting both the differences and similarities in individual perception. This focus on individual perception as opposed to objective linearity helps us vicariously participate in a protagonist's existential experience in a way that forces us into a posture of deeper participation.

Resisting Formulas and Inviting Empathy

These modern and, later, postmodern artistic forms (or antiforms) are not always indicative of the claim that we live in an empty, meaningless universe, although in many cases, they are. But this subversive form shift from realism to the avant-garde can also point to a deeper, God-given meaning in the ways that it offers a more close-up, unique, and challenging capacity to experience the life of the other from the inside out. In trying to imagine living in the mind and shoes of another, works with a form mimicking the nonformulaic subjective human experience provide a kind of direct intimacy with their characters. Three works of art that utilize more experimental narrative forms, Toni Morrison's *Beloved*, Krzysztof Kieślowski's *Three Colors: Blue*, and Mark Haddon's *A Curious Incident of the Dog in the Night-Time*, require dedication and careful, measured analysis from their readers and viewers. Their form forces us to slow down, to contemplate, to try to put together the pieces along with the story protagonists. In doing this, we wrestle with the existential experience of being human and experiencing joy and suffering in a unique, personal way. None of these stories can be understood without an embodied commitment from the reader or viewer. As we experience life through the fractured, often frantic, lenses of protagonists Sethe, Julie, and Christopher, we get a small taste of what it feels like to *be* them, thus expanding our empathetic imagination.

BELOVED

The decidedly postmodern narrative form of *Beloved* situates itself in a familiar artistic genre: the ghost story. Perhaps it is strange to consider a novel that might also fit within the category of horror a work of art that encourages and expands empathy. Yet the ghost story, in particular, can have a profound symbolic meaning as it explores the lifelong impact of psychological trauma as a kind of haunting. This is the case in Netflix's recent series *The Haunting of Hill House*—a harrowing portrait of intergenerational family dysfunction that leads to addiction, obsession, and death—which is loosely based on the novel of the same name by Shirley Jackson. Both the ghost genre and the overlapping horror genre are subversive, fitting means by which to explain the often silent, lingering impact of systemic racism. Jordan Peele's two recent hit films, *Get Out* and *Us*, both deconstruct the American dream to disclose the rot hiding just below the shiny surface. Reading *Beloved* as a ghost story, a predecessor to the recent, imaginative works of horror that actuate more painful lament than titillating screams, helps the reader edge closer to the narrative's complex purpose: humanizing an enslaved woman who has been forgotten by history.

The novel is populated by the ghost of the Beloved, the daughter killed by Sethe's own merciful hands, as well as the ghosts of the "sixty million and more."[5] Morrison explains that it is not possible to reimagine the impact of the amoral world of slavery without summoning ghosts: "To invite readers (and myself) into the repellant landscape (hidden, but not completely; deliberately buried, but not forgotten) was to pitch a tent in a cemetery inhabited by highly vocal ghosts."[6]

When local resident Stamp Paid steps onto the porch of number 124, "he [believes] the undecipherable language clamoring around the house was the mumbling of the black and angry dead."[7] The "undecipherable" voices surrounding the house are the "unspeakable thoughts, unspoken" from members of the African diaspora, combined with the haunted thoughts of the women in the house.[8] In order to help her readers both understand and empathize with the experience of the enslaved and their descendants, Morrison recognizes that she must push them into an uncomfortable space that cannot be explained fully through the logic of language. In this, readers feel their security slipping while participating in the raw edge of psychological and spiritual pain: "In trying to make the slave experience intimate, I hoped the sense of things being both under control and out of control would be pervasive throughout; that the order and quietude of everyday life would be violently disrupted by the chaos of the needy dead; that the herculean effort to forget would be threatened by memory desperate to stay alive. To render enslavement as a personal experience, language must get out of the way."[9] Although Sethe has escaped slavery herself, she carries the weight of her ancestors on her shoulders and in her mind along with her own personal trauma that is still very much alive. As Morrison invites readers to participate in Sethe's trauma, to feel somewhat haunted ourselves, she is feeding our imaginations the words, pictures, and emotions that we need to feel connected with the very humanity of those who have been lost to the historical record. Reading *Beloved* is an embodied experience, more visceral than describable.

The mental and physical abuse that Sethe has endured is repeatedly replayed in both her mind and body, and Morrison emphasizes that this trauma belongs not just to Sethe but to the "sixty million and more" enslaved human beings whose thoughts and voices were never recorded.[10] The novel's form is disorienting, jagged, and non-linear. Although we start in the present day, the narrative quickly switches from present to past without any warning, and the distinctions between present-day reality and memories from the past are purposefully blurred, reemphasizing that the past and present are never clearly separated in the human consciousness. This is particularly true in the bruised mind of a trauma survivor like Sethe who continually experiences repetitions of buried memories that dictate the motions of her life just as much as her daily tasks do. Her body and unconscious mind have absorbed the sinister impact of the institution of slavery, and these visceral, disruptive recollections, what her mother-in-law calls "rememories," do not just exist in her mind but materialize outside of her.[11] In fact, Morrison emphasizes that these tangible "rememories" are a particular type of haunting that all ex-slaves experience, that Sethe sometimes "bumps into a rememory that belongs to someone else."[12] In continually conflating the past and the present, Morrison is asking readers to recognize that the trauma inflicted by the institution of slavery has never fully been exorcised. When *Beloved* was published in 1987, there had never been a memorial erected to the voiceless victims of the transatlantic slave trade, so Morrison created her own.[13] And in spending focused time participating in the memorialization of these passed souls, the reader also begins to get a profound sense of the unmeasurable, unspeakable impact of the dark past on the present-day descendants of the enslaved.

Readers become much more aware of the intergenerational impact of trauma when reading about Sethe's lonely daughter, Denver, choking under the weight of Sethe's rememories. Denver and Sethe are alone, isolated from the community, their only contact Sethe's dying mother-in-law, Baby Suggs. Denver is a victim of secondary trauma; although she cannot remember the horrors of an enslaved life, she experienced them in her infancy and feels the impact upon every interaction with her mother. Her only playmate is the greedy ghost of her murdered newborn sister, Beloved. Although the small family is isolated, the house is never silent. The infant ghost is an angry ghost, "not evil but sad," and she throws fits to get attention, including hurling furniture and making noise.[14] When Denver eventually learns via local gossip that her own mother killed her sister, the same sister who is her ghost playmate, her fragile unconscious mind can no longer take the pain and fear. A classmate at Lady Jones's school, Nelson Lord, asks her, "Didn't your mother get locked away for murder? Wasn't you in there with her when she went?"[15] Denver goes home and asks her mother these questions, but in order to protect her heart and mind from receiving this hidden, nefarious truth, Denver "[goes] deaf rather than [hears] the answer."[16] Like a victim of shell shock, Denver's body unconsciously protects her fragile mind. She only regains her hearing once the ghost of her sister becomes manifest in her house; the first sound she perceives is the gleeful noise of a baby climbing up the stairs. But this cooing baby girl soon becomes angry, resentful, and jealous—and the sounds of destruction replace the sounds of joy. Denver is one of the most pained, sympathetic figures in the novel. She is a child who, more than anything, wants a safe family. Through Denver, Morrison illustrates the all-too-real impact of parental trauma on a child who does not even know how to narrate or understand her own pain. This empathetic portrait is so poignant and familiar that all readers can, on some level, relate to the natural fears and desires of childhood, thus recoiling in horror at their perversions.

Denver's world becomes more crowded and threatened upon the arrival of Paul D, another formerly enslaved man from Sethe's past. Denver does not want to share her mother or her ghostly sister, but Sethe's unspeakable pain is temporarily soothed because she and Paul D share a story, a past, that they both inhabit: "Her story was bearable because it was his as well—to tell, to refine and tell again."[17] Like *What Is the What, Beloved* emphasizes the rehumanizing aspects of retelling a story in order to share experience and emotional space. We see the transformative power of empathy and the sharing of stories when Sethe and Paul D occupy the same physical and emotional space. But there is also a tension in this for Sethe in her need to speak the unheard, aching story into being—to process and make sense of it. At the same time, the telling of these stories is also unbearable, paralyzing. "Saying more might push them both to a place they can't get back from," Morrison writes, deciphering the unspoken fears between the side-by-side stories of Paul D and Sethe.[18] Their shared stories are both liberating and suffocating. Morrison's text reflects this paradoxical complexity as readers have moments of clarity alongside moments of confusion when reading. Important details are omitted, fact blurs into fantasy, and settings abruptly change. As much as we are invited in, we are also pushed out. We have to fight to try to find the plot and come to know the characters. And all of this is intentional, as it replicates the experience of trying to understand the lived traumatic experience of another, someone who both wants to be known but is terrified by the implications of it.

The central pieces that both the reader and the novel's protagonists must attempt to connect into a whole are the shards of a decentered, dehumanized self. Morrison places the impact of racist dehumanization and objectification on the forefront so that the novel's readers must dwell within the dysfunction, negotiating an ever-splitting self. Although they have technically escaped their oppressors, Paul D and Sethe are unable to live into their freedom. After being identified as property, losing any identity or sense of self, they struggle with what the concept of self even means. When Paul D arrives, Sethe is reminded of the way that her enslavement defined and owned her, and she wonders what she even has left to give. She finds herself "crying because she has no self."[19] Denver inherits this aspect of intergenerational trauma, never seeing herself as a "self." When her mother becomes sick and needy, Denver recognizes that she must take care of herself in order to help carry and heal her mother, but the concept is strange and puzzling: "It was a new thought, having a self to look out for and preserve."[20] In one of the novel's most bright, powerful scenes, we see a flashback of Sethe's mother-in-law, "an unchurched preacher," Baby Suggs Holy, preaching in a clearing in a sun-drenched forest. A large group of former slaves dances around her as she challenges them to love their bodies, their minds, their hearts. She tells them that "they do not love your neck unnoosed and straight. So love your neck; put a hand on it, grace it, stroke it and hold it up."[21] And most importantly, she says, "love your heart. For this is the prize."[22] Although a powerful leader and preacher, Baby Suggs eventually surrenders to the "wild things" that the white folks planted inside of her. She "dismissed her great heart and lay in the keeping room floor," where her only interest was in looking at various colors, and then dies.[23] Sethe's grief is profound over her loss, and she knows the ultimate cause of this loss of self, heart, and life: "Those white things have taken all I had or dreamed . . . and broke my heartstrings too. There is no bad luck in the world but whitefolks."[24] In her use of language, she attempts to reclaim a sense of self by dehumanizing her white abusers, seeing them as Baby Suggs does, merely as "white things," mechanical monsters that feed off her loss.[25] She decides that she must "protect self and love small," especially after the "thick" love for her baby led to its murder.[26]

Understandably, Sethe's main impulse is to hold back, to protect her body, her heart, her vulnerability. But once the daughter she killed returns to her, she opens up out of love, need, and guilt. Although in a woman's body, Beloved's incomplete sentence formation, obsession with her mother's attention, and greediness remind us that she is a baby. A trauma victim herself, her moans and childish utterances transcend language. Once again, Morrison plays with our expectations as she subverts traditional narrative form. Beloved's speech is perplexing, odd, and disorienting. Morrison writes that Beloved "lapped up her mother's devotion like cream."[27] The initial joyful harmony that Denver has with her mother and sister eventually becomes a deeper sense of misery and isolation. Denver is locked out of their games, their conversations, their love. Sethe's sense of guilt and deep need to be forgiven for the murder leads to her consumption by Beloved. Beloved takes everything dear to her mother, including Paul D. She seduces him and becomes pregnant, and "the bigger Beloved got, the smaller Sethe became."[28] This dysfunctional family model has its roots in the perverse damage of white supremacy: the separation of families, the attempts to extinguish the other's sense of self, the deep wound of loss and grief that seems it can never be healed. Sethe knows that, at any point, "anybody white could take your whole self for anything that came to mind."[29] Along with their power to "work, kill, or maim you," they could also "dirty you. Dirty you so bad you couldn't like yourself anymore."[30] Sethe's fierce protection of her daughter—her instinctual need to shield her from dehumanization, abuse, and rape—led her to murder. The evils of her enslavement led her to behave, on some level, like the animal they—"whitefolks"—always claimed her to be.[31] And as she desperately tries to rehumanize herself by "loving" her newly returned daughter, she loses more and more of herself, so much so that Denver has difficulty telling her mother and sister apart; they have seemingly merged into one.

In the second half of the novel, Morrison takes the reader deeper into Sethe's existential chaos, creating narrative disruptions and a confusion of identities. This harrowing section is, to some extent, the core of the novel that truly allows the reader to experience not just Sethe's pain but the pain of her ancestors and her children. Morrison attempts to capture the cry of the oppressed that goes beyond language, what theologian Cornel West calls "a guttural cry and a wrenching moan."[32] It's a cry "not so much for help as for home, a moan less out of complaint than for recognition."[33] This description of the inherited "moan" is reminiscent of Jemar Tisby's claim that the cry "'Black Lives Matter' is an assertion that the image of God [is] present in Black people."[34] Both body and voice express a deep, unrelenting lament at this lost recognition: "The deep black meaning of this cry and moan goes back to the indescribable cries of Africans on the slave ships during the cruel transatlantic voyages to America and the indecipherable moans of enslaved Afro-Americans on Wednesday nights or Sunday mornings near god-forsaken creeks or on wooden benches at prayer meetings in makeshift black churches. The fragile existential arsenal—rooted in silent tears and weary lament—supports black endurance against madness and suicide."[35] Morrison's use of literary abstraction forces readers to pause, contemplate, and look closely into the heart of this very human "moan."[36] And as we do that, attempting to string together the fragments of lost identity, we can just visualize the human form of some of the forgotten victims of the Middle Passage and the institution of slavery.

In four experimental sections, readers become lost within the mind of Sethe, the mind of Denver, and the mind of Beloved—the final of which embodies the collective mind of those on the Middle Passage and the merging minds of Sethe and her two daughters. In the first portion, Sethe tells herself, "BELOVED, she my daughter, she mine."[37] And the interloping reader is ushered into spaces of affliction and grief that Sethe has not even yet realized herself. As we continue reading, we see the complexity of this broken women's soul, her image-bearing self. Although she is illiterate and degraded by those around her, she is still marvelously and wonderfully made. Morrison also shows us Denver's bruised internal world: "BELOVED is my sister."[38] She taps into her deepest fears of her mother, a murderer. "She cut my head off every night," Denver says of her nightmare fears.[39] She acknowledges to herself that "I spent all my outside loving Ma'am so she wouldn't kill me," and she waits for her "angel man," her father, to come rescue her.[40] The root of all the inherited trauma is in the next section, where we hear the voices of the Middle Passage, collectively embodied in the manifest ghost of Beloved, crying out. This is the space where "language must get out of the way," so Morrison takes out many of the sense-making aspects of language: punctuation, finely measured spaces between words, rational descriptions:[41]

I AM BELOVED   and she is mine . . . her face is my own and I
    want to be there in the place where her face is and to be looking
    at it too a hot thing
I would bite the circle around her neck bite it away
I am going to be in pieces say me my name[42]

The words are jumbled, piled up, and incomplete, like the bodies stacked on a slave ship. We read of the "men without skin" who are branding these human beings, who have put metal collars around their necks.[43] The acute pain shatters the conventions of language. More than anything, the nameless, childlike voice wants to be acknowledged, to have an identity, to "say me my name."[44]

The final piece of this disordered portion of the novel restores at least some sense of order via a dialogue poem between Beloved, Sethe, Denver, and other nameless voices talking about being taken by the "men without skin." The frenzied diction of the previous section resolves itself in the smoothness of a poem disclosing profound human longing:

Beloved
You are my sister
You are my daughter
You are my face; you are me
I have found you again; you have come back to me
You are my Beloved
You are mine.[45]

The wording of this section is reminiscent of the novel's opening epigraph from Romans 9:25: "I will call them 'my people' who are not my people; and I will call her 'my loved one' who is not my loved one." This verse, a New Testament repetition of Hosea 2:23, refers to the transformation of those who have been despised, enslaved, and "soiled" due to being chosen and loved by God. In the midst of such affliction and wretchedness, there is beauty and worth. Morrison reminds us to see these forgotten souls, as well as their ancestors, as the Beloved, those who are loved, wanted, and infinitely beautiful and valuable. And as we trace the lines of her disjointed renderings, we learn how to better see these souls through the eyes of love.

Only through the act of radically loving those whose voices have often been silenced, what Cornel West calls the "politics of conversion," can one dispel the tendency toward what West defines as "nihilism" in certain segments of the Black community.[46] The pervading sense of hopelessness "is not overcome by arguments or analyses; it is tamed by love and care. Any disease of the soul must be conquered by the turning of one's soul. This turning is done through one's own affirmation of one's worth—an affirmation fueled by the concern of others. A love ethic must be at the center of a polities of conversion."[47] West recalls a scene from the end of *Beloved* as an example of this "conversion" back to identity and reconciliation.[48] When Sethe has once against lost everything and claims that she cannot hold the parts of herself together, Paul D explains that "she gather me, man. The pieces I am, she gather them and give them back to me in all the right order."[49] Once the scattered "pieces" of these characters have been collected and reassembled, they each have a story. Morrison then tells us, "He wants to put his story next to hers."[50]

The readers of *Beloved* must be haunted by the collective voices of the Middle Passage, whose stories can only be expressed in chaotic poetry—the facts of their trauma long forgotten, beaten back as a defense, or ignored. In "Human Personality," philosopher Simone Weil explains that "in those who have suffered too many blows . . . that place in the heart from which the infliction of evil evokes a cry of surprise may seem to be dead."[51] "But," she remarks, "it is never dead. It is simply unable to cry out anymore."[52] As we journey into the collective psyches of the novel's characters, we see the life there, we hear the voices. "Even in those who have the power to cry out," Weil continues, "the cry hardly ever expresses itself, either inwardly or outwardly, in coherent language."[53] Morrison asks a lot of her readers. We must participate in the reintegration of the subject as the past disrupts the present, and we, like the shocked and disoriented woman at the center of the novel, must encounter truth only via haunting. Only the nonlinear fictionalized rendering of this story can compel the reader to embody trauma in this way, preventing us from distancing ourselves from the subject, thus objectifying her.

THREE COLORS: BLUE

Just as novelist Toni Morrison asks for the focused, unflinching attention of her readers as they wrestle with nonlinear word sequences and jarring flashbacks in *Beloved*, Polish filmmaker Krzysztof Kieślowski almost demands our contemplation and devotion as we navigate the sad yet sublime river of grief-related images in his masterpiece, *Three Colors: Blue*. The protagonist of the film that Kieślowski scholar Joe Kickasola calls "a requiem composed in images" is an affluent, successful, attractive, white French woman, clearly not a victim of oppression.[54] The film, however, focuses on the common human denominator of grief and suffering, something that levels the playing field for all human beings, revealing a shared need for compassion and empathy. *Blue* is the intimate study of a singular character, Julie, as she floats on a pool of grief, afraid to take a deep dive. The film's use of lush visual abstraction, silence, and evocative choral music transcends the limiting power of language in order to enable viewers to feel as Julie feels in the wake of unthinkable tragedy.

Blue's atypical opening scene contains no music or dialogue, only images and raw sounds. Viewers first see a black screen and hear an increasingly loud, mechanical soaring sound. Perhaps a plane taking off? The wind whistles intensely, a mournful moan. As the black screen finally turns blue, we realize that we are viewing the back underside of a steadily rolling car tire. The very commonplace has become abstract, disorienting, rich with mystery. As the car goes into a tunnel, the screen turns black again. Horns honk and the tire is rolling very fast; cars and motorcycles fly by, and the anxiety builds as we wonder where we are and why we are here. Finally, a sign of life appears as a small child's hand reaches out of the window; she holds a blue-tinted metallic candy wrapper that flaps in the now fierce wind. It flies away, and the camera quickly refocuses on the face of the child, framed not in blue but in the red tint of headlights as she leans up against the car's back window. The camera is now above and in front of multiple cars, roaring at high speed through a dark tunnel. Nothing is stable, and the sense of indefinable anxiety is palpable. The car stops on the roadside, awash in the blue light of dusk, and the child happily jumps out of the car to run behind the tree for a bathroom break. Her father stands, stretching his arms, and the camera quickly takes us underneath the car to see brake fluid drip, drip, dripping from a damaged brake line. This is not good.

Behind the focused image of the dripping fluid, we see an unfocused image of the child running back to the car and finally hear a human voice, that of the child's mother: "Get back in."[55] The car door slams, and the family moves on, their car merging into traffic. The camera now, jarringly, focuses on a young man sitting alone playing a game, catching a wooden ball on a stick over and over and over, echoing the dripping of the brake fluid. The monotonous repetition of the dripping brake fluid and the bobbing ball are ominous and relentless. In the midst of a very heavy fog that prevents us from seeing distinguishable images, we hear a car honking. The young man, who we later know as Antoine, lifts his head to see the front lights of an approaching car. He looks down, finally succeeding at winning his game. As he smiles, we hear a loud crash, and Antoine looks up to see that the family's car has violently crashed into a tree. The child's inflated ball falls out of the car door and onto the ground, a sad last reminder of stolen childhood. Smoke from the destroyed vehicle mixes with the dense fog, and Antoine picks up his skateboard to run to the scene of the horrific accident. We hear grass crunching under his feet, then the textured sounds of the pavement as he throws his board aside and runs even more quickly toward the crashed car. As the camera draws back, it lingers for a few thick seconds, and we can see that the car, tragically, has hit the one and only tree on the edge of a foggy field. The screen once again turns black.

This description of the first four minutes of *Blue* illustrates the ways that Kieślowski can use images and sounds (and later, music) to evoke such a strong sense of both mystery and dread. By giving the viewer just a few nonverbal cues, the film coaxes us to engage on a deeper level as we must watch very *intentionally* in order to find the clues. Significantly, these clues do not necessarily work on a rational level, but by tapping into our intuitive aesthetic sensibilities, they remind us of the ways that sound and image are so closely connected to emotion. We are immediately engrossed in the detailed mystery on the screen, so much so that we participate with an almost visceral connection. The viewers' intuitive connection with the film grows more intense as they witness different forms of self-inflicted violence that Julie uses to kill the pain still trying to manifest within her.

When we first encounter Julie postaccident, we only hear her rhythmic, belabored breathing as it causes a feather to float up and down. Its plodding monotony is reminiscent of the mysterious, repetitious rhythms of the opening scene. A close-up of the feather is in the foreground, while the background is out of focus. We finally realize that the feather is from Julie's pillow, but we still don't see her face, just a close-up of her eye. In a tragic, beautiful scene, the reflection of the doctor is in Julie's pupil as she is told for the first time about the loss of her husband and daughter. Kieślowski is reminding us that we are going to experience grief from the eyes of Julie's stricken soul, a soul that ultimately wants to destroy itself. When we finally see her face, it is bruised, scabbed, and dully reflective of unspeakable grief. Moments later, she leaves her hospital bed and slams her fist into a glass window so that she can enter the ward where the drugs are kept. She pours out a bottle of white pills and crams them into her mouth, their chalkiness leaving residue on her already pale face. Again, we can feel the glass shards cutting her skin and the chalky pills crammed in her mouth.

Julie initially tries to extinguish her grief by extinguishing herself, but her suicide attempt is unsuccessful. After this, she decides that she must freeze the grief that is raging within her and, to do this, divorce any attachments to relationships with places or people. Just as she burrows into her newly frozen self, secrets about her husband's life are revealed. Patrice, Julie's husband, was a famous composer in the midst of writing a symphony of dedication to the reunification of Europe. Through garish media sources screaming into her cloistered silence, Julie learns that her husband was having an affair. The grief of losing her husband and her daughter is also now the grief of Patrice's betrayal as well as Julie's public humiliation.

The film relies far more on images than dialogue and, in this sense, it asks for a different sort of participation from the viewer than most dialogue/plot-driven movies do. Julie has temporarily silenced the pain of her soul, so the film itself is often silent. Ironically, her life's work was alongside that of her husband, partnering and supporting him as he created sound. There are even rumors that she, not her husband, is the genius behind his musical compositions. Although there is much silence in the film, there is also much music. Music and images, more than words, are the language of Julie's grief. And the more abstract the images are, the more the viewer must work intentionally to translate them into a story. This willful participation on the viewer's part creates an intimacy between character and film reader, enabling a sort of pregnant contemplation that births true empathy.

Three Colors: Blue is the first in Kieślowski's trilogy based on the colors of the French flag: *Blue, Red,* and *White*. Each film corresponds to the analogous concept of liberty, fraternity, and equality. Julie's story is, therefore, under the banner of freedom, which initially seems very odd. But in the film, Kieślowski questions and even redefines what freedom might look like in the context of grief. After the death of her family, Julie wants to be free of life, and when this does not work, she resolves to be free of any life-giving relationships because they will only ever end in death and grief. According to this logic, freedom from relationships means freedom from pain, the only seemingly safe way to survive. To outside observers, Julie seems cold and uncaring, but this is a means of self-preservation. The sharp contrast between Julie's internal and public worlds is significant, reminding us that there is a teeming world within every human being that defines their problematic behavior. Julie's seeming aloofness and desire for distance is a response to pain, not a sign of hatred or inhumanity. The color blue reflects her deep sadness, her frozen inner self that prevents any true healing within. It also represents the eventual, much healthier understanding of freedom that begins to liberate her.

As much as the film is full of ethereal, abstract images, it is also grounded in the reality of embodiment in a physical world. In one memorable scene, Julie briskly walks alongside a brick wall, purposefully dragging and scraping her knuckles on it. It is painful to watch, and when she sucks her skinned knuckles, we feel her pain, both physical and emotional. Although at one point Julie says, "I want no possessions, no money, no friends, no lovers. They are all traps," she eventually sleeps with her husband's assistant, Olivier, after his constant pursuit of her.[56] But this is also an act of desperation and violence rather than love. She believes that if she has meaningless, casual sex with a man whom she admires and then does not develop any attachment, then her internal world is dead. And she invites this death. As viewers witness and feel Julie's self-destructive behavior, we both are repelled by her and have compassion for her. This step of empathy is not earned, as Julie is not a traditionally admirable or needy character, but we identify with the very human impulse to want to be free from pain and the paradoxical desire to inflict it on oneself in order to overpower the deeper, lingering presence of grief.

Kieślowski's pervasive use of vivid blue represents both freedom and despair, echoing the very paradoxical heart of the human condition. It signifies a desire for independence and recognition that love is the absence of a certain type of freedom, including the freedom from relational pain and loss. When Julie finally returns to the elaborate home of her past family life, she walks briskly through until she arrives in a room painted blue—her daughter's room. It houses a blue crystal chandelier; she is stilled for a moment, staring vacantly at the fixture, and the blue refractions of light dance upon her face. The grief, symbolized by these reflections, is upon her and all around her, but she refuses to fully internalize it. She finds one of her daughter's lollipops; it has a blue, metallic wrapper just like the one held outside of the car window before the crash. She strips off its wrapper and immediately chews it up, not savoring, but devouring. The taste of the candy is sweet and intense, and like any other pleasure, she wants to rid herself of it as quickly as possible. She takes the chandelier with her and leaves the home, deciding immediately that she must sell it and never set foot there again. When she is leaving, she finds her maid hiding in a corner, weeping, and asks, "Why are you crying?" The grief-stricken maid replies, "Because you are not."[57]

The acts of denial and self-destruction continue as Julie leaves any familiarity behind and moves into an anonymous apartment building in Paris. In another desperate act of destruction, she destroys the sheet music for the symphony that her husband was writing. Her attempt to remove the music from her life is not successful, however, as it is the soundtrack of her internal world, a product of her creative partnership with her husband. The music represents the spiritual, imaginative life within her, and she is unable to easily stifle it. In unpredictable moments, the music often revisits her in waves, attempting to undo her emotional paralysis. As she hears the music, so do the film's viewers, following the ebb and flow of Julie's inner seascape. We also see an internal wincing manifest upon her face, and as we focus on this, her pain is laid bare. Another way that Julie frequently attempts to escape the presence of pain is by swimming in a blue-tinted pool in a local gym. As she dives under, she is in an altered reality while feeling the weighty, powerful physical presence of water washing over her, momentarily overpowering the even more acute waves of her loss.

On one occasion, however, she completes her laps and, shortly after, a group of small children wearing water wings runs and jumps in the pool. The symphony music swells, the blue light spills upon her face, and she fights back tears, jumping up out of the pool, desperate to leave. This triggering maternal image is followed by yet another as she later finds that a mouse has given birth in the closet of her new bedroom. She asks to borrow her neighbor's cat to eat the mice, but she confesses that she feels unable to deal with the cleanup herself. Her kind neighbor, Lucille, an exotic dancer ostracized by other residents of the apartment building, offers to do this for her. Julie's small request for help is a turning point in her story. Although Julie fears and resists her maternal longings, she leans into them when she responds to Lucille's late-night call for comfort and companionship when the young sex worker spots her father in the audience of her own strip club. Julie's most shocking act of maternal care is a response to her deceased husband, Patrice's, mistress, whom she discovers is pregnant with his child. In an act of extravagant empathy, she decides to leave her luxurious home to Patrice's lover and their child.

The concluding moments of the film are a dramatic, image-based meditation on the very love that Julie fears, a love that connects all human beings in both interdependence and empathy. Through a distorted yet stunningly beautiful camera eye, we see a montage of faces all retaining their colorful humanity under the influence of a blue tint. The connecting thread between these images is that each face belongs to someone who has been touched by Julie's surprising capacity for love during her period of internal paralysis. We see the forlorn Lucille, a sex worker who has been rejected by most but for whom Julie becomes a surrogate parent. We see Julie's mother, lost to dementia, but still a home to her faithful daughter. And most importantly, we see the ultrasound image of her husband's preborn illegitimate child as well as a close-up of the face of the mistress whose betrayal leads Julie not to hate but to love. All these images are accompanied by the glorious sounds of the finished symphony that was not fully destroyed even after Julie's attempts to do so. Only then do we realize that the composition's libretto, sung in Greek, contains passages from 1 Corinthians 13, the great biblical chapter on sacrificial love. All is awash in blue, the color of freedom that comes from both sacrifice and empathy, two bonds that forge human relationships. The final shot is a close-up of Julie's blue-tinted face, a lone tear streaming down her cheek. She now has the freedom to feel, to cry, to remember her own humanity. And after being ushered into her inner world through the use of visual abstraction, sound, and silence, so do we.

THE MYSTERIOUS INCIDENT OF THE DOG IN THE NIGHT-TIME

Although Julie intentionally denies her own humanity, Christopher John Francis Boone is a young man whose full humanity is often denied by others. In telling Christopher's story, novelist Mark Haddon cleverly uses a postmodern narrative technique to enable readers to see life from the perspective of a neurodivergent teenager. *The Mysterious Incident of the Dog in the Night-Time* is part detective story, part family drama, part coming-of-age tale. It is a novel about the writing of a novel, and we not only read words written by Christopher but learn about his process of thinking and writing. Unlike *Beloved* and *Blue*, Haddon's novel emphasizes the importance of language and order—ironically, to the point of near abstraction. This is because he is giving the reader access to the world through Christopher's lens, a lens that privileges logic over emotion and more traditional forms of interpersonal communication. In doing this, the novel provides us with the opportunity to grow our capacity for empathy for someone whose brain functions in a manner that seems foreign to many of us. As we learn of the logic behind Christopher's fixations, we see more of his connectedness rather than his difference. And we also see the eccentric beauty of his orderly, safe way of perceiving the world.

The novel opens with Christopher's discovery that Wellington, the small dog belonging to his neighbor, has been impaled on a gardening fork. Christopher likes dogs, and he is determined to solve the mystery of the dog's death. In the process, he plans to document his findings and turn them into a detective story. The entire novel is Christopher's written account of his "detecting."[58] In this sense, it has similarities with the postmodern narrative genre called metafiction, what Patricia Waugh defines as "fictional writing which self-consciously and systematically draws attention to its status as an artefact in order to pose questions about the relationship of fiction to reality."[59] Metafiction subverts our customary suspension of disbelief and constantly reminds us that fiction is a construct, that the author is the one behind the scenes pulling the strings. Most works of metafiction surprise the reader with an intrusion from the author themselves popping their head into the narrative, disrupting the process of reading with a reminder that the work is fiction. With *Curious*, Haddon himself is silent in the background, but the process of writing fiction, done by a fictional character, is a constant reminder of the novel's break from reality. This continually reinforces Christopher's own agency, positioning him not as a victim but as the very purposeful creator of his own story.

Christopher only likes to write true stories and is strongly opposed to any kind of lying. In fact, he does not know how to lie and only ever tells the truth. For this reason, he hates "proper novels."[60] He does not understand why one would write a book "about lies about things which did not happen," and this confusion makes him "feel shaky and scared."[61] Again, he finds comfort in structure, logic, literal descriptions, and directions. The creative world of the novel is a foreign and frightening place for Christopher, so he frequently seeks advice from his teacher friend, Siobhan. She tells him that he must describe things, but not everything, as he writes his own novel. She has also taught him how to read faces in order to identify human emotions and react appropriately. As Christopher seeks to learn how to do things that are considered normal and human, Haddon highlights his own atypical, beautiful humanity.

Siobhan is Christopher's guide not just for writing the novel but also for navigating a world that does not understand him just as much as he does not understand it. She provides him with security and helps him create structure out of chaos. Her words accompany him as he writes the story and, more importantly, as he writes his life. As a teenager who is quite self-aware, he now understands that he struggles with what we would call empathy. At one point, he tells a story from his early childhood when a teacher shakes a Smarties candy tube and asks him what is inside. Christopher guesses "Smarties" and then sees the teacher dump the contents of the tube onto a desk: a red stapler.[62] She then asks Christopher what his "mummy" would guess is inside the tube if she saw it, and he quickly responds, "A red stapler."[63] This recollection is Haddon's ingenious way of showing us Christopher's inability to read the thoughts and feelings of another human being or even understand that they have a different perception of reality. He explains that "when I was little, I did not understand about other people having minds," but he does not find this difficult anymore because he now thinks of trying to understand other people as a "puzzle," and "if something is a puzzle there is always a way of solving it."[64] The entire world of Christopher's experience, the act of navigating a society made for neurotypicals, is a continual, exhausting puzzle for him. Haddon's portrayal of this exhaustion is deeply moving, largely because Christopher does not fully understand it himself. The world is alive with chaotic images, sounds, and body language that he must put in order in order to attempt to read properly. As he tries to read the world, we learn more about how to read him through the eyes of empathy that ascribe not pity but dignity and joy to his unique experience of reality.

Haddon does not ever reveal what Christopher's particular diagnosis is—although the original book jacket description mentions that the book is about a young man with Asperger's, a description that Haddon later said he regretted approving. On this point, the novel is controversial, with members of the autism/Asperger's communities divided in their praise and condemnation of the portrayal of the young man at the center of it. Haddon claims that he did little research into autism, yet many sources claim that he previously worked with autistic children. This all raises an ethical question about representation as critics ask whether this is Haddon's story to tell or whether the novel is an exploitative gimmick. On his website, Haddon resists labeling the character of Christopher with any particular diagnosis. Instead, he claims to have written the novel to encourage readers to resist labels:

> If anything, it's a novel about difference, about being an outsider, about seeing the world in a surprising and revealing way. It's as much a novel about us as it is about Christopher.
>
> Labels say nothing about a person. They say only how the rest of us categorise that person. Good literature is always about peeling labels off. And treating real people with dignity is always about peeling labels off. A diagnosis may lead to practical help. But genuinely understanding another human being involves talking and listening to them and finding out what makes them an individual, not what makes them part of a group.[65]

Haddon's discussion of the capacity and function of "good literature" for disclosing the truth that lies underneath human labels is one of the prime reasons that the arts can help us become empathetic.[66] Haddon treats Christopher with dignity, even as he details both his day-to-day thinking process and his reaction to extreme trauma. And the novel's form, the orderly edifice of Christopher's inner world, enables us to see the world through his eyes, peeling off the labels and replacing them with shared experience.

By enabling the reader to interpret reality via Christopher's perspective, Haddon subverts the dichotomy of normal/abnormal and challenges us to do the same as we consider the full humanity of his protagonist. In *Discipline and Punish*, philosopher Michel Foucault argues that in contemporary Western society, we are constantly being surveilled, not just by cameras but by those who have been given the authority to determine what is and is not considered normal. "The judges of normality are present everywhere," writes Foucault. "We are in the society of the teacher-judge, the doctor-judge, the educator-judge, the social worker-judge."[67] When considering disabilities, it is easy to slip into both thinking and rhetoric that see a mind like Christopher's as abnormal. Foucault would say that the "doctor-judge" and "psychiatrist-judge" have conditioned us to think this way rather than realizing that Christopher's perspective is not abnormal but simply "different."[68] By providing readers with the tools to feel and see the world like Christopher, projecting order on a disorderly world, we can relate to his desires and see the very normality of them.

In *Disabilities Studies Quarterly*, Sarah Ray claims that Haddon's novel successfully collapses the unhealthy binaries that Foucault himself critiques: "The most important way that the novel achieves its message that disability is a social construction is through point of view and using form to critique the dominant novel form: the novel is written from Christopher's perspective, rather than being *about* Christopher."[69] By presenting disability as a social construction, a category that is not inherently abnormal but has been created for the sake of labeling and determining a norm, she argues that Haddon humanizes Christopher. Unlike the feel-good viral videos championing a "normal" person for taking a disabled student to the prom, Haddon's novel allows us to see the world through Christopher's categories, centering his story and allowing it to be told the way he wants to tell it.

The novel's metafictional narrative technique is significant, as it reminds us that our interpretations of the world, those that we often assume are facts, are, in fact, always partially fiction. We see reality through Christopher's eyes in a dramatic, revealing way. At one point, he explains that he does not like to travel to new places (especially France!) because "I see everything."[70] He first lists what a neurotypical person sees when looking at a field in the countryside:

1. I am standing in a field that is full of grass.
2. There are some cows in the field.
3. It is sunny with a few clouds.
4. There are some flowers in the grass.
5. There is a village in the distance.
6. There is a fence at the edge of the field and it has a gate in it.[71]

Christopher explains that this list of "typical" observations proves that "the information in their head is really simple."[72] He knows this to be true because this is a list he received from Siobhan. He writes that this lack of detail, this skimming of the surface, what he has been told is called "glancing," reflects laziness on the part of the viewer.[73] Christopher's list is, of course, much more detailed, nuanced, and long. In fact, his list contains thirty-eight items and detailed descriptions of each. Although Siobhan tells him that he does not need to write them all in his book, he does note a few:

1. There are 19 cows in the field, 15 of which are black and white and 4 of which are brown and white.
2. There is a village in the distance which has 31 visible houses and a church with a square tower and not a spire.
3. There are ridges in the field, which means that in medieval times it was what is called a *ridge and furrow* field and people who lived in the village would have a ridge each to do farming on.
4. There is an old plastic bag from Asda in the hedge, and a squashed Coca-Cola can with a snail on it, and a long piece of orange string.[74]

In seeing these lists on the page, readers can now understand how amazing and overwhelming it must be to live inside Christopher's head. His power of observation and photographic memory capacity are both astonishing—but they are also deeply tiring. Christopher dreads traveling to new places because the amount of sensory information is overwhelming. He explains this brilliantly by comparing his brain to a computer that is "doing too many things at the same time," which causes the blocking of the "central processing unit," taking up all the space left, preventing him from thinking "about other things."[75] Christopher relates his experience of being in a new place, seeing and meeting new people, and perceiving new sensory data as a system overload that can only be remedied by pressing CTRL + ALT + DELETE. For Christopher, this looks like crouching down, putting his hands over his ears, and groaning.[76] In doing this, he is attempting to make his internal world once again safe and calm. It works even better if he can find a snug place to hide, shielding himself from the barrage of new sensory data. More than anything, Christopher wants safety.

Christopher also hides when he experiences trauma that leads to fear and a feeling of being unsafe. The novel begins with a minor trauma, the death of the neighbor's dog. Although Christopher liked the dog, he is not truly traumatized but propelled to solve the puzzle of the dog's death. But at the novel's halfway point, Christopher finds out that the dog's killer is his own father. Around the same time, he discovers letters from his estranged mother that have been hidden away in a wardrobe by his father. Christopher had been told that his mother died of a heart attack. When he reads the letters from his mother and his father finally tells him the truth about the dog, the novel's superficial mystery is solved. But Christopher keeps writing, and we realize that the main puzzle to be solved, the central mystery, is how Christopher can survive and thrive when his central life guides, his parents, are not trustworthy. Haddon's humanization of someone who is so often mislabeled or ignored becomes even richer as we learn that Christopher is not as emotionless as many would assume—but that his deep well of emotion is yet something else that is too overwhelming for him to communicate in more traditional ways. Again, we see how his character is profoundly human and profoundly deserving of informed empathy rather than misinformed stereotypes.

Christopher is further traumatized when he reads the letters from his mother, now living in London, and discovers his father's lies. We initially see little emotional response as he tries to rationalize things, wondering if the letters were from another mother to another Christopher. The puzzle pieces don't fit, can't fit. But the more letters he reads, full of details about their past life together, the more he must process the truth. He does not write of any emotional pain, but he is unable to think because "my brain wasn't working properly."[77] He eventually gets in bed and vomits on himself, a somatic response to the deep trauma that he is unable to verbalize. When his father sees and understands what has happened, he confesses his sins and explains the backstory: Christopher's mother was having an affair with the owner of the dog, and after she left them, Christopher's father killed the dog out of spite. In hearing this, Christopher's main emotion is fear because he believes the same father he trusted for safety to actually be a liar and a murderer: "That meant he could murder me, because I couldn't trust him."[78] At this point, Christopher's impulse is to run and hide and, eventually, attempt to travel to London in order to find his mother. His entire world has collapsed, and he is not safe.

It is clear that Christopher's father was trying to protect him by not explaining to him that his mother had not died but left the family to run away with a neighbor. And as Christopher records the letters he reads, his mother comes into focus as more of a needy child than a comforting, nurturing parent. In one letter, she admits, "I was not a very good mother, Christopher."[79] But instead of apologizing, she shifts blame, making excuses: "Maybe if things had been different, maybe if you've been different, I might have been better at it."[80] In another letter, she describes, in detail, the reasons it was difficult for her to live with and care for Christopher, including a lengthy retelling of an embarrassing (for her) shopping excursion when Christopher broke down, screaming, in a department store. She seems to have little capability to form a true, empathetic attachment with her son, to think of things via his very different and fragile perspective. The letters appear to be written more for her benefit than his, a means to assuage her guilt for leaving.

But Christopher only knows that he is now afraid of his father so he must leave. The nuances of the letters do not impact him the same way that they do the readers of the novel that he (and Haddon) is writing. This is just one example of the many times that the readers must fill in the gaps between what Christopher says and objective reality.

We follow Christopher's thought processes as he attempts to put ordered form onto spiraling trauma by memorizing the address on the letters and undergoing an odyssey that seems impossible, both to the reader and to Christopher. Yet Christopher has such a knack for the careful following of directions from signs, charts, and timetables that he manages to successfully navigate the train to London and then the London Underground. This is all quite terrifying and overwhelming to him. Haddon includes timetables, tube maps, and the math equations that Christopher says over and over in his head in order to calm himself while surrounded by such strange, extreme overstimulation. Once he arrives in London, he is so terrified in the tube station that he sits on a bench for five hours as, over and over, he watches a sea of people flow onto the platform and into the tube and disappear. He finally follows a map and finds his way to his mother's apartment. She is both delighted and alarmed to see him, but her lover, Roger, is not so happy. He is a clearly abusive man who threatens Christopher and constantly complains about his presence. In a very quick and perhaps unlikely character change, Christopher's mother gains enough confidence to take Roger's car and drive both her and her son to their real home in Skipton, with a plan to leave Roger and live there again. The rest of the story highlights the damage done by Christopher's mother and father and their many attempts to repair things with him, to make him feel safe and loved. He is still terrified of his father and refuses to live with him, so he and his mother live together in a room in a boarding house. He returns to school and his routine, and he excels on his A level math exam, even with all the emotional and mental disruptions.

Although we learn quite a lot about Christopher's psyche from the book he is still writing, we go even deeper when he describes a dream that he has. It is a sleeping dream, but when he remembers it upon waking, he is delighted by it; it is his ultimate fantasy. In the dream, a strange virus spreads among human beings. It is unusually contagious, and you can even catch it by watching another person in real life or on television. When someone gets the virus, they are unable to take care of themselves, to eat, to drink, and so on. So they eventually die, and the only people left in the world are the "special people" like Christopher, people who "don't look at other faces" and who don't know how to read emotions.[81] And these people do not congregate together because they are like "okapi in the jungle . . . a kind of antelope and very shy and rare."[82] Christopher's dream reminds us that his understanding of reality makes sense to him; it is based on an internal logic that forms a system of self-preservation and comfort. Christopher wants to be alone in his world because the world that he was born into will always treat him like a foreigner.

According to Christopher, the world outside of him is where the problem lies, and Haddon's novel actually supports this thesis as it points a finger back at readers, reminding us that we are the very ones making life difficult for someone like Christopher. The deserted world of Christopher's dream is the real normal: "And I can go anywhere in the world and I know that no one is going to talk to me or touch me or ask me a question."[83] His joys are simple and very contained in the small, safe world of his creation. He likes solving puzzles; he likes figuring things out that make literal, logical sense; and he likes routine. When he had a detective mystery to solve, he was happy with the new puzzle: "When I got home I said hello to Father and went upstairs and fed Toby, my rat, and felt happy because I was being a detective and finding things out."[84]

But after his independent trip to London, he gains greater confidence in navigating the outside world alone. He matures and comes of age when he sees that he can do "normal" things that "normal" people can do. And he can do them alone. He wants to go to university, get a degree, and become a scientist: "And I know I can do this because I went to London on my own, and because I solved the mystery of Who Killed Wellington? and I found my mother and I was brave and I wrote a book and that means I can do anything."[85] These things are all true. Along with Christopher, we know this now as well. And we learn that Christopher, and image bearers like him, are not "abnormal" or mistakes but human beings trying to make sense of reality along with the rest of us.

The multilayered, nontraditional structure of each of these works of art helps us make sense of the individual life experience of Sethe, Julie, and Christopher. The form serves the content, and both are equally important for the sake of deeper participation on the part of the reader and viewer. As we interpret reality through the individual grid of each character, we begin to think more like them and care more for them. The time we must spend trying to understand the motives, behaviors, and existential reality of these characters is forcefully elongated and slowed down. And this practice helps us see not just these characters but our real-life neighbors with the same amount of patience and curiosity that, hopefully, gives birth to deeper empathy.

Chapter Six

GROWING EMPATHY
FOR OUR ENEMIES

THE GREATEST ACT OF EMPATHY

Friedrich Nietzsche found the story of Christ's sacrifice on the cross both despicable and obscene.[1] He could not comprehend why this religious leader would willfully give up his life, betraying the survival impulse of human evolution. Nietzsche was a preacher's kid through and through—his father and grandfather were both Lutheran ministers—so he knew the textbook theological answers to these questions. At the same time, he found this level of self-denial to the point of physical death disgusting and, according to his terms, immoral. Nietzsche's idea of the good is to continually follow our impulses for self-preservation and the acquisition of power. The idea of the first being last is, according to him, utter performative nonsense. More than anything, Nietzsche was appalled by the transformative empathy both practiced and taught by Christ. Jesus's cry, "Father, forgive them; for they know not what they do," is a profound statement of empathy contained in the most powerful narrative known to humanity.[2] Christ chose to take on human flesh and become one of us to feel our pain, reside within our struggles, and save us.

This was the most fully embodied act of empathy ever to exist, and it has been passed onto Christ's followers in artful, narrative form in the Gospels, allowing us to witness it and dwell upon it. Christ taught that this profound act of empathetic love, the act of sacrificing ourselves even to love our enemies, is at the heart of the gospel message that we, his followers, are to emulate and practice in our daily lives. We are told that while we were his enemies, Christ died for us, thus enabling us to be transformed from enemies to friends. This is a truly supernatural calling, a contrast to the natural human responses of both revenge and self-preservation in an almost Darwinian sense. As we try in desperation to achieve this type of success, we must speed up, looking for the best way to advance. Yet the way of Christ is the way of inclusion via his sacrifice. And it is illustrated to us in the biblical narrative that asks us to slow down, contemplate, and learn to see and hear.

EMPATHY FOR ENEMIES: THE HEART OF THE GOSPEL

We struggle with loving our enemies, especially as we struggle to see them as God sees them, beloved by him and made in his image. We see Christ's anger and deep love together in Matthew 23, when he rebukes the religious leaders, calling them "hypocrites," "whitewashed tombs," and a "brood of vipers."[3] He does not mince his words. But the chapter ends like this: "Jerusalem, Jerusalem, you who kill the prophets and stone those sent to you, how often I have longed to gather your children together, as a hen gathers her chicks under her wings, and you were not willing. Look, your house is left to you desolate. For I tell you, you will not see me again until you say, 'Blessed is he who comes in the name of the Lord.'"[4] Both the rebuke and the tender picture of maternal care are acts of love, as Christ is speaking the truth boldly in order to allow a chance for repentance. As we know from Scripture (and maybe from life), the religious people who don't know their own spiritual sickness are often the ones who struggle the most to change. Matthew 23 is prominently featured in the appendix to *Narrative of the Life of Frederick Douglass*, where the formerly enslaved author quotes large portions of it when exposing the hypocrisy of religious slave owners who used decontextualized Scripture as a justification to brutalize, rape, and turn human beings into commodities. In doing this, he discerns a prophetic distinction between the "Christianity of this Land" and the "Christianity of Christ."[5] Douglass is deeply, righteously angry, but his anger—at least on paper—never devolves into hatred of his enemy. Even his rebukes are full of mercy. He realizes that power corrupts, and, at one point, he says that "the institution of slavery is just as damaging for the slaveholder as it is for the slave."[6] The spiritual damage of the oppressor's heart is something to be pitied. And the oppressor could be any one of us when we get a taste of power. Kevin Smith, a pastor of New City Fellowship, Chattanooga, claims that "God loves the oppressed *and* the oppressor." This is quite a hard pill to swallow. The love, strength, and forgiveness that we see in the history of the Black church—America's true persecuted church—is an example of love for our enemies that is truly humbling to witness.

Jesus called Matthew, a tax collector, a man who had aligned himself with the oppressors and was benefiting from their power while harming his own people. He was a traitor, but Jesus still saw his intrinsic value. Jonah was an arrogant, self-righteous racist, but the Lord called him. Saul was, to some degree, a religious terrorist, but Jesus appeared to him on the road to Damascus, an apocalyptic intervention that dramatically altered the course of his life. It is important to reflect on this lavish grace and these miraculous transformations in order to see and hear from a kingdom perspective.

Engaging stories through the lens of the most powerful narrative moment in history—the crucifixion of Christ—is a means to enlarging our ability to truly love our neighbors, even those whom we view as enemies. This is especially helpful when reading or watching stories of those whom we dislike, fear, or even despise. Dwelling within their stories helps us keep their fully image-bearing humanity in the forefront of our minds, reminding ourselves that Christ himself asked the Father to forgive them because "they know not what they do."[7] Perhaps some of the hardest figures to love and empathize with are those who use the name of Christ to fuel their love of money, esteem, or power. At the same time, the Lord has pity and love for these hypocrites. Douglas Coupland's prophetically perceptive novel *Hey Nostradamus!* primes us to hate Reg, a religious hypocrite, but then surprisingly shows us his capacity for change. In this, we are reminded that even a charlatan is loved by God, can be forgiven, and has worth and value. Craig Thompson's melancholy, beautiful graphic novel *Blankets* is the autobiographical story of a young man growing up under the teachings of a church culture that embodies hypocrisy, judgment, and unforgiveness. Because of this, Craig leaves the faith, making him an enemy in the eyes of some of the supposed faithful. But Thompson's story humanizes a young man so often labeled only as a backslider, a threat to those around him, and a stain on his former faith community. Paul Thomas Anderson's sprawling film *Magnolia* is a mélange of stories about the inheritance of parental abuse, and many of its characters initially appear inherently despicable. But Anderson traces the lineage of this abuse as well as shows miraculous moments of redemption that humanize the abused and, in some cases, their abusers. All of these narratives continually remind us that all human beings, regardless of their brand of sin, are created to be loved. While reading and watching through the vantage point of the cross, we are challenged to grow our imaginations for the sake of seeing the image of God in the other.

HEY NOSTRADAMUS!

In Matthew 23, Christ's righteous anger is palpable as he rebukes the religious leaders who tithe, follow the law, and look outwardly righteous but have "neglected the more important matters of the law—justice, mercy and faithfulness."[8] It is clear that religious hypocrisy, and the use of the name and law of the Lord for individual gain, leads to the most passionate examples of Christ's outrage. At the same time, we see the anger of Christ, as well as his passion for justice, tempered with mercy. Douglas Coupland's novel *Hey Nostradamus!* provides one of the most profound and powerful examples in literature of the humanization of a Christian hypocrite. Fascinatingly, Coupland himself is a self-described outsider to the Christian faith who illustrates grace and mercy when considering the wounded heart of a cruel, legalistic Christian named Reg. Reg is the abusive father of Jason, a heroic victim of a Columbine-like school shooting. Coupland's novel highlights the victims of this tragedy, both in the moment and, more importantly, in its aftermath. It is divided into four sections, each with a different narrator, yet Reg, not present during the shooting, gets the final word.

Reg's son, Jason, is secretly married to the novel's first narrator, Cheryl, a devout yet doubtful Christian teenager who is killed in the shooting. She is in the cafeteria when the gunmen come in, and she falls prey to their violence before Jason arrives on the scene. When Jason learns about the shooting, he rushes to the cafeteria to rescue her but is too late. He does, however, manage to kill the final living shooter, thus preventing many more deaths. In response to the police who are calling his son a hero, Reg says, "What I understand is that my son experienced murder in his heart and chose not to rise above that impulse. I understand that my son is a murderer."[9] Rather than focusing on the lives saved, Reg labels his son as a villain, a sinner, and a killer. This sets the tone for Coupland's gracious critique of North American evangelicalism through the eyes of empathy and under-standing rather than anger or hate. As much as Reg appears to be irredeemable, Coupland closes the novel with his unexpected redemp-tion, reminding his readers that there is always something within a person to love.

Before examining Coupland's treatment of Reg's character, it is important to look a bit more closely at the North American evangeli-cal subculture that is featured in the novel. Jason and Cheryl are both members of a youth group called "Youth Alive!" who are profoundly superficial in their faith, more like a Christian sorority than a disci-pleship group.[10] They form the "Out to Lunch Bunch," a clique of popular girls that leaves campus for lunch rather than eat alongside the hoi polloi in the school cafeteria.[11] The voice of Cheryl, speaking from the dead in the book's first chapter, describes the group's val-ues: "The Out to Lunch Bunch talked about going to heaven in the same breath as they discussed hair color. Leading a holy life inside a burgundy-colored VW Cabrio seems like a spiritual contradiction. Jason once joked that if you read Revelations closely, you could see where it says that Dee Carswell counting the calories in a packet of Italian dressing is a sign of imminent apocalypse."[12] The Out to Lunch Bunch counts calories and sins, and just as they form a purity pact, they also collectively decide to only eat two French fries each for lunch. In an interview with Tony Watkins, Coupland talks about the very hierarchical structure of the high school he attended in affluent West Vancouver. The Out to Lunch Bunch reflects his observation that "every high school has the good-looking girl gang" and that the lives of these cliques have a certain "tabloid" quality in the high school community.[13] He continues by mentioning that the members of the "good-looking girl gang" frequently "became evangelical."[14]

In two different interviews, Coupland shares one of his own high school interactions with evangelicals that seems to have left a deep imprint upon his life. He was one of the many Vancouver youths who was "raised without religion" in a house with parents who were decidedly secular.[15] Although not a Christian, teenage Coupland wanted to attend a Young Life barbecue after seeing posters up around school. Yet when he asked to join the group, he was told not to come—and on more than one occasion. It became clear to him that the members of the group had talked about him and made a collective decision to reject him. This early exposure to the evangelical subculture was wholly negative, as its members seemed to be self-righteous, judgmental, and exclusive to the point of cruelty. When explaining this to Watkins, Coupland ends by saying that perhaps his life would have been different if "they'd have, like, just invited me to a barbecue or something."[16] This story is significant because Coupland, a non-Christian, has written a book that critiques the evangelical system that rejected him but empathizes with the human beings who have used Scripture as a status symbol, a means to power, and a claim to exclusivity. In his interview, Watkins tells Coupland that the *Observer*'s review of *Hey Nostradamus!* claims that it was "an attack on religion," to which Coupland responds, "Oh, no, no. I don't think so at all. I would never do that. . . . It's a non-censorious critique."[17] Coupland's novel speaks the truth in love, and the author's empathy for his deeply flawed characters is even more powerful than its critique.

Although the characters of both Cheryl and Jason were members of a youth group modeled after this painful memory from Coupland's youth, they resist its exclusivity and cruelty. Jason wants to be nothing like his brutal, legalistic father, Reg, who cares only about the rules that prove his righteousness. Reg neglects the second of the two greatest commandments, making Christianity into a self-improvement ideology rather than a religion based on the importance of sacrificial relationships with God and others. Jason says that Reg will "always sell you out to his religion" and insightfully adds that "he's actually a pagan that way . . . he has to make sacrifices."[18] Reg sacrifices his own family upon the altar of his rule-based ideology.

Unlike Jason, Cheryl is from a family of nonbelievers, and she feigned faith in order to win Jason. With admirable and endearing candor, she admits, "I had, and continue to have, a nagging suspicion that I used the system simply to get what I wanted. Religion included. Does that cancel out whatever goodness I might have inside me?"[19] Unlike her friends, Cheryl eventually begins to take her faith to heart, practicing it in a deeply human way. She recognizes the pride and legalism of Reg and of her friends, and she sees the ways this calcifies into judgment and a lack of kindness: "There can be an archness, a meanness in the lives of the saved, an intolerance that can color their view of the weak and the lost. It can make them hard when they ought to be listening, judgmental when they ought to be contrite."[20] The "saved" that she is speaking of show a lack of empathy, a lack of understanding in the wretchedness and human frailty that they share with others. But Cheryl's faith is honest and transparent, so much so that she even feels safe to doubt. And at the moment Cheryl is shot and killed, she is scribbling these two phrases over and over again on her notebook: "GOD IS NOWHERE; GOD IS NOW HERE."[21] After her death, each camp—believers and nonbelievers alike—tries to appropriate the phrase as evidence that Cheryl belonged to them. But Coupland presents Cheryl's genuine questions through empathetic eyes, a contrast to those of her religious peers.

The beauty of Cheryl's character lies most in her honesty about her shortcomings and her capacity for the acceptance of grace: "I believe that what separates humanity from everything in this world—spaghetti, binder paper, deep-sea creatures, edelweiss and Mount McKinley—is that humanity alone has the capacity at any given moment to commit all possible sins. Even those of us who try to live a good and true life remain as far away from grace as the Hillside Strangler or any demon who ever tried to poison the village well. What happened that morning only confirms this."[22] Cheryl recognizes that, except for grace, she could be like her cocky friends, like hypocritical Reg, or even like the young killers. Her faith makes her soul crystal clear, whereas Reg's seems to blacken his. This capacity for grace is connected to a growing capacity for empathy. When seeing an enemy through the eyes of grace, Cheryl, and hopefully the novel's reader, comes to understand that "all have sinned and fall short of the glory of God."[23] True faith in the grace of God leads to the conclusion that no one can boast for their own goodness, and this provides a base upon which to build compassion and empathy for the other, even if the other is an enemy.

On all accounts, Reg is Cheryl and Jason's enemy. He is a cruel man who uses his religion as a weapon to empower himself through berating others. Reg's identity lies in what he hates: anyone or anything that pushes the lines strictly outlined by the book (not the Bible, but the book of Reg's righteousness). Cheryl remembers that "Reg often said, 'Love what God loves and hate what God hates' but believes that what he really meant was 'Love what Reg loves and hate what Reg hates.'"[24] Along with this, Reg lacks any curiosity and expresses contempt for any new ideas, labeling this rigidity "being traditional."[25] This lack of curiosity and presence of contempt is the fruit of an arrogant attempt for an airtight faith.

The contrast between the ways that Cheryl and Reg embrace the Christian faith creates a grace versus legalism dichotomy, an interesting lens through which to read the book. Coupland illustrates that the presence of legalism is a barrier to empathy, whereas the presence of grace is essential for empathy. This is especially effective when we are asked in the book's final chapters to have grace for its central villain, Reg, when his cruel legalism is challenged. When reading the inner monologues of both Cheryl and Jason, we get an accurate picture of Reg's harshness, his inability to have a relationship that is not damaged by his constant attempt to expose sin in the lives of others without seeing his own sin. But the book's third section enables us to see Reg through a new set of eyes, those of Heather, Jason's girlfriend during his restless adult years. Although Reg has never shown any vulnerability or a need for Jason in his life, the cracks in his self-drawn caricature begin to appear when his son suddenly disappears. The last words we read from Jason are a confession that although there is beauty in the world, he knows that there is "chilled black ink pumping through my veins," and he feels like "the unholiest thing on earth."[26] And Jason's self-hatred is largely because he believes that he has been made in the image of his sadistic, self-righteous father.

Once Jason disappears, his girlfriend Heather begins to visit Reg more frequently. She is deeply in love with Jason and will try anything to feel close to him, even befriend the cold-hearted father whom Jason has never really known. The longer Jason is gone, the more Reg's hard facade begins to crack. He begins asking questions about the very small life he created in the name of holiness. Although Heather originally sees Reg as a religious freak, he eventually stops trying to convert her because he becomes "far too preoccupied with the state of his own soul."[27] She notes that "his honesty about his doubts has made him genuinely spiritual," and this has led her to become "far more open to his ideas."[28] The more Reg learns about his son from Heather, the more he grieves the relationship he forfeited for the sake of his angry religion. And in this process, he becomes increasingly more human.

The novel's brief last section takes us directly into Reg's tormented inner world. Although he is grieving the loss—both physical and emotional—of his son, there is a surprising amount of redemptive hope in the book's final pages. Reg's process of rehumanizing is an unexpected transformation, not unlike that spoken of in the biblical epigraph that Coupland chose for the novel: "Behold, I tell you a mystery; we shall not sleep, but we shall all be changed, in a moment, in the twinkling of an eye, at the last trumpet; for the trumpet will sound, and the dead will be raised imperishable, and we shall be changed."[29] Reg's internal shift, his true conversion, is the novel's astounding and completely unexpected change. Only when he loses the very son he abused does he begin to regain his soul and offer it up and out. His weary soul finally relaxes after years and years of tension, pressure, and the need to keep things all together for the sake of his own salvation. He must lose before he can win, and he realizes this as he composes a letter to the son whom he has lost. He begins to gain eyes to see the wretched state of his own heart, especially as he considers the way he mistreated Jason. Because Jason was so smart and sensitive, Reg believed that he had been chosen for a mission, and only now can Reg admit that "he was jealous that God had given a mission not to him, but to his son."[30] And part of that mission was the act of violence that it took to save the lives of many children. But in his tight-fisted resentment and pride, Reg labeled his son's goodness as evil, and this left a mark that would stain Jason for the rest of his life. As readers walk through Reg's movements toward true conversion, it becomes easier to pity him, to see the fear and sadness underneath his impenetrable veneer of man-made holiness. He finally realizes his own need for empathy that has been present, yet unacknowledged, all along.

Reg recognizes that his intense loneliness and isolation were because of his own "pride" and "vanity."[31] Tragically, this isolation and loneliness were inherited by his son. As Reg confesses, he likens the words spilling onto the page to "bile and poison," a necessary step before any healing.[32] The mention of Reg's "bile and poison" is directly connected to Jason's belief that he has "black ink" pumping through his veins.[33] Although Jason rebelled in order to avoid it, he still swallowed the poison that was festering within his father. While writing his letter to Jason, Reg recognizes that "it wasn't until I felt emptied of lies and weaknesses that, as with recovering from a poisoning, I felt mended again."[34] While Jason's last memories of his father lead to him feeling like "the most unholiest thing on earth," Reg marvels over the stories that Heather tells him about Jason's creativity, whimsy, and curiosity—the very traits that Reg previously hated.[35] And when she tells him of the animal characters that the couple created in order to share secret stories together, Reg says, "They're almost holy."[36] For the first time, Reg allows himself to recognize the beauty of childlike wonder when seeing it in these memories of his son.

Once Reg gains a sense of empathy for his son, he also begins to see the glory in creation, becoming almost childlike in this newfound sense of wonder. In this sense, he is like Coleridge in "This Lime-Tree Bower My Prison" and Mr. O'Brien in *The Tree of Life*. In the Watkins interview, Coupland acknowledges that Reg is a "miserable bastard you hate, hate, hate . . . and yet he's the one who actually ends up being humanized."[37] He continues, explaining that "the moment he shatters a legalistic doctrinaire thinking and actually begin questioning things for himself, suddenly he became real."[38] When Reg becomes "real," this contemporary novel has a surprising ending reminiscent of the final apocalyptic moment of Flannery O'Connor's "A Good Man Is Hard to Find." Although much less likable, Reg shares the shallow faith, judgmentalism, and self-righteousness of O'Connor's manipulative grandmother who eventually causes her own family to get killed. Like many of O'Connor's protagonists, she wears the name of Christ like a fashion, and she is only truly converted when she faces the great tragedy that is the result of her own manipulative carelessness. She grieves the death of her son, and then she becomes more fully human when looking into the eyes of The Misfit, feeling his pain. Just as she finally feels empathy for another person, seeing him as one of her own children, she meets her end. When The Misfit says, "She would of been a good woman . . . if it had been somebody there to shoot her every minute of her life," he acknowledges that the goodness buried in her soul was only finally unearthed when she was faced with tragedy, reduced to her essence.[39] Both O'Connor's grandmother and Reg are ultimately redeemed as a result of a tragedy of their own making. And although they are the authors of great familial pain, we empathize with them as we see them finally break.

As the story ends, most readers want to weep for Reg. In the most paradoxical, Christian sense, he becomes full once he recognizes that he is empty and then empties himself even more. In the novel's final pages, we learn that Reg has been at Kinko's typing his letter to Jason. He then makes copies in order to tack them to the trees of the forest that he believes might have swallowed his lost son. He has faith, real faith, that his son is not lost and that Jason will find one of these letters, each containing the painful inscription of Reg's soul. The last words of the novel, a direct quote from Luke 15, are full of longing and hope: "Awake! Everyone listen, there has been a miracle—my son who was once dead is now alive. Rejoice! All of you! Rejoice! You must! My son is coming home!"[40] Reg imagines himself running, rejoicing, and crying out the happy news that the son who was lost has now been found. This allusion to the parable of the prodigal son brings a layer of dramatic irony to the novel. Although Reg has faith in the return of his lost son, the real rebirth is his own. He is the one who is finally "coming home," raised from the dead.[41] He is both the prodigal and the older brother in the story. In fact, this could be a story of the internal world of the older brother who relied upon his own righteousness rather than humbly seeking the good of the lost son.

The end of Coupland's novel is stunning and totally unexpected. Reg is an enemy who causes damage for all around him. It is easy to hate him. His grotesque, depraved character is the result of pride masquerading as faith. He profanes the name of God over and over in word and deed, yet in the end, he is saved. This undeserving hypocrite is now just as human as Cheryl, the teenage convert. Both have achieved a "purity of heart" that hopefully compels the reader to see the pain and frailty in the heart of the oppressor.[42] This is yet another invitation to imagine our neighbor, even our abusive neighbor, as ourselves, seeing the glory inside of him. As we empathize with his inability to see his own blindness, we also rejoice once he gains new eyes.

BLANKETS

Although Reg is finally broken enough to begin healing, he has done much damage to his family. Jason's self-hatred and ultimate rejection of his father's faith, which he believes is Christianity, are both devastating and unresolved. The autobiographical graphic novel *Blankets*, written by Craig Thompson, tells the story of Thompson's upbringing in a fundamentalist evangelical home similar to Reg's stifling household. *Blankets* is also the story of Thompson's process of eventual de-conversion. Now that Thompson is self-avowedly outside of the fold, there are some within it who would see him not just as a lost soul but as an enemy. This is obvious when watching the Twitter wars between so-called exvangelicals and some pockets of conservative evangelicals. Regardless of the bitterness and snark in some of the exvangelical responses, it is important to look at the root of their pain and remember that they are also image bearers, deserving of love and empathy, even if they don't claim it. Thompson's story is both unique and shared by many, and its commonality is tragic.

Blankets is a story of devastating spiritual abuse that is also connected to physical abuse and neglect. As it is autobiographical, the author himself is providing intimate access to his own process of apostasy. The novel is a gift for people of faith who want to understand those who leave the faith; it provides a very round portrayal of an oft-flattened experience. When reading *Blankets*, taking in both the dialogue and the gorgeous illustrations, it is almost impossible to see Thompson merely as a rebellious, backsliding stereotype. Instead, we see that he is a brilliant, talented young man, always eager to do the right thing, to please God, to show kindness. His glorious value warrants our deepest empathy, and his transformation often evokes sadness and discomfort from Christian readers. This is a good discomfort, one that we must wrestle with in order to know how to better love those who have, sometimes understandably, left the faith tradition of their youth.

During his childhood, Craig, like all kids, bases much of his perception of God on the behavior of his legalistic parents who, at a young age, are like God to him. His father is especially domineering and abusive, and his mother is submissive to the point of self-harm. As much as Craig's parents care about the need for their two sons, Craig and Phil, to follow the rules of their faith, they seem to care very little for their actual spiritual and physical well-being. The first examples from *Blankets* showing this lack of attachment between parent and child revolve around the bedroom and bed that Craig and

Phil must share. In Thompson's vivid illustrations, we see Craig toss-
ing and turning, unable to sleep, mainly because his little brother is
constantly moving, stealing covers, and kicking him in the head. This
sleepy sibling rivalry is almost comic until Craig runs to ask his father
why he is required to share a bed with his annoying little brother.
In the next frame, we see the shadowy, hulking back of his father
(whose face we rarely see) towering over Craig and yelling, "Don't
question your parent's authority!"[43] To discipline both children, their
father forcefully removes Phil from the bed and takes him to the much
feared "cubby hole," a tiny room that is hidden behind the paneling
in the boys' playroom.[44] As Phil is forced into the dreaded space, he
yells, "Daddy no, no!!" while Craig cowers in bed, full of guilt and
anger.[45] Phil is locked in and made to spend the night in this room
that was "uninsulated, unlit, and uninhabited—except by spiders and
vermin . . . and a few dust-filled cardboard boxes."[46] The room represents both the children's deep fear of their parents and the rot and
filth at the core of their suburban evangelical home, a space that looks
normal to outsiders.

The more we learn about Craig's church community, the more we
realize that this view of fear-based discipline and spiritual training is
the norm. The description of the "cubby hole" and the children's fear
of being left alone in it are reminiscent of the "red room" section of
Charlotte Brontë's *Jane Eyre*, one of the first fictional condemnations
of the spiritual abuse of children.[47] Like Phil and Craig, Jane is subject
to great psychological damage at the hands of supposedly Christian
leaders. In Thompson's account, Craig suffers even as much as his
brother because he feels guilt and shame for prompting his brother's
punishment. Even worse, he feels unable to protect his brother from
sexual abuse when their babysitter takes them one by one into a closet
to supposedly tell them each a joke. Craig is taken first and knows
what really happens, but he is paralyzed with fear when Phil gleefully
takes the babysitter's hand for his closet visit. Although this sexual
assault was not enacted by their parents, they are culpable because
of their neglect and lack of attentiveness to the needs of their own
children. Craig's parents lack both sensitivity and empathy in their
parenting, a reflection of their legalistic theology.

Home is not the only place that is frightening and disempowering
for Craig; he is constantly bullied at school for being too skinny, too

poor, too religious. He is afraid of running away because he has been taught that "the *real world* could only deliver new threats."[48] As much as his home life is steeped in fear and shame, he has been indoctrinated to believe that home is safe while the outside world is the real danger. His only two getaway cars are dreaming and drawing, and his frequent experiences of creating a safe and beautiful world through drawing are "the only wakeful moments of my childhood that I can recall feeling life was sacred or worthwhile."[49] Yet Craig's parents and the leaders at his church see drawing not as a "sacred" act but as, at best, ornamental. As Francis Schaeffer notes in *Art and the Bible*, "many evangelicals treat the *arts* as secondary ornamentation for the truth rather than a window into reality."[50] In Craig's church, the arts are considered frivolous, and the artist is not a spiritual leader but a frivolous, perhaps even transgressive, outsider.

Craig's misfit status is solidified when, as a child, a Sunday school teacher asks his class what they think they would be doing in heaven. One child yells, "Playing football!" while another asks, "Snowmobiling?"[51] The teacher nods her head in happy approval. Then Craig excitedly tells her that he envisions himself drawing in heaven. His teacher's countenance changes, and she mockingly asks, "Oh Craig, *drawing* for all eternity?"[52] Craig is confused because he has been told heaven is a perfect place, and he imagines that, in a perfect place, he will be doing what he loves. His teacher then explains that "in heaven our *new lives* will be devoted to *praising and worshiping god!* We will *love* every second of it."[53] This does not sound joyful or appealing to Craig, who confesses he can't sing and does not want to sing, even in heaven. He then asks a question that perhaps, more than anything, defines his future relationship with the Christian faith: "Couldn't I praise God with my *drawings?*"[54] His teacher scoffs, asking, "How can you praise God with drawings?" When Craig responds, "Draw his creation—like trees and stuff," she tells him that there is no use or need for this, as "he's already drawn it for us."[55] The Sunday school teacher's response is not only ignorant but also devoid of empathy. There is no understanding of the relationship between the acts of the Creator and the human desire to create, nor is there a willingness to see that this is an essential part of what it means for Craig to be a spiritual human being as he uses his gifts to increase beauty and point to truth. Craig's church community is unable to love who he really is;

they only love the idea of his fitting into their fundamentalist mold. In reading about experiences like this one, it is easy to see how the very snark and mockery that have been ingested by former evangelicals will eventually be vomited back up. And it is important to look past the acerbic responses to the root of the wounding in order to be willing to both self-critique and empathize.

Craig eventually realizes that "drawing is out" because it is not considered a Christian vocation, and he has been taught that it would be selfish to do something that he loves so much if it is not considered a ministry.[56] Craig's church's inept, legalistic theology of vocation is very damaging, and it puts limits not only on the artist but on God. In his church's collective thinking, a vocation is a job in the traditional ministry, such as preaching, leading Bible studies, and so on. And according to these rigid categories, Craig is deserving not of empathy, only rebuke. He is not fulfilling his God-given calling; rather, he is rebelling and transgressing. This theology goes hand in hand with the belief in a problematic sacred/secular dualism, the belief that being spiritual is limited to going to church, preaching, reading the Bible, praying, and consuming Christian media—and that anything outside of these narrow boundaries is useless, at best, or dangerous, at worst. Yet according to Jim Paul, director of the English branch of L'Abri Fellowship, when we want to understand what it means to be spiritual human beings, we must look at all of the aspects of creation that God made and called "good," looking at Christ as the ultimate example of what it means to be human.[57] And in looking at Christ for the ultimate example of humanity, we also grow our empathy, seeing his actual lived experience as good and looking for this in other image bearers. As James Paul notes, it is telling that one of the few recorded sentences from Christ after his resurrection is "come and have breakfast."[58] Eating and creating community can be sacred acts, and so can the creation of art, especially as the artist is made in the image of the ultimate Creator. The artist often has a prophetic sensibility when viewing the culture, communicating the truth of beauty and the deadliness of falsehood. Yet this prophetic gifting can also seem threatening to those living within the rigid lines of religion rather than the teachings of Christ. The fear of this bold, prophetic understanding of humanity is a barrier to compassion and empathy.

On looking back at his traumatic childhood experiences, the adult Craig sees that the dogma of this version of Christianity "denies the beauty of being *human*."[59] Sadly, he was never taught to see life, faith, and human existence as church father Saint Irenaeus famously did: "The glory of God is a human person fully alive." Because of this, Craig's family, church leaders, and congregants do not see a world "charged with the grandeur of God" and humans made in his glorious, endlessly creative image.[60] Instead, they see a list of fears and threats. This is apparent when teenage Craig tells his pastor that he is planning to go to art school, and he is advised strongly against it. The pastor claims that his brother went to art school and had to "draw from life," which led to an addiction to pornography and, eventually, homosexuality.[61] To encourage Craig, a church friend tells him to go to a "Christ-centered college" where they "reject any text that strays from biblical truth."[62] Once again, Craig feels both selfish and ashamed of the gifts that bring him great joy. Although this mistreatment is not physical, it is still damaging, dehumanizing abuse, a lack of love and empathy that leads to self-righteousness and chastisement.

Tragically, the fearful mindset of Craig's home church is contagious and drives a guilt-stricken Craig to burn all his drawings: "I've wasted my God-given time on escapism . . . the most secular and selfish of worldly pursuits."[63] As his beloved creations go up in flames, he "[acts] as if I was sacrificing a burnt offering before God."[64] The fire of legalistic abuse has momentarily crushed the God-given creative part of him. Although deeply hurt, Craig is still very earnest and devoted in his faith after this supposed cleansing, reassuring himself that "the world is not my home; I'm just passing through."[65] He says this in his mind over and over again, a mantra to enable him to transcend the cruel taunts of his high school hallways and church camp peers who call him "faggot" and make fun of his long hair. These same normal, good Christian kids speak of their female classmates as objects that they want to consume. In his sensitivity and great sense of empathy, Craig does not fit in, and ironically, this is seen as a bad thing. He begins to love the idea of heaven and long for it: "I grew up striving for that world—that would wash away my temporary misery."[66] He also begins to believe that his body is temporary and, therefore, not sacred and that anyone who embraces the beauty of the world would be cast into hell, where they would be constantly in pain. Thompson's recollection of the Sunday school sermons on hell is not unlike the pages-long fire-and-brimstone diatribes that were used to torment the young Stephen Dedalus in James Joyce's *A Portrait of the Artist as a Young Man*. Both Craig Thompson and James Joyce were ultimately driven away from the faith of their childhood because of the sort of fear-inducing Gnosticism that they absorbed in their young, devout years. Ultimately, they left abusive communities devoid of empathy to look for beauty, goodness, and empathy elsewhere.

When at a dreaded church camp during his high school years, Craig is once again surrounded by peers who are accepted by the church community yet secretly much less devoted to the faith than Craig is. He finds friends in a group of misfits, including a beautiful, mysterious, artistic young woman named Raina. As the story continues, Craig begins to wrestle with his faith, seeking heaven in a relationship with Raina. In her, he finds a temporary sense of freedom, a momentary fulfillment of his real need for affirmation, and an earthly source of beauty that speaks to his artist's heart. With Raina, he senses something sacred, and he does not understand how this can be reconciled with his faith, yet he trusts that it is good. Soon, however, the two drift apart and Craig is heartbroken, left alone with his deep pain and sense of worthlessness. As Craig sits in a high school classroom learning about Plato's Allegory of the Cave, he realizes that he has been like one of the prisoners, chained up and facing a wall, believing that a distorted shadow in front of him is reality.[67] This attention to Plato's story foreshadows Craig's departure from his faith, abandoning the confining, distorted images of reality that he inherited.

In the book's last section, an adult Craig is making a rare visit home, his backdrop a kitchen decorated with the kitschy slogans of his parents' faith: "Jesus is the Reason for the Season."[68] He is afraid of informing his parents that he is no longer a Christian, and he tells his brother, Phil, that "I envision them on their deathbeds, solely concerned with the salvation of their children."[69] As abusive as his childhood was, he does not want to hurt his parents. He explains that after he left home, "[his] faith came crumbling down so easily."[70] The first time he went into a library after his de-conversion, he was "like a kid in a candy store" because he was "allowed to read any book."[71] He admits that he then "[gorges] himself" on all of this forbidden knowledge, so much that "[his] tummy aches."[72] Although he feeds himself with all the culture that he had been deprived of, he admits that he is "still hungry," and the book's final words and images reflect this longing and ambiguity.[73] During his visit, Craig takes a lonely walk in the Wisconsin snow, where he draws a small figure of himself in the midst of several blank pages. Across these pages, he writes the following: "How satisfying it is to leave a mark on a blank surface to make a map of my movement—no matter how temporary."[74] Although Craig has denied the faith that initially defined him, he is now defining himself, leaving his artistic mark on this sacred earth, if only for a short time. His departure seems both liberating and tragic, especially as the leaving could perhaps have been prevented if his peers and religious instructors could have stepped outside of their constructed notions of the Christian life to see Craig's desire for God and love of beauty—both profound, prophetic sensitivities. There was no one to listen to Craig, to enjoy the beauty of God's universe and his talent with him, to see Christ in him. Instead, he was seen as only a transgressor, a backslider, and an enemy who deserves neglect and abuse, by both his parents and the community that claimed to be the hands and feet of Christ.

MAGNOLIA

The kinds of parental abuse and neglect that we see in *Blankets* are some of the most primal, damaging manifestations of the absence of empathy. Paul Thomas Anderson's labyrinthine film, *Magnolia*, also emphasizes the long-term impact of parental abuse and neglect and, in doing so, asks us to empathize with abuse victims who have themselves become abusers. Both parents and, in some cases, children in the film are enemies to themselves, to one another, and to the community. Some of these enemies are predators, perhaps the most reviled of sinners, yet Anderson shows us the need that even these characters have for forgiveness, redemption, and a sort of empathy that makes their goodness visible even amid their badness. Like Coupland, Anderson asks us to look beyond the behavior of these characters to their capacity for grace and transformation. Some of them accept this grace; others don't. All are beautiful and broken humans who challenge our all-too-easy labels and surprise us with their paradoxical frailty and strength.

Magnolia runs close to three hours, weaving together multiple life stories that are all somehow connected to big-name television producer Earl Partridge. Partridge is a cruel, amoral, elderly man who is now bedridden, succumbing to cancer. One of Earl's main projects is a popular evening game show called *What Do Kids Know?*, a trivia face-off between a team of children and a team of adults.[75] The host of this show is Jimmy Gator, who has also been recently diagnosed with cancer. Both Earl and Jimmy are wealthy, successful, and estranged from their children—and Anderson's central focus is to explore the reasons for this estrangement and the many ways that the children are punished "for the sin of the parents."[76] Earl and Jimmy are both adulterers who have climbed up the corporate ladder, self-styled Nietzschean supermen stepping on any below them who got in their way, including their own family members. Anderson does not romanticize or glamorize the impact of these behaviors; rather, he exposes the brutality of their intergenerational impact. The film has a hard R rating, mainly because of the barrage of violent, dehumanizing, and obscene language that we hear coming from the mouths of the deeply broken characters. Understandably, many viewers, especially Christians, did not finish the film for this reason. But if you wade through the film's filth (which is all mostly verbal rather than visual), the profane meets the sacred in compelling, moving, potentially life-changing ways.

There is a method to the film's profane madness, and this is governed by its undeniable moral core. Many seemingly discerning filmgoers who will watch a tame, PG-rated romantic comedy balk at the notion of watching a film like *Magnolia*. Yet *Magnolia* is a film that tells the truth more honestly and in a far more convicting, revealing fashion than most formulaic romantic comedies, many of which argue that the supreme value is "following your heart," even if this means committing adultery. *Magnolia*, on the other hand, reveals many ways that "the heart is deceitful above all things" as we bear witness to the damage wrought from the selfishness inherent in both adultery and sacrificing family for the bottom line.[77] In a sense, Anderson's film is an anti-Hollywood movie, an attempt to deconstruct the mythology of happiness bought by wealth, illicit sex, and privilege. Formulaic, mainstream films often present an artificial invitation to shallow empathy, providing us with airbrushed images of false perfection rather than the reality of human wretchedness and glory. A film like

Magnolia helps us expand our potential for empathy as we wrestle through the awkward experience of caring for a thief, a drug addict, a seduction artist, and a gold-digging wife. All these characters have acted out of their misunderstood deepest needs, reaching for false remedies that leave them wallowing in suburban anguish.

Anderson wants us to feel pain as we watch this movie tell the truth about the consequences of interpersonal sin. At the same time, he asks us to be empathetic with the broken, fragile, yet successful men at the heart of the film's trauma. It is telling that the game show in the center of the movie's web of connections is called *What Do Kids Know?*, as Anderson's central focus is on ways that children absorb the behaviors of their parents. Along with Earl's estranged son, Frank, and Jimmy's estranged daughter, Claudia, we meet both a former and a current contestant on the game show. Quiz Kid Donnie Smith, a lonely, middle-aged barfly, was a former champion of the show. His parents took all his earnings and squandered them. Stanley Spector is an introverted, socially awkward kid genius whose father continually pushes him into competitions for the sake of making money off him. His father does not listen to his needs, only seeing his son as a possible paycheck. All these interconnected stories of abuse are central to the plot—but the lives of Frank T. J. Mackey, Earl's son, and Claudia Gator, Jimmy's daughter, are the most harrowing and challenging as we watch and ask how to have empathy for these victims, now abusers themselves.

Earl Partridge abandoned his only child, Frank, after the child's mother was diagnosed with cancer. Frank spent many of his years caring for a dying mother, losing both his childhood and his capacity for love and empathy. As an adult, Frank is a men's self-help guru, specifically focusing on teaching men how to seduce women. Every night, as he becomes the stage character Frank T. J. Mackey, his persona is both comical and despicable as he struts onstage, flexing his muscles while Richard Strauss's "Thus Spake Zarathustra" blasts the ears of his participants.[78] Frank has a poster behind him with the words "Seduce and Destroy" written across it, and his first lecture is titled "How to Fake like You Are Nice and Caring."[79] The more he speaks, the more it is clear that he is teaching men not how to date women but how to become sexual predators. His language is objectifying, dehumanizing, and vile—and the more profane and aggressive he becomes, the more his all-male audience cheers him on. His meetings are predecessors to what we now call incel communities—groups of men who feel rejected and emasculated by women and desire to get revenge and overpower them. Frank's ridiculous use of "Thus Spake Zarathustra" as an entry song is significant, considering the piece's reference to the philosophy of Friedrich Nietzsche. Like his father did, Frank is advocating and living his own life according to the rules of Nietzsche's central philosophy where "might makes right" and the strong have every right (and, in fact, a moral obligation) to overpower and dominate the weak. Frank follows this pattern, empowering himself by devouring women just as his father devoured his mother. Frank also devours the men entrusting him with their money and time as he teaches them to become like him. He is a vicious cult leader and a predator, and it is almost unbearable to watch these portions of the film. Yet we are asked to bestow empathy upon him.

Frank's story shifts in a surprising way when he receives an unexpected phone call during an interview. A female reporter has just gently but firmly confronted Frank for the lies he has told about his family and his past. He grows increasingly angry and aggressive, and the film's tension rises very quickly. In another scene, we see a miserable, moaning Earl Partridge cry out, not just because of his physical pain but because of his regret. He confides in his nurse, Phil, that he repeatedly cheated on his beloved first wife. Perhaps worse than the cheating is Frank's cruel abandonment of his young son, Frank, to take care of a terminally ill mother. His own selfish drive for pleasure and fame destroyed his family as well as his son's life. Tears run down Phil's face as he feeds morphine pills to Earl, who continues his lament: "Now I'll die, and I'll tell you what . . . the biggest regret of my life . . . I let my love go. What did I do? I'm sixty-five years old. And I'm ashamed. A million years ago . . . the fucking regret and guilt."[80] The scene is agonizing to watch. Anderson interjects this sacred and profane moment with an internal shot of Earl's body as the cancer devours it. Until this moment, Phil has not even been aware that his dying patient had a son. Earl has since remarried, and his young wife, Linda, agreed to their union for the sake of Earl's money—but now she is also consumed with guilt over her actions. The luxurious Los Angeles home is thick with the spiritual realities of guilt, shame, and death.

Phil, Earl's nurse, is one of the two deeply empathetic intercessory figures in the film and one of our guides in the motions of patience and love. The violence of Earl's soul is hard to comprehend, but in these moments, we see it through the grace that Phil extends as he sees this deeply needy human "as God sees him."[81] When Earl cries out for his son, Jack, Phil begins researching to try to gain contact with the man he soon realizes is, sadly, just like his father. Phil sheepishly orders pornographic magazines to be delivered from the drugstore so that he can find an ad for Frank T. J. Mackey's seminars. When he finally locates it, he calls and begs Frank's handlers to pass the phone to him. In an almost metafictional turn, Phil relates this unbelievably dramatic scene to the stuff of Hollywood movies:

> I know this sounds silly, and I know that I might sound ridiculous, like this is the scene of the movie where the guy is trying to get ahold of the long-lost son, you know, but this is that scene. This is that scene. And I think they have those scenes in movies because they're true. You know, because they really happen. And you gotta believe me: this is really happening. I mean, I can give you my number and you can go check with whoever you gotta check with, and call me back, but do not leave me hanging on this, all right? Please—I'm just—please. See, see this is the scene of the movie where you help me out.[82]

Anderson's anti-Hollywood movie is both ironically and earnestly including a favorite formulaic film trope—but in a much more dark, real, and intense way. The music pulses and tension grows as Frank's many employees pass the call from person to person to try to find him. As they do this, he is still sitting, facing the female reporter, staring intensely and hatefully into her eyes, refusing to speak. But then the truth breaks through in the form of a phone call beckoning Frank to the bedside of his estranged, dying father.

Frank rage-drives through a violent nighttime storm to his childhood home, then threatens to kick the dogs that come to greet him at the door. He has to catch his breath before seeing his father, the shadowy figure from his broken past. Phil gently leads him to the bedside, where Frank bends over, clasping his hands, seething with anger. He rocks back and forth, screaming with fiery glee at a man who cannot hear him because he is so far gone into his own physical pain: "Earl. It hurts, doesn't it? Huh? You in a lot of pain? She was in a lot of pain. Right to the end, she was in a lot of pain. I know because I, I was there. Earl. You didn't like illness then, did you? I was there. She waited for your call. For you to come. I am not going to cry. I am not going to cry for you! You ****, I know you can hear me. I want you to know that I hate your mother****ing guts. You can just ****ing die. . . . And I hope it hurts."[83] The words become more intense, and anger breaks into grief and pain as Frank rocks back and forth, weeping. He cries out, "Why didn't you call? I ****ing hate you."[84] Then, like a whimpering, abandoned child, he begs, "Don't go away, you ****ing asshole! Oh, God, don't go away, you ****ing asshole!"[85] Frank is no longer a predator: he is an abused son, a child crying out for his daddy. The poison that he was forced to drink as a child has been coming back up for years in his angry, arrogant misogyny, but inside, he is that abandoned child, wanting nothing more than the love and acceptance of a father. Soon, Earl dies, and Frank's entire demeanor changes as he quietly and gently works with Phil to make arrangements. The tears on his face appear to have purified him of the vileness that has been lodged deep inside of him. This deeply moving, powerful scene asks us to see the wounded man inside of the bully, to try to understand the ways in which he became the man he is. Frank's breakdown, his moment of nonverbal forgiveness and humility, just may lead to his redemption.

Although Frank Mackey and Claudia Gator have never met, their fathers worked together, both neglecting and abusing their individual families. Claudia is an addict, one who many might see as worthless and weak—perhaps even a threat, an enemy. In one of the film's early segments, Officer Jim Kurring has received a complaint about the loud music and screaming coming from Claudia's apartment. When she answers the door to Jim, her comments are erratic, her body movements jerky; she is clearly high. He ignores this, merely asking if she is safe. Once he is assured that she is, he leaves then immediately comes back, asking if she would like to go to dinner with him. She accepts, and the dinner date that follows is painfully awkward. Claudia is still high, and Jim is a naive, sweet, yet socially anxious man. He is deeply caring, a protector, and an honorable cop. He is also a devout Catholic, and we see him regularly kneeling at the side of his bed, under a crucifix, praying. Like Phil, he is gentle and kind; he does not seem to belong to the world of this film. And also like Phil, he guides us through grace-filled motions of compassion, forgiveness, and empathy. Although their dinner is uncomfortable, Jim is smitten by Claudia's beauty and senses her deep insecurity. Rather than taking advantage of it, he speaks words of truth and kindness to her, words that she cannot accept.

The film's title, *Magnolia*, is in reference to Claudia, a beautiful yet deeply fragile flower who can either blossom or shrivel up. Anderson created her character based on songs already written by Aimee Mann, and in the dinner date scene, Claudia screams out this self-destructive line from a song called "Deathly": "Now that I've met you / would you object to never seeing each other again?"[86] The portrayal of Claudia as a beautiful, bruised young woman who feels so unworthy of love is the heart of the film. "Deathly" is just one of the eight songs from Mann that make up the soundtrack, but it provides our initial insights into Claudia's deeply needy character: "Cause I'm just a problem / for you to solve and / watch dissolve in the heat of your charm. . . . One act of kindness could be deathly, deathly."[87] Before meeting Jim, we see a quick scene of Claudia recklessly having sex with a nameless stranger whom she has met in a bar. Her addiction to anonymous sex and cocaine both give her temporary pleasure but fuel her insecurity. She believes she deserves to be thrown away, and these self-destructive behaviors are consistent with her sense of worthlessness. In his groundbreaking study on addiction, *In the Realm of Hungry Ghosts: Close Encounters with Addiction*, psychiatrist Gabor Mate discloses that at least ninety-five percent of the addicts he has worked with were sexually molested as children, thus creating their deeply entrenched feelings of dirtiness and unworthiness and their desire to escape through drug use.[88] Claudia's character fits this profile. Although she is high throughout most of the film, Anderson manages to show us her beauty, her sad frailty, and her large potential for grace. And as we continually see her through Jim's eyes, like the eyes of God, she is worthy of being loved.

As the film progresses, we discover that Claudia's father, Jimmy, molested her and refuses to admit it, continually denying it and gaslighting her. Like many abused children, Claudia grew up believing that this secret was her fault, that she was the dirty one. On her first date with Jim, we see the deep fear of intimacy that was birthed out of her hidden abuse: "I'm really nervous that you're gonna hate me soon. You're gonna find stuff out about me and you're gonna hate me."[89] Jim does not understand this because he finds her exquisite, sweet, beautiful. She continues: "You have so much—so many good things. And you seem so together. You're a police officer and you seem so straight and put together—without any problems."[90] In an act of great kindness, empathy, and humility, Jim responds by telling her how ashamed he is that he lost his gun earlier that day. He feels like a failure as a cop. Although this is clearly problematic for Jim, his confession seems quite minor, even innocent, compared to Claudia's dark secret—but this doesn't matter. Jim's act of confession creates a sense of shared vulnerability, a gesture of love and kindness that builds trust, at least in the moment.

Phil and Jim, the film's great empathizers, are never given a backstory, as they seem to be significant only in their capacity to provide grace to the most deeply wounded characters. We see Frank through Phil's eyes and Claudia through Jim's eyes, and we realize that these very lost adults are also deeply wounded children who need hope for redemption. The muck and mire of their lives were initially and violently foisted upon them, but it has since accumulated, partially from their own making (especially in Frank's case). Near the end of the film, the rain over LA reaches biblical proportions, washing the grime off the streets but replacing it with the bodies of dead frogs. The surreal inclusion of this biblical allusion to the plagues of Egypt is daring, unexpected, and strange. The hardened hearts of the pharaoh-like parents are challenged, and some, not all, are softened. But the children experience a sense of redemption and hope after the cleansing rain. In a touching poststorm scene, Officer Jim is helping the adult Quiz Kid Donnie Smith return money that he has stolen, even though Donnie should be taken to jail. Jim's brief monologue captures the film's central tensions about the nature of forgiveness and redemption:

> A lot of people think this is just a job that you go to. Take a lunch hour . . . job's over. Something like that. But it's a twenty-four-hour deal. No two ways about it. And what most people don't see . . . is just how hard it is to do the right thing. People think if I make a judgment call . . . that's a judgment on them, but that is not what I do. And that's not what should be done. I have to

take everything . . . and play it as it lays. Sometimes people need a little help. Sometimes people need to be forgiven. And sometimes they need to go to jail. And that is a very tricky thing on my part . . . making that call. I mean, the law is the law. And heck if I'm gonna break it. You can forgive someone. Well, that's the tough part. What can we forgive? Tough part of the job. Tough part of walking down the street.[91]

The "tough part" of Jim's job and the even more "tough part" of being human is knowing when and how to forgive. In a film about the devastating sins of the fathers, we see that an inability to forgive can lead to more damage. More than anything, we see the need that both Frank and Claudia have to forgive themselves for the false guilt that they have been carrying.

The film's final scene is filmed in a very dramatic, atypical manner. The only voice we hear belongs to Jim, but his back is turned to the camera. He is standing over and facing Claudia, who is curled up on her bed. We can barely hear the words Jim is speaking to her, but we see the tears well up in her eyes. Jim's words are almost drowned out by the film's final song, Aimee Mann's "Save Me." The lyrics are deeply relevant, and they add to the pathos of the concluding scene: "You look like a perfect fit / for a girl in need of a tourniquet / But can you save me / from the ranks of the freaks / who suspect they could never love anyone."[92] Claudia feels like an unlovable "freak," and she does not know how to stop the hemorrhaging that results from her abuse. Mann continues the narrative, singing, "You struck me dumb like radium / Like Peter Pan or Superman / You will come to save me."[93] This is the song's most telling line, as the reference to "Peter Pan" alludes to a story about the "Island of Lost Children" and a fantasy character who is forever a child. Superman, on the other hand, is a traditional, all-powerful hero who rescues the weak and needy. The film contrasts this notion of Superman with the Nietzschean idea of a Superman who follows his natural desires for domination, regardless of the fallout. Earl and Jimmy were Nietzschean supermen, not heroes but destroyers. Frank inherited and adapted this sinister behavior, whereas Claudia was merely crushed by it. But the film's final shot presents a different type of Superman, someone who is humble, self-effacing, and kind yet gently stern in his truth-telling. Like Phil, Jim moves the plot forward through his acts of empathy, causing the very lines of "spiritual motion" that O'Connor says we need to be looking for in a good story. The final lines of the film, almost overwhelmed by the music, are Jim's prompting for Claudia to see herself through the same eyes of grace and love that he does: "You are a good and beautiful person, and I won't let you walk out on me. And I won't let you say those things—those things about how stupid you are and this and that. I won't stand for that. You want to be with me . . . then you be with me."[94] As the dramatic music wells up and Jim's final words are spoken, Claudia looks to the camera and, with tear-filled eyes, smiles for the first time perhaps in a lifetime. The scene fades out, and the film is over. Anderson is asking us to see the frailty and humanity of both Frank and Claudia, two desperate figures who are on opposite ends of the outside of acceptable society. Though children of privilege, they have been disempowered seemingly beyond redemption. But redemption often comes from unexpected places. As we watch this film, we are asked to see past their behavior, their violent language, and their addictions in order to see their needs. We are asked to see them, like Phil and Jim, through the eyes of Christ.

Each of these pieces of art asks us to extend radical empathy to characters who would be, perhaps understandably, judged and rejected by many. Wrestling with these difficult stories can help move us toward the revolutionary grace modeled by Christ as he became one of us, empathizing in the most profound and intimate way possible. This is the sort of love that Friedrich Nietzsche found absurd. In *The Antichrist*, he describes this savior whose self-sacrifice he defined as "decadent" and "evil": "But this god of the 'great majority,' this democrat among gods, has not become a proud heathen god: on the contrary, he remains a Jew, he remains a god in a corner, a god of all the dark nooks and crevices, of all the noisesome quarters of the world!"[95] Nietzsche means these scathing lines as an insult—instead, they are a powerful description of the beauty of Christ's sacrificial goodness, the embodied empathy that transcends a human capacity for love. Yes, Christ is Lord of all the "dark nooks and crevices," the hidden places filled with hypocrites, backsliders, predators, and junkies. Even in these "noisome quarters," there is an opportunity for the followers of Christ to be like him, "a great democrat" as we see all human beings as equally worthy of love, grace, and the extension of our empathy.

CONCLUSION

Up on a mountain our Lord is alone
Without a family, friends, or a home
He cries ooh ooh ooh
Will you stay with me?
He cries oh oh oh
Will you wait with me?

Up on a mountain our Lord is afraid
Carrying all the mistakes we have made
And he knew . . . ooh . . . ooh
It's a long way down
Do you know . . . oh . . . oh?
It's a long way down

Up in the heavens our Lord prays for you
He sent his spirit to carry us through
So it's true . . . ooh . . . ooh
That you're not alone
Do you know . . . oh . . . oh?
He came all the way down

So it's true . . . ooh . . . ooh
That you're not alone
Do you know . . . oh . . . oh?
He came all the way down[1]

Monique Aiuto's lilting, gentle voice is that of a very human Christ, a Christ who embodies divine empathy. As she sings "Up on a Mountain," a folk hymn written by her husband, Vito, the expression of Christ's suffering is tender, relatable, sad, and glorious. The song is a picture of the Christ who understands loneliness, rejection, and pain—the same Christ who volunteered to share these deeply human experiences when "he came all the way down."[2] The song begins with Monique's lonely voice, but she is soon joined by Vito singing backup. As the song continues, the community grows as a chorus of voices joins in, backed by a rich flourish of instrumentation. Although initially focusing on Christ's unavoidable loneliness, the greatest sacrifice ever made, the hymn ends with a collection of buoyant voices assuring listeners "that you're not alone."[3]

EMPATHY IN COMMUNITY

As we sit in an Italian coffee shop on a sunny Brooklyn day, Monique answers all my questions about her music by speaking about her love of and need for community. She and Vito have now created and put out three albums of hymns and indie-folk songs about everyday life, love, and faith under the moniker the Welcome Wagon. Monique explains that her main love is creating and sharing art in the context of a community because, in doing this, she learns more about the people in that community. As they listen, react, and share pieces of their lives, she knows more about what it feels like to be them. It strikes me that Monique's focus, as well as the focus of the song, is the importance of an empathy rooted first in Christ's sacrificial love.

And just as "Up on a Mountain" is about Christ's voluntary vulnerability, we can also hear the vulnerability in the track's human voices. Monique shares that performing "puts me in a vulnerable place" because of "moments of chance and contingency" and "sharing my life as part of a married couple" in front of a community.[4] This vulnerable sharing, and the reflexive vulnerability that occurs when the community of listeners responds, is a beautiful picture of the way the arts can bring human beings together on a deeper level. Although we often experience art in isolation—reading a book, listening to an album—we are never truly alone but always in conversation with the artist, as long as we are willing to listen and respond.

This reflexive relationship between artists and audience is grounded in the need to hear and be heard, to share stories and life experiences. The more we have ears to hear and eyes to see the image bearer both behind the work of art and modeled within even its fictional characters, the more we can grow in our understanding of how to love them. "I am alive and you are alive so we must fill the air with our words," says Valentino Achak Deng on the final page of *What Is the What*.[5] He must tell his story to others because "to do anything else would be something less than human." Human beings were created through the words of the Creator, and we have a natural desire to share the words that we have within us. "Up on a Mountain" meditates upon the great story of Christ's sacrifice, contextualizing all of our empathy within the true-life example of empathy shown on the cross.

EMPATHY IN THE GREATEST STORY

The recent streaming series *The Chosen* also focuses on Christ's life of empathy, leading up to the cross. Dallas Jenkins masterfully creates a series of biblically based stories focusing on the relationships, daily life, and teachings of Jesus, brilliantly emphasizing both his human-ity and his divinity. In the moving last episode of season one, Jesus purposefully encounters an outcast Samaritan woman at Jacob's Well. The episode fills in quite a bit of cultural context and background to the biblical narrative, emphasizing the divide between Jews and Samaritans. The unnamed woman is shocked that a Jewish man would speak to her, especially as her own people have rejected her for being "unclean" in her relationships and behaviors. Jesus begins to tell her things about her life, and she initially assumes he is a prophet sent to preach to her and scold her. But the more details he provides about her life—the more he gives words to her painful story of rejection and abuse—the more she has eyes to see who he is. By telling her the story of her life, Jesus shows that he both knows and loves her, regardless of what she has done. Her story is sacred when he gives words to it because he is the source of all stories. At this moment, her countenance brightens; she believes that Jesus is the promised Messiah when he says, "I, the one speaking to you—I am he."[6]

As she rejoices, Jesus's eyes fill with tears as he feels the joy that she is feeling. In a conversation between *The Chosen* show creator, Dallas Jenkins, and Jonathan Roumie, the actor who plays Jesus, the two talk about this unscripted moment. Roumie teared up each time they filmed the scene because "she opened herself up to the infinite, eternal love" within Christ, and "to be filled with this spirit of joy is infectious."[7] He also saw a picture of all humanity in her figure: "The Messiah has converted her heart and taken away all this pain . . .

transforming the circumstances of her life—what God wants for all of us."[8] Roumie believes that Christ himself would have cried in that moment, tears of deep, empathetic love for a woman whose pain has turned to gladness. Jenkins and Roumie also comment on the way the show portrays Christ's decision to willfully feel what humans feel, including their pain. In one scene, Jenkins recalls, we see Jesus bandaging a wound on his hand rather than healing it. Jenkins includes these moments to reflect that Christ "put aside his God-head" so that he would feel what we feel.[9] In playing Jesus, Roumie tried to feel every emotion on a "much more intense level . . . a much more tactile scale" as he attempted to step into the feelings that Jesus might have had.[10]

In this powerful work of art, Jenkins and Roumie remind us that Christ's empathy, from such a place of pure and profound love, is our great model for empathy. And this retelling of Christ's story is also a reminder of the almost magical ability a story has to capture our imaginations and hearts. Of course, Jenkins is retelling the greatest and truest story ever told—but all good stories, to some degree, point back to the humanity of Christ in trying to depict the humanity of its characters. As we make space for the art we encounter, we also make space for the artist(s) and the human stories that the art contains. This space is pregnant with the possibility for imaginative empathy, even for those we find the most challenging, different, difficult. It is important to remember that Christ died for his enemies, spilling his own blood in order to convert them into his friends. And in this regard, we are asked to model our lives after him.

THE ARTS AS A MEANS TO AGAPE LOVE

The decision to take time to read, watch, and listen to the stories of those who don't fit our comfortable molds is a sacrificial act of love. In seriously engaging these stories, we must resist the comfort of familiarity and the lure of simple stereotypes, instead making space for childlike wonder and curiosity about the unknown other, made in God's image. In a sermon given on loving our enemies, Martin Luther King Jr. claimed that "love is creative, understanding goodwill for all men."[11] Love itself is an act of abundant creativity birthed out of a connection to the Creator. In seeking to have eyes to see the *imago Dei* in all human beings, we are also wanting "goodwill" for them. King continues, emphasizing the most profound reason that we should love our neighbors as ourselves: "We should love everybody because God loves them."[12] As we work to love our neighbors, to see Christ in them, we will "have *agape* in [our] soul."[13] This agape love is a self-less love that makes room for the other, taking valuable time as well as intellectual and emotional effort to get to know their stories. The arts create an opportunity to grow our empathy and thus our agape love for one another.

ACKNOWLEDGMENTS

This book grew out of a lecture I first delivered in 2018 at Regent College in Vancouver, BC, during my time there as a scholar-in-residence. I want to thank the Regent College community for creating a nurturing, challenging space where I could both work and share my work. I am also deeply indebted to three other vibrant communities that have taught me so much about the relationship between the arts and spiritual formation: Covenant College, L'Abri Fellowship (England), and Calvin University. Many heartfelt thanks to former Calvin University staff member, dear friend, and visionary mentor Ken Hefner for years of devoted work on his brainchild, the Festival of Faith and Music. I am so honored to have been a part of the community grown out of Ken's love for God and the arts.

Thank you to Dr. Joseph Kickasola, my brilliant colleague, friend of many years, and chief pep-talk giver. I am so thankful to both Joe and Baylor University for providing me with the space for a much needed postvaccination writing retreat in New York City during the summer of 2021. Thank you also to Lee University for providing funding to enable time in NYC to research and finish the book.

I would also like to thank the friends who read and commented on portions of this book: Linnea Kickasola, Mary Frances Giles, James Paul, Rachel Lorenz Morales, Cody Nailor, Ann Pleiss Morris, Bill Rice, Laura and Harry Jones, Lauren Bentley, Matthew Nelson, Tucker McClelland, Becki Whetsel, and Catharyna Vail Britt. Your insights were invaluable during my final revision process. Thank you especially to Carol Baker, who read almost all of my book chapters (in a lightning-fast amount of time, no less) and provided extensive and insightful comments.

My editor, Emily King, has been a joy to work with. Thank you, Emily, for having such faith in my work, and thank you for your copious, gracious comments. They have helped me become a better writer.

I am profoundly thankful to Monique Aiuto, Lili Taylor, and Scott Teems for taking the time to talk with me and/or respond to my questions via email. Your beautiful contributions reflect the heart of this book's central argument about empathy and the arts. I am also very grateful to Rev. Vito Aiuto for granting permission to use the song "Up on a Mountain" by the Welcome Wagon.

Finally, thank you to my mother, Frances Walker McCampbell. This book is dedicated to her. From a very young age, I learned about compassion and empathy from watching her interactions with other people. And more recently, her continual encouragement as well as her endless prayers for my work have been a great boon during the entire process.

NOTES

INTRODUCTION

1 Graham Greene, *The Power and the Glory* (London: Penguin, 1940), 131.
2 Ibid.
3 Ibid.
4 Ibid., 132.
5 Ibid., 131.
6 Agnieszka Tennant, "Electing to Be Open, a Christian Writing Festival Invites Nonbelievers, Too," *Wall Street Journal*, May 16, 2018, https://on.wsj.com/3AaMIGv.
7 David Dark, *Everyday Apocalypse: The Sacred Revealed in Radiohead, the Simpsons, and Other Pop Culture Icons* (Grand Rapids, MI: Brazos, 2002), 10.
8 Paul Bloom, "Against Empathy," *Boston Review*, September 10, 2014, https://bit.ly/3lAoVfc.
9 Luke 10:27.
10 John 1:14.
11 John 11:35.
12 Luke 10:25.
13 Luke 10:27.
14 Luke 10:29.
15 Luke 10:31.
16 Luke 10:33.
17 Luke 10:36.
18 Luke 37.
19 Howard Thurman, *Sermons on the Parables* (Maryknoll, NY: Orbis, 2018), chap. 5.
20 Ibid.
21 Ibid.
22 Pope Benedict XVI, *Deus Caritas Est*, encyclical letter, Vatican website, December 25, 2005, https://bit.ly/3iq5un5, section 15.
23 Ibid.
24 Ibid., section 31.
25 Matt 25:40.

26 Timothy Fry, ed., *The Rule of St. Benedict in English* (Collegeville, MN: Liturgical Press, 1981), 83.

27 Ibid.

28 Ibid.

29 Christina Pohl, *Making Room: Recovering Hospitality as a Christian Tradition* (Grand Rapids, MI: Eerdmans, 1999), 62.

30 Ibid.

31 Blaise Pascal, *Pensées and Other Writings* (Oxford: Oxford University Press, 1995), 12.

32 C. S. Lewis, *The Weight of Glory* (New York: Harper One, 1980), 45.

33 Ibid.

34 Ibid., 46.

35 Gerard Manley Hopkins, "God's Grandeur," Poetry Foundation, accessed September 20, 2021, https://bit.ly/3Cr9w6N.

36 Gerard Manley Hopkins, "As Kingfishers Catch Fire," Poetry Foundation, accessed September 20, 2021, https://bit.ly/3CjNmmU.

37 Ibid.

38 Ibid.

39 Ibid.

40 Ibid.

41 Ibid.

42 Jeremy Begbie, "The Sound of Freedom: The Music of Liberation" (lecture, Camp House, Chattanooga, TN, January 29, 2015). I am deeply indebted to Dr. Jeremy Begbie whose discussion of the way music can act as an agent of rehumanization after dehumanization has greatly influenced both my teaching and the writing of this book.

43 Alice Walker, *In Love and Trouble: Stories of Black Women* (New York: Harcourt Brace, 1973), 82.

44 Ibid.

45 Matt 25:45.

46 Pohl, *Making Room*, 64.

47 Walker, *In Love and Trouble*, 94.

48 The spiritual was recorded by Clara Ward as "Walk and Talk with Jesus" on the 1962 album *Come in the Room*. Alice Walker dedicated "The Welcome Table" to "Sister Clara Ward." Lyrics retrieved from "I'm Going to Walk and Talk with . . . ," Musixmatch, accessed September 20, 2021, https://bit.ly/3lu6LeW.

49 Matt 25:40.

50 Langston Hughes, "I, Too, Sing America," in *The Poetry of the Negro: 1746–1970*, ed. Arna Bontemps and Langston Hughes (New York: Anchor, 1970), 97.

51 Ibid.; Martin Luther King Jr., "I Have a Dream," NPR, accessed September 20, 2021, https://n.pr/3yuYN8Q.

52 Walter Brueggemann, *The Prophetic Imagination: 40th Anniversary Edition* (Minneapolis: Fortress, 2018), 9, 21.

53 Ibid., 11.

54 Ibid., 48.

55 Flannery O'Connor, "The Grotesque in Southern Fiction," in *O'Connor: Collected Works*, ed. Sally Fitzgerald (New York: Literary Classics, 1988), 816.

56 Flannery O'Connor, "Revelation," in Fitzgerald, *O'Connor*, 635.

57 Flannery O'Connor, "A Good Man Is Hard to Find," in Fitzgerald, *O'Connor*, 138.

58 Brueggemann, *Prophetic Imagination*, 9.

59 O'Connor, "Good Man," 147.

60 Ibid., 152.

61 Ibid.

62 Ibid.

63 Greene, *Power and the Glory*, 132; Flannery O'Connor, *Mystery and Manners*, ed. Sally Fitzgerald (New York: Farrar, Straus & Giroux, 1970), 111–12.

64 O'Connor, *Mystery and Manners*, 111–12.

65 Ibid.

66 O'Connor, "Good Man," 147.

67 "A Good Man Is Hard to Find," track 9 on Sufjan Stevens, *Seven Swans*, Asthmatic Kitty Records, 2004.

68 O'Connor, "Good Man," 148.

69 O'Connor, *Mystery and Manners*, 111–12.

70 David Foster Wallace, *This Is Water* (New York: Little, Brown, 2008), 38.

71 Ibid., 78.

72 Ibid., 50.

73 Ibid., 93.

74 Ibid., 98.

75 Benedict XVI, *Deus Caritas Est*.

76 Ellis Potter, "Is Art a Commodity or Relationship?" (lecture, L'Abri Fellowship, UK, n.d.), https://bit.ly/3AK4VKH. I am deeply indebted to Ellis Potter as well as the English L'Abri workers for the conceptualization of art as a relationship. My first encounter with this idea was when sitting in the L'Abri library in England listening to the lecture on a tape recorder.

77 Scott Huelin, "Peregrination, Hermeneutics, Hospitality: On the Way to a Theologically Informed General Hermeneutics," *Theology & Literature* 22, no. 11 (2008): 243.

78 Ibid.

79 I first began to explore how both cynicism and romanticism were equally problematic ways of avoiding reality when listening to a lecture given by Marsh Moyle at L'Abri Fellowship (UK) titled: "Cynicism, Romanticism & Other Ways We Escape Reality." The lecture can be found in the L'Abri library in the Greatham, England Manor house. Or you can listen online here: https://bit.ly/3GQYnyd.

CHAPTER ONE

1 O'Connor, *Mystery and Manners*, 111–12.

2 Ibid.

3 Paul Fiddes, *The Promised End: Eschatology in Theology and Literature* (Oxford: Wiley-Blackwell, 2000), 5.

4 O'Connor, *Mystery and Manners*, 134.

5 *Friday Night Lights*, directed by Jeffrey Reiner, written by Peter Berg, featuring Connie Britton and Kyle Chandler, aired 2006–11 on NBC.

6 Mark 12:31.

7 Samuel Taylor Coleridge, "This Lime-Tree Bower My Prison," Poetry Foundation, accessed September 20, 2021, https://bit.ly/3lDPTlU.

8 Ibid.

9 Ibid.

10 William Wordsworth, "Lines Composed a Few Miles above Tintern Abbey, on Revisiting the Banks of the Wye during a Tour," Poetry Foundation, July 13, 1798, https://bit.ly/3CnfxkG.

11 Coleridge, "This Lime-Tree Bower."

12 Ibid.

13 Ibid.

14 Ibid.

15 Ibid.

16 *A Beautiful Day in the Neighborhood*, directed by Marielle Heller (Pittsburgh, PA: Sony Video, 2019), Amazon Prime.

17 Ibid.

18 Ibid.

19 Ibid.

20 Mary Hartzell and Daniel J. Siegel, *Parenting from the Inside Out: How Deeper Self-Understanding Can Help You Raise Children Who Thrive* (New York: Penguin, 2004), 21.

21 *Beautiful Day in the Neighborhood*.

22 Ibid.

23 Ibid.

24 Ibid.

25 Ibid.

26 Ibid.

27 Henri J. M. Nouwen, *Life of the Beloved: Spiritual Living in a Secular World* (New York: Crossroad, 2002), 134.

28 "Henri Nouwen: The Catholic Priest Who Embraced His Demons," CBC. CA, January 13, 2017, https://bit.ly/3fCHn2L.

29 Henri J. M. Nouwen, *Love, Henri*, ed. Gabrielle Earnshaw (New York: Convergent, 2016), 210.

30 Ibid.

31 *Beautiful Day in the Neighborhood*.

32 Ibid.

33 Phil 2:3.

34 *Beautiful Day in the Neighborhood*.

35 Ibid.

36 Ibid.

37 Ibid.
38 Matt 18:3.
39 *Beautiful Day in the Neighborhood.*
40 Nouwen, *Life of the Beloved*, 134.
41 Raymond Carver, *A Small, Good Thing* (Portland: Scriptor, 2006), 5.
42 Ibid.
43 Ibid.
44 Ibid., 6.
45 Ibid., 11.
46 Ibid., 18.
47 Ibid., 21.
48 Ibid., 24.
49 Ibid., 25.
50 Ibid., 5.
51 Ibid., 27.
52 Ibid., 28.
53 Ibid.
54 Ibid.
55 Ibid.
56 Ibid., 29.
57 Ibid.
58 Matt 25:40.
59 Luke 21:1–4.
60 Mark 14:8.
61 Craig Detweiler, "*Lars and the Real Girl* Study Guide," Grace Hill Media, accessed September 21, 2021, https://bit.ly/3lDro8E.
62 *Lars and the Real Girl*, directed by Craig Gillespie (Alton, ON: Metro-Goldwyn-Myer, 2007), Amazon Prime.
63 Ibid.
64 Ibid.
65 Ibid.
66 Detweiler, "*Lars and the Real Girl.*"
67 *Lars and the Real Girl.*
68 John 8:7.
69 *Lars and the Real Girl.*
70 Mary Hulst, "Lars and the Real Girl Go to Church," *Think Christian*, December 8, 2008, https://bit.ly/3CwtuNF.
71 *Beautiful Day in the Neighborhood.*
72 Detweiler, "*Lars and the Real Girl.*"
73 Ibid.

CHAPTER TWO

1 Jean-Paul Sartre, *No Exit and Three Other Plays* (New York: Vintage, 1989).
2 Jean-Paul Sartre, "Existentialism Is a Humanism," in *Existentialism from*

Dostoyevsky to Sartre, ed. Walter Kaufman (New York: New American Library, 1975), available at https://www.marxists.org/reference/archive/sartre/works/exist/sartre.htm.

3 Ibid.

4 Ibid.

5 Pascal, *Pensées*, 10.

6 Ibid.

7 Ibid., 37.

8 *The Walking Dead*, season 2, episode 11, "Judge, Jury, Executioner," directed by Greg Nicotero, written by Frank Darabont, Robert Kirkman, and Tony Moore, featuring Andrew Lincoln, John Bernthal, and Sarah Wayne Callies, aired March 4, 2012, on AMC, Netflix.

9 *The Walking Dead*, season 2, episode 1, "What Lies Ahead," directed by Ernest R. Dickerson and Gwyneth Horder-Payton, written by Frank Darabont, Robert Kirkman, and Tony Moore, featuring Andrew Lincoln, John Bernthal, and Sarah Wayne Callies, aired October 16, 2011, on AMC, Netflix.

10 Pascal, *Pensées*, 41.

11 Ibid., 42.

12 Ibid.

13 Dark, *Everyday Apocalypse*, 10.

14 Pascal, *Pensées*, 14.

15 Jas 2:17.

16 Flannery O'Connor, "Good Country People," in Fitzgerald, *O'Connor*, 263.

17 Flannery O'Connor, "A Temple of the Holy Ghost," in Fitzgerald, *O'Connor*, 197.

18 Ibid.

19 Ibid., 200.

20 Ibid., 202.

21 Pascal, *Pensées*, 14.

22 O'Connor, "Temple of the Holy Ghost," 199.

23 Ibid.

24 Ibid.

25 Ibid., 204.

26 Ibid., 205.

27 Ibid., 204.

28 Ibid., 205.

29 Ibid., 207.

30 Ibid.

31 Ibid., 208.

32 Ibid.

33 C. S. Lewis, *Till We Have Faces* (New York: Mariner, 2012), 70.

34 Ibid., 75.

35 Ibid., 73.

36 Ibid., 49.

37 C. S. Lewis, *The Four Loves* (London: Geoffrey Bles, 1960), chap. 6, https://bit.ly/3CiFoup.

38 Lewis, *Till We Have Faces*, 122.

39 Ibid., 171.

40 Lewis, *Four Loves*, chap. 5.

41 Ibid.

42 Lewis, *Till We Have Faces*, 76.

43 Ibid.

44 Ibid., 82.

45 Ibid., 163.

46 Ibid., 115.

47 Ibid., 124, 97.

48 Ibid., 266.

49 Ibid.

50 Ibid., 294.

51 Ibid., 306.

52 Greene, *Power and the Glory*, 131.

53 "Futile Devices," track 1 on Sufjan Stevens, *The Age of Adz*, Asthmatic Kitty, 2010.

54 Pascal, *Pensées*, 14.

55 "Futile Devices."

56 Ibid.

57 "Too Much," track 2 on Stevens, *Age of Adz*; "All for Myself," track 9 on Stevens, *Age of Adz*.

58 "Age of Adz," track 3 on Stevens, *Age of Adz*.

59 Ibid.

60 Pascal, *Pensées*, 10.

61 Zadie Smith, introduction to *The Burned Children of America*, ed. Dave Eggers (London: Hamish Hamilton, 2003), xv.

62 Sufjan Stevens and Deborah Johnson, "Too Much," Asthmatic Kitty, November 24, 2010, YouTube video, 6:43, https://bit.ly/37osKvx.

63 Ibid.

64 "Impossible Soul," track 11 on Stevens, *Age of Adz*.

65 Ibid.

66 Thomas Merton, *No Man Is an Island* (New York: Mariner, 2002).

67 *Breaking Bad*, season 2, episode 8, "Better Call Saul," created by Vince Gilligan, directed by Terry McDonough, written by Peter Gould, featuring Bryan Cranston, Aaron Paul, and Bob Odenkirk, aired April 26, 2009, on AMC, Netflix.

68 Joseph Stanichar, "The Reason Bob Odenkirk Made Better Call Saul Isn't What You Think," Looper, April 17, 2021, https://bit.ly/3yHdmqh.

69 *Better Call Saul*, created by Vince Gilligan and Peter Gould, featuring Bob Odenkirk, Jonathan Banks, and Rhea Seahorn, on AMC, Netflix.

70 Ibid.

71 *Better Call Saul*, season 1, episode 9, "Pimento," created by Vince Gilligan and Peter Gould, featuring Bob Odenkirk, Jonathan Banks, and Rhea Seahorn, aired March 30, 2015, on AMC, Netflix.

72 Ibid.

73 Ibid.

74 Ibid.

75 Ibid.

76 Ibid.

77 Ibid.

78 *Better Call Saul*, season 1, episode 6, "Five-O," created by Vince Gilligan and Peter Gould, featuring Bob Odenkirk, Jonathan Banks, and Rhea Seahorn, aired March 30, 2015, on AMC, Netflix.

79 Luke 15:29–30.

80 Luke 15:32.

81 *Better Call Saul*, season 3, episode 10, "Lantern," created by Vince Gilligan and Peter Gould, featuring Bob Odenkirk, Jonathan Banks, and Rhea Seahorn, aired June 19, 2017, on AMC, Netflix.

82 Ibid.

83 Pascal, *Pensées*, 10.

84 Lorraine Hansberry, *A Raisin in the Sun* (New York: Vintage, 1988), 24.

85 Martin Luther King Jr., "The Other America," Civil Rights Movement Archive, accessed September 20, 2021, https://bit.ly/3Cnnvus.

86 W. E. B. Du Bois, *The Souls of Black Folk* (Garden City, NY: Dover Thrift, 2012), 4.

87 Hansberry, *Raisin in the Sun*, 142, 143.

88 Ibid., 144.

89 Ibid., 143.

90 Ibid., 144.

91 Ibid., 142.

92 Ibid., 144.

93 Ibid., 145.

94 Ibid.

95 Ibid.

Chapter Three

1 1 Sam 13:14.

2 2 Sam 12:5.

3 2 Sam 12:13.

4 William Shakespeare, *Hamlet*, Folger Shakespeare Library Online, accessed September 20, 2021, https://bit.ly/3fCTDjW, 2.2.628–29.

5 Ibid., 3.2.261.

6 Ibid., 2.2.633–34.

7 Mark 2:17.

8 *The Tree of Life*, directed by Terrence Malick (Houston, TX: Fox Searchlight, 2011), DVD.

9 Ibid.

10 Ibid.

11 Ibid.

12 Ibid.

13 Ibid.

14 Ibid.

15 Ibid.

16 Ibid.

17 Ibid.

18 Ibid.

19 Richard Winter, "The Glory and Ruin of Man," in *Francis A. Schaeffer: Portraits of the Man and His Work*, ed. Lane Dennis (Wheaton: Crossway, 1986), 86.

20 *Tree of Life*.

21 Ibid.

22 Job 38:4, 7.

23 Joseph G. Kickasola, "The Mystery Dialectic in Cinema: Paradox, Mystery, Miracle," *Christian Scholars Review* 40, no. 4 (2011): 432.

24 Ibid.; Theodor Adorno, *The Culture Industry: Selected Essays on Mass Culture*, ed. J. M. Bernstein (New York: Routledge, 2001), 21.

25 *Tree of Life*.

26 Ibid.

27 Ibid.

28 Ibid.

29 Ibid.

30 Ibid.

31 Ibid.

32 Ibid.

33 Ibid.

34 Ibid.

35 Ibid.

36 Ibid.

37 Ibid.

38 "Agnus Dei," A Collection of Prayers, accessed September 20, 2021, https://bit.ly/2X3JmH5.

39 *Tree of Life*.

40 O'Connor, *Mystery and Manners*, 111–12.

41 *Tree of Life*.

42 Ibid.

43 Rev 21:5.

44 Stephanie Goodman, "Walking in and Walking Right Back Out of *The Tree of Life*," *New York Times*, June 30, 2011, https://nyti.ms/3xrnmlJ.

45 Roy Anker, "Terrence Malick's *The Tree of Life*," Religion & Ethics NewsWeekly, September 6, 2011, YouTube video, 9:17, https://bit.ly/3xsWrX0.

46 O'Connor, *Mystery and Manners*, 111–12.

47 Pascal, *Pensées*, 64.

48 *The Addiction*, directed by Abel Ferrara (New York: Fast Films, 1995), DVD.

49 Ibid.

50 Pascal, *Pensées*, 7.

51 Ibid., 34.

52 Carol Senf, *The Vampire in Nineteenth Century English Literature* (Madison: University of Wisconsin Press, 1988), 166.

53 *Addiction.*

54 Ibid.

55 Chuck Palahniuk, *Fight Club* (London: Vintage, 1996).

56 Gerald G. May, *Addiction and Grace: Love and Spirituality in the Healing of Addictions* (New York: Harper One, 2009), 4.

57 *Addiction.*

58 Ibid.

59 Friedrich Nietzsche, *The Antichrist* (New York: Alfred Knopf, 1918), section 2, https://bit.ly/37oOcQX.

60 Lili Taylor (actress in *The Addiction*) in discussion with the author, email dated February 20, 2012.

61 Ibid.

62 Ibid.

63 Matt 25:40.

64 *Addiction.*

65 This first came to my attention in a conversation with my friend, Dr. Jennifer Williams, a vampire story aficionado, who noted the absence of the wine.

66 O'Connor, *Mystery and Manners*, 111–12.

67 Palahniuk, *Fight Club.*

68 Douglas Coupland, *Life after God* (New York: Washington Square, 1994), 161.

69 Ibid., 143.

70 Ibid., 273.

71 Ibid., 38, 304.

72 Ibid., 225, 219.

73 Ibid., 272.

74 Ibid.

75 Ibid.

76 Ibid., 273.

77 Ibid.

78 Ibid., 161.

79 Ibid., 273.

80 Ibid.

81 David Foster Wallace, "E Unibus Pluram: Television and U.S. Fiction," in *A Supposedly Fun Thing I'll Never Do Again: Essays and Arguments* (London: Abacus, 1997), 66.

82 Ibid.

83 Ibid., 67.

84 John Butler, "Writing His Own Rules: Jon Butler Talks to Douglas Coupland," interview in *Eleanor Rigby* by Douglas Coupland (London: Harper Perennial, 2005), 4.

85 Ibid.

86 Coupland, *Life after God*, 221.
87 Ibid.
88 Ibid., 271.
89 Ibid., 286.
90 Ibid.
91 Ibid., 286.
92 Ibid., 287.
93 Ibid.
94 Ibid., 280.
95 Ibid., 321.
96 Ibid., 326.
97 Ibid., 341.
98 Ibid.
99 Ibid., 338.
100 Ibid., 344.
101 Ibid., 352.
102 Ibid., 353.
103 Ibid., 272.
104 Ibid., 357–58.
105 Isa 55:12.
106 Coupland, *Life after God*, 359.
107 Ibid., 360.
108 Ibid.
109 Ibid.

CHAPTER FOUR

1 Dave Eggers, *What Is the What* (New York: Vintage, 2006), 5.
2 Ibid., 142.
3 Ibid.
4 Jer 5:21.
5 Eggers, *What Is the What*, 162.
6 Ibid.
7 Zech 7:9–12.
8 Ibid.
9 Marilynne Robinson, *When I Was a Child, I Read Books* (New York: Farrar, Straus & Giroux, 2012), 19.
10 Martin Buber, *I and Thou* (New York: Touchstone, 1970), 62.
11 Eggers, *What Is the What*, ix.
12 Ibid., 142.
13 Ibid., 535.
14 Ibid., 29.
15 Ibid., 6.
16 Buber, *I and Thou*, 67.

17 Eggers, *What Is the What*, 27.

18 Ibid., 57.

19 Ibid., 125.

20 Ibid., 160.

21 Ibid.

22 Ibid., 287.

23 Ibid.

24 "25 Functions of Art That Make Us Better Human Beings," The Artist, accessed September 20, 2021, https://bit.ly/3fIhK0y.

25 Cathy Caruth, *Unclaimed Experience: Trauma, Narrative, and History* (Baltimore: Johns Hopkins University Press, 1996), 8.

26 Heb 13:3; Matt 25:40.

27 Greene, *Power and the Glory*, 131.

28 Ibid.

29 Ibid.

30 *Rectify*, season 1, episode 1, "Always There," created by Ray McKinnon, directed by Keith Gordon, written by Ray McKinnon, featuring Aden Young and Abigail Spencer, aired April 22, 2013, on Sundance Channel, Netflix.

31 Ibid.

32 Scott Teems (writer and director of *Rectify*) in discussion with author, February 3, 2021.

33 Ibid.

34 Sigmund Freud, *Beyond the Pleasure Principle*, trans. C. J. M. Hubback, accessed September 20, 2021, https://bit.ly/3CsTIAf.

35 Scott Teems (writer and director of *Rectify*) in discussion with author, February 3, 2021.

36 *Rectify*, season 1, episode 6, "Jacob's Ladder," created by Ray McKinnon, directed by Romeo Tyrone, written by Ray McKinnon, featuring Aden Young and Abigail Spencer, aired May 20, 2013, on Sundance Channel, Netflix.

37 *Rectify*, season 1, episode 5, "Drip, Drip," created by Ray McKinnon, directed by Keith Gordon, written by Ray McKinnon, featuring Aden Young and Abigail Spencer, aired May 13, 2013, on Sundance Channel, Netflix.

38 Scott Teems (writer and director of *Rectify*) in discussion with author, February 3, 2021.

39 Ibid.

40 Ibid.

41 Ibid.

42 Ibid.

43 *Rectify*, season 2, episode 1, "Running with the Bull," created by Ray McKinnon, directed by Stephen Gyllenhaal, written by Ray McKinnon, featuring Aden Young and Abigail Spencer, aired June 19, 2014, on Sundance Channel, Netflix.

44 Ibid.

45 Ibid.

46 Bryan Stevenson, *Just Mercy: A Story of Justice and Redemption* (New York: Spiegel & Grau, 2014), 18.

47 *Rectify*, "Jacob's Ladder."

48 Ibid.

49 *Rectify*, "Running with the Bull."

50 Ibid.

51 *Rectify*, season 4, episode 1, "A House Divided," created by Ray McKinnon, directed by Patrick Cady, written by Ray McKinnon, featuring Aden Young and Abigail Spencer, aired October 26, 2016, on Sundance Channel, Netflix.

52 Ibid.

53 Ibid.

54 Ibid.

55 *Rectify*, season 4, episode 8, "All I'm Sayin'," created by Ray McKinnon, directed by Patrick Cady, written by Ray McKinnon, featuring Aden Young and Abigail Spencer, aired December 14, 2016, on Sundance Channel, Netflix.

56 Scott Teems (writer and director of *Rectify*) in discussion with author, February 3, 2021.

57 Matt 25:36, 40.

58 Rom 12:15.

59 King, "Other America."

60 Angie Thomas, *The Hate U Give* (New York: Balzer & Bray, 2017).

61 Ibid.

62 King, "Other America."

63 Thomas, *Hate U Give*, 30.

64 *The Hate U Give*, directed by George Tillman Jr. (Atlanta, GA: Fox Searchlight, 2018), Amazon Prime.

65 Thomas, *Hate U Give*, 17.

66 Cornel West, "Justice Is What Love Looks like in Public," Patrick Moore, August 27, 2010, YouTube video, 9:59, https://bit.ly/3xvld8W.

67 Thomas, *Hate U Give*, 20.

68 Ibid., 25.

69 Frederick Douglass, *Narrative of the Life of Fredrick Douglass* (New York: Dover, 1845), 21.

70 Thomas, *Hate U Give*, 94.

71 Ibid., 101.

72 Ibid., 157.

73 Ibid., 248.

74 *Hate U Give*.

75 Ibid.

76 Ibid.

77 Ibid.

78 Resmaa Menakem, *My Grandmother's Hands: Racialized Trauma and the Pathway to Healing Our Hearts and Bodies* (Las Vegas: Central Recovery, 2017), xix.

79 Ibid.

80 Ibid.

81 *Hate U Give.*

82 Ta-Nehisi Coates, *Between the World and Me* (New York: Spiegel & Grau, 2015), 11.

83 Thomas, *Hate U Give.*

84 Prov 31:8.

85 Gal 6:2.

86 *Unbelievable*, season 1, episode 7, directed by Susannah Grant, written by Susannah Grant, featuring Toni Collette, Merritt Weaver, and Kaitlyn Dever, aired September 13, 2019, on Netflix.

87 Freud, *Beyond the Pleasure Principle.*

88 Bessel van der Kolk, *The Body Keeps the Score: Mind, Brain and Body in the Transformation of Trauma* (New York: Penguin, 2014), 97.

89 *Unbelievable*, season 1, episode 7.

90 Ibid.

91 *Unbelievable*, season 1, episode 2, directed by Lisa Cholodenko, written by Susannah Grant, featuring Toni Collette, Merritt Weaver, and Kaitlyn Dever, aired September 13, 2019, on Netflix.

92 van der Kolk, *Body Keeps the Score*, 97.

93 *Unbelievable*, season 1, episode 7.

94 van der Kolk, *Body Keeps the Score*, 97.

95 Prov 31:8.

Chapter Five

1 Toni Morrison, *Beloved* (New York: Vintage, 2004), 3.

2 Ibid., 43.

3 Ibid., xviii.

4 "25 Functions of Art."

5 Morrison, *Beloved*, vi.

6 Ibid., xvii.

7 Ibid., 234.

8 Ibid.

9 Ibid., xviii–xix.

10 Ibid., vi.

11 Ibid., 43.

12 Ibid.

13 The National Memorial for Peace and Justice is the USA's first memorial "dedicated to the legacy of enslaved Black people." It opened on April 6, 2018, in Montgomery, Alabama. See its website, https://museumandmemorial.eji.org/memorial. A National Slave Memorial to be built in Washington, DC, is still in the proposal stage.

14 Ibid., 10.
15 Ibid., 123.
16 Ibid.
17 Ibid., 116.
18 Ibid., 86.
19 Ibid., 145.
20 Ibid., 297.
21 Ibid., 104.
22 Ibid.
23 Ibid.
24 Ibid., 104–5.
25 Ibid., 104.
26 Ibid., 191.
27 Ibid., 286.
28 Ibid., 294.
29 Ibid., 295.
30 Ibid.
31 Ibid., 104–5.
32 Cornel West, "Black Strivings in a Twilight Civilization," in *The Cornel West Reader* (New York: Basic Civitas, 1999), 101.
33 Ibid.
34 Jemar Tisby, *The Color of Compromise: The Truth about the American Church's Complicity in Racism* (Grand Rapids, MI: Zondervan, 2019), 222.
35 West, "Black Strivings," 101.
36 Ibid.
37 Morrison, *Beloved*, 236.
38 Ibid., 242.
39 Ibid., 243.
40 Ibid., 245–46.
41 Ibid., xix.
42 Ibid., 248.
43 Ibid.
44 Ibid., 251.
45 Ibid., 255.
46 Cornel West, *Race Matters* (Boston: Beacon, 1993), 12.
47 Ibid., 18–19.
48 Ibid.
49 Morrison, *Beloved*, 321.
50 Ibid., 322.
51 Simone Weil, "Human Personality," in *Simone Weil: An Anthology*, ed. Sian Miles (New York: Grove, 1986), 52–53.
52 Ibid., 53.
53 Ibid.
54 Joseph Kickasola, *The Films of Krzysztof Kieslowski: The Liminal Image* (New York: Continuum, 2004), 263.

55 *Three Colors: Blue*, directed by Krzysztof Kieślowski (Paris: France 3 Cinema, 1993), Amazon Prime.

56 Ibid.

57 Ibid.

58 Mark Haddon, *The Curious Incident of the Dog in the Night-Time* (London: Vintage, 2003), 30.

59 Patricia Waugh, *Metafiction: The Theory and Practice of Self-Conscious Fiction* (London: Taylor & Francis, 1984), 2.

60 Haddon, *Curious Incident*, 19–20.

61 Ibid.

62 Ibid., 115.

63 Ibid., 116.

64 Ibid.

65 Mark Haddon, "Asperger's & Autism," MarkHaddon.com, July 16, 2009, https://bit.ly/37tfYfq.

66 Ibid.

67 Michel Foucault, *Discipline and Punish: The Birth of the Prison* (New York: Pantheon, 1977), 326.

68 Ibid.

69 Sarah Jaquette Ray, "Normalcy, Knowledge, and Nature in Mark Haddon's *The Curious Incident of the Dog in the Night-Time*," *Disabilities Studies Quarterly* 33, no. 3 (2013), https://bit.ly/3fKlazN.

70 Haddon, *Curious Incident*, 140.

71 Ibid.

72 Ibid.

73 Ibid.

74 Ibid., 141.

75 Ibid., 143.

76 Ibid.

77 Ibid., 112.

78 Ibid., 122.

79 Ibid., 106.

80 Ibid.

81 Ibid., 198–99.

82 Ibid., 199.

83 Ibid.

84 Ibid., 32.

85 Ibid., 221.

CHAPTER SIX

1 Nietzsche, *Antichrist*.

2 Luke 23:34 KJV.

3 Matt 23:13, 27, 33.

4 Matt 23:37–39.

5 Douglass, *Narrative*.

6 Ibid.

7 Luke 23:34 KJV.

8 Matt 23:23.

9 Douglas Coupland, *Hey Nostradamus!* (New York: Bloomsbury, 2003), 77.

10 Ibid., 33.

11 Ibid.

12 Ibid.

13 Douglas Coupland, "Interview with Douglas Coupland" by Tony Watkins, TonyWatkins.co.uk, original interview conducted in 2004, https://bit.ly/3jzRd6T.

14 Ibid.

15 Douglas Coupland, *Life after God* (New York: Washington Square, 1994), 161.

16 Ibid.

17 Ibid.

18 Coupland, *Hey Nostradamus!*, 84.

19 Ibid., 7.

20 Ibid., 28.

21 Ibid., 111.

22 Ibid., 3.

23 Rom 3:23.

24 Coupland, *Hey Nostradamus!*, 22.

25 Ibid.

26 Ibid., 146.

27 Ibid., 204.

28 Ibid.

29 1 Cor 15:51–52.

30 Coupland, *Hey Nostradamus!*, 235.

31 Ibid., 236.

32 Ibid.

33 Ibid., 236, 146.

34 Ibid., 241.

35 Ibid., 146.

36 Ibid., 241.

37 Coupland, "Interview with Douglas Coupland."

38 Ibid.

39 O'Connor, "Good Man," 148.

40 Coupland, *Hey Nostradamus!*, 244.

41 Ibid.

42 Ibid., 243.

43 Craig Thompson, *Blankets* (Marietta: Top Shelf Productions, 2003), 13.

44 Ibid., 15.

45 Ibid., 17.

46 Ibid.

47 Charlotte Brontë, *Jane Eyre* (London: Penguin, 1847), 19.

48 Thompson, *Blankets*, 57.

49 Ibid., 44.

50 Francis Schaeffer, *Art and the Bible*, IVP Classics (Downers Grove, IL: IVP, 2009).

51 Thompson, *Blankets*, 137.

52 Ibid.

53 Ibid.

54 Ibid.

55 Ibid., 138.

56 Ibid., 140.

57 James Paul, *What on Earth Is Heaven* (London: Inter-Varsity, 2021), 7.

58 John 21:12.

59 Thompson, *Blankets*, 533.

60 Hopkins, "God's Grandeur."

61 Thompson, *Blankets*, 516.

62 Ibid., 518.

63 Ibid., 58.

64 Ibid.

65 Ibid., 56.

66 Ibid., 52.

67 Ibid., 496.

68 Ibid., 558.

69 Ibid., 531.

70 Ibid., 551.

71 Ibid.

72 Ibid., 552.

73 Ibid.

74 Ibid., 579–81.

75 *Magnolia*, directed by Paul Thomas Anderson (Los Angeles: New Line Cinema, 2000), DVD.

76 Exod 20:5.

77 Jer 17:9.

78 *Magnolia*.

79 Ibid.

80 Ibid.

81 Scott Teems (writer and director of *Rectify*) in discussion with author, February 3, 2021.

82 *Magnolia*.

83 Ibid.

84 Ibid.

85 Ibid.

86 "Deathly," track 4 on Aimee Mann, *Magnolia: Music from the Motion Picture*, Warner Brothers, December 1999.

87 Ibid.

88 Gabor Mate, *In the Realm of Hungry Ghosts: Close Encounters with Addiction* (Berkeley, CA: North Atlantic, 2011).

89 *Magnolia.*

90 Ibid.

91 Ibid.

92 "Save Me," track 9 on Mann, *Magnolia.*

93 Ibid.

94 *Magnolia.*

95 Nietzsche, *Antichrist.*

Conclusion

1 "Up on a Mountain," track 1 on the Welcome Wagon, *Welcome to the Welcome Wagon*, Asthmatic Kitty, 2008.

2 Ibid.

3 Ibid.

4 Monique Aiuto (member of the Welcome Wagon) in conversation with the author, August 2, 2021.

5 Eggers, *What Is the What*, 562.

6 *The Chosen*, season 1, episode 8, "I Am He," directed and written by Dallas Jenkins, featuring Jonathan Roumie, Shahar Isaac, and Elizabeth Tabish, aired November 26, 2019, Amazon Prime.

7 Dallas Jenkins and Jonathan Roumie, "The Immense Weight of Playing Jesus," The Chosen, YouTube video, posted on April 11, 2020, 54:36, https://bit.ly/2U1ifuX.

8 Ibid.

9 Ibid.

10 Ibid.

11 Martin Luther King Jr., "Loving Your Enemies," sermon delivered on November 17, 1957, Dexter Avenue Baptist Church, Montgomery, AL, https://stanford.io/3fLUHlE.

12 Ibid.

13 Ibid.

INDEX